THE TRIAL OF

Born in Edinburgh, Ludovic Kennedy was educated at
Eton and Christ Church, Oxford. He served in the
Royal Navy during the war and was Private Secretary
and ADC to the Governor of Newfoundland. An active
member of the Liberal Party for many years, he was
President of the Young Liberals from 1959 to 1961. He
is one of Britain's most distinguished broadcasters,
having worked on numerous current affairs pro-
grammes and having made a number of docu-
mentaries. Since 1980 he has been the presenter of
BBC2's *Did You See?*. Well known as a campaigner for
the righting of judicial wrongs, he is the author of a
number of books. These include *Ten Rillington Place*
(1961), *A Presumption of Innocence* (1976) and *Wicked
Beyond Belief* (1980). Married to Moira Shearer,
Ludovic Kennedy has one son and three daughters.

By the same author:

SUB-LIEUTENANT
NELSON'S BAND OF BROTHERS
ONE MAN'S MEAT
MURDER STORY
TEN RILLINGTON PLACE
VERY LONELY PEOPLE
PURSUIT
A PRESUMPTION OF INNOCENCE
MENACE
THE PORTLAND SPY CASE
WICKED BEYOND BELIEF
THE AIRMAN AND THE CARPENTER

THE TRIAL OF
STEPHEN WARD

by

LUDOVIC KENNEDY

LONDON
VICTOR GOLLANCZ LTD
1987

First published in Great Britain 1964
by Victor Gollancz Ltd,
14 Henrietta Street, London WC2E 8QJ

First published in Gollancz Paperbacks 1987

British Library Cataloguing in Publication Data
Kennedy, Ludovic
    The trial of Stephen Ward.
    1. Ward, Stephen—Trials, litigation, etc.
    2. Trials (Pimps)—England—London
    I. Title
    344.2105'2534'0924   KD373.W/

    ISBN 0-575-04194-3

Printed and bound in Great Britain
by Richard Clay Ltd, Bungay, Suffolk

"The English system leans heavily on the arrival of a verdict by way of general impressions rather than scrupulous examination of the testimony."

Louis Blom-Cooper: *The A.6 Murder*

PREFACE

In the early summer of 1987 the publication of two books, *An Affair of State* by Phillip Knightley and Caroline Kennedy, and *Honeytrap* by Anthony Summers and Stephen Dorril, renewed public interest in what became known as the Profumo affair of 1962-3 and the subsequent trial and conviction of Stephen Ward. For their necessarily truncated accounts of that trial both lots of authors relied on the original edition of this book, and both are in broad agreement that Ward should never have been brought to trial, let alone convicted. *An Affair of State* quotes Sir David Tudor-Price, Ward's junior defence counsel and later a High Court judge, as saying that it left him with a burning sense of injustice, and Lord Goodman (who read the original edition of this book for libel) as describing Ward as "an historic victim of an historic injustice". When you consider (what is known for certain now but was only guessed at then) that all the principal prosecution witnesses were pressurised by the police into giving false evidence, it is hardly surprising.

Recently, however, in a letter to *The Times*, Lord Denning (whose 1963 report on the security aspects of the affair is reviewed on pages 241-244) declared that Ward was fairly and properly prosecuted, tried and convicted, and that the conduct of the trial judge, Sir Archibald Marshall, was beyond reproach. So that readers may judge the matter for themselves, so too that they may have an idea of what it was like to be an eye-witness of that extraordinary trial and all its richly variegated participants, this book is now republished.

Ludovic Kennedy
June 1987

THE TRIAL OF STEPHEN WARD

INTRODUCTORY

THIS IS NOT the place to recount in detail all the complex
events that led to the trial of Stephen Ward. But a brief word of
explanation may be helpful.

Stephen Ward, a man of fifty at the time of his trial, was an
osteopath and artist who practised in Devonshire Street, W.1.
His patients consisted of many rich and famous people. He was
a son of a Canon of the Church of England and had been
brought up in Torquay. He liked the company of peers and
prostitutes, singly and together. He was a great name-dropper.
The only time I ever met him, his first words were: "We've so
nearly met at 'B's'" (the name of a mutual peer), which in fact
was untrue. He had been married once, briefly; but his sex life
had never been satisfactory, and the older he grew the more
dissolute he became. He was said to be very kind and also rather
mean. He had a plausible manner and enormous charm.

The story may be said to have started in 1956 when Lord
Astor, who had been a patient and friend of his since 1950,
arranged for him to have the lease (at peppercorn rent) of a
cottage in the grounds of his estate at Cliveden. In July 1961
Lord Astor was entertaining a house-party which included among
the guests Mr. John Profumo, the Minister for War, and his
wife, Valerie Hobson, the actress. Ward also had guests that
weekend, including Captain Ivanov, the Russian Naval Attaché,
and the girl Christine Keeler, whom Ward had first met at the
Cabaret Club some two years before and who was now living
(but not sleeping) with him at his flat in Wimpole Mews. After
dinner Mr. Profumo met Miss Keeler at the swimming-pool, was
attracted to her, telephoned her when he returned to London
and started an affair with her. According to Miss Keeler she was
also having an affair with Captain Ivanov, but many people

have doubted this. The Security Service got to know of Profumo's association with Ward, and in view of Ward's known friend-ship with Ivanov, they informed Sir Norman Brook, the Secre-tary of the Cabinet. Sir Norman had a word with Profumo who, imagining the authorities had got wind of his affair with Miss Keeler, at once took steps to break it off. It was a brief affair and not, one imagines, a particularly enriching one; yet it was to cost Mr. Profumo his career, and Ward his life.

There the matter might have ended but for two things: Ward's continued association with Ivanov and a penchant he had for playing at politics, which made the Security Service keep an eye on him; and secondly the activities of Christine Keeler. Among her many lovers were two West Indians, Lucky Gordon and John Edgecombe. In October 1962 Christine was at a night-club in Wardour Street, Soho, with Lucky Gordon when John Edgecombe came in. There was a fight, and Gordon's face was slashed. Edgecombe fled, and later Christine went to live with him at Brentford. Early in December Christine left Edgecombe and took the lease of a flat at Great Cumberland Place. On December 14th she was visiting her friend Marilyn (Mandy) Rice-Davies who was now living in her old room at Ward's flat in Wimpole Mews: Miss Rice-Davies had also been in the Cabaret Club and had subsequently shared a flat with her in a place called Comeragh Road. For the past two years she had been the mistress of a slum-property racketeer called Peter Rach-man and lived with him in a flat at Bryanston Mews. Edgecombe heard where Christine was, and came round breathing fire and thunder in a mini-cab. When the girls would not let him in, he pulled out a gun and fired several times at the door. Again he fled, this time in the mini-cab, but the police caught and arrested him.

This incident naturally brought both Ward and Christine Keeler into the public eye and particularly to the attention of the Press. Soon several people knew, because Christine told them, that she had been to bed with Profumo: her claims also to have slept with Ivanov clearly provided the groundsheet for a first-class scandal. It looked as though the scandal would break in one, or both, of two ways; by Christine revealing what she knew in the witness-box at Edgecombe's trial and/or in an article in the newspapers. In fact Edgecombe's trial was postponed because of the illness of the mini-cab driver, and when it was at last held on March 14th and 15th she had gone to Spain for a holiday. She did manage to sell her story to the *Sunday Pictorial*, but frenzied efforts by a number of people resulted in the *Sunday Pictorial* dropping the story and publishing one by Ward instead.

But the rumours had now reached the Houses of Parliament, and on March 21st, a week after Edgecombe's trial (he got seven years) Mr. George Wigg rose to ask the Home Secretary either to deny the rumours circulating about a member of the Government Front Bench or else to appoint a Select Committee to investigate them. Although Mr. Profumo had already seen the Attorney-General, the Chief Whip and other senior Government officials and assured them that he had done nothing wrong, they thought that the time had now come for him to refute the rumours publicly. Accordingly he made a personal statement to the House of Commons the following day, denying that he had had any hand in Christine Keeler's not attending Edgecombe's trial or that there had ever been any impropriety between them. He also threatened to issue writs if any further allegations or rumours were repeated. Having established a pattern of lying about his affair some time before, Mr. Profumo now had no alternative, if he was to stay above water, but to continue to lie. It was reprehensible but understandable. His conscience was clear about spiriting Miss Keeler away to Spain and his relationship with Ivanov, and he may well have asked himself why he should jeopardise his entire career because of half a dozen tumbles in the hay eighteen months before.

His brazenness almost paid off. Two foreign magazines did libel Mr. Profumo and he successfully sued both of them. Ward and Christine Keeler both confirmed that what he said in the House of Commons was true. And there the matter might have ended, had not the authorities, irritated no doubt by what had happened and especially irritated by it coming so soon after the Vassall case, decided to make inquiries about Ward. It was on March 22nd that Profumo made his statement to the House. Just five days later the Home Secretary asked the Commissioner of Police if there was a police interest in Ward. The Commissioner said there might be, if they could get the full story, but this he doubted. On April 1st the police began their investigations. From this moment, ironically, Profumo was doomed.

At first Ward was co-operative with the police, but as the investigations went on, as his friends and patients were interviewed over and over again, the strain began to tell. He felt, naïvely perhaps but not altogether unreasonably, that as he had done his best to protect the Government's War Minister, the Government might do their best to call their dogs off him. He wrote to the Home Secretary, his local M.P., Sir Wavell Wakefield, and the Leader of the Opposition, Mr. Harold Wilson. To Mr. Wilson he wrote: "Obviously my efforts to conceal the fact that Mr. Profumo had not told the truth in Parliament have made it look as if I myself had something to hide. It is quite clear now that they must wish the facts to be known, and I shall see that they are." He sent copies of some of these letters to the papers.

These activities of Ward's resulted in the tabling of further questions in the House. Mr. Harold Wilson urged the Prime Minister to take some action. The Prime Minister called for more information from the Security Services, and as a result of what they told him, he asked Lord Dilhorne, the Lord Chancellor, to undertake an inquiry into the whole affair. This was on May 29th. For Profumo the sands were now fast running out. The Press were constantly at his heels, for they knew now that he had lied to the House of Commons, and that if the pressure was kept up on him, it could only be a matter of time before he admitted to it. Three days later in Venice Profumo broke the news to his wife. They returned immediately to England, and after issuing a statement that he had lied to the House, he handed in his resignation both as Minister and M.P.

The hunt for Ward meanwhile continued unabated. All through April, May and most of June, the police pursued their inquiries, interviewing vast numbers of witnesses, many of them several times. On June 5th Lucky Gordon was tried at the Old Bailey for assaulting Christine Keeler on April 18th. At his trial Christine Keeler was a prosecution witness and gave perjured evidence. Gordon, loudly protesting his innocence, was sentenced to three years' imprisonment. Three days later Stephen Ward was arrested in Watford and taken into custody. At the end of June he appeared before the Marylebone magistrate on no less than eight charges. He was committed for trial at the Old Bailey and it is there, on July 22nd, 1963, that the story of this book begins.

PART I

THERE WERE CROWDS outside the Old Bailey ten deep. They were there because Christine Keeler was expected to give evidence and they wanted to see her and Dr. Ward for themselves. They were prepared to wait long hours in the sun for this, just as people at funfairs are prepared to queue for freaks; only here the freaks were sexually not physically deformed. Round the corner nearly a hundred people were queuing for the tiny public gallery. Some had been there all night. One of them said: "I got here at one. It was a lovely night. I had a nice four hours' kip on the pavement. Bar accidents I'm in." Beyond the crowd and the marshalling policemen was a space of open road and beyond that, lining either side of the main entrance like a guard of honour at a wedding, were the cameramen. I never saw so many cameramen, not even at the American elections. They were fearful of missing anybody important and snapped promiscuously at every likely arrival.

As I went up the marble steps, I heard a great hum and clatter of conversation from above. Normally the hall outside the main courts is empty, but now it was alive with people; journalists mostly, alert tumbledown fellows with weather nostrils cocked to the prevailing wind; lawyers wigged and robed, modestly expressing in their dress the national obsession for charades; a sprinkling of beefy policemen to prevent unseemly behaviour; and the rude mechanicals themselves, soberly dressed and with stolid anonymous faces, from whom the jury would be chosen.

At the Public Office they were issuing Press tickets. There was a crowd in there too, all jostling impatiently behind a long wooden counter. It was a small Dickensian sort of place. I saw Wayland Young and Rebecca West, pioneers in the tangled byways of, respectively, sex and treason; Sybille Bedford too, whose title for her brilliant book on the trial of John Bodkin Adam—*The Best We Can Do*—is as succinct a comment as one could find on this or any other country's system of justice. A woman from New York was clamouring for a ticket without success. A man from one of the agencies smiled at me: I smiled back: later I found out he had a nervous tick and smiled at everybody. Beyond the counter a tall, sober man in spectacles and morning coat did his best to create calm. He explained that there were only twelve tickets for the Commonwealth Press and nobody had told him how to allocate them. I asked for my ticket and was informed, after much routling, that it wasn't there: it came to light eventually marked Victor Gollancz. Beside me, in pepper and salt trousers, were three small black barristers from some steamy clime. They asked diffidently if they could have some tickets, and were told firmly there were none left. What were they thinking of our wicked white society?

Court No. 1 at the Old Bailey is a famous court. Thompson and Bywaters, Hatry and Bottomley, Evans and Christie, Birkett, Hastings, and Marshall Hall are among its many ghosts. Yet it is a court which, it would seem, is expressly designed to prevent all laymen except the merely curious from hearing or seeing what is going on. From the stage where he sits in pomp under the coat of arms of Edward VII and the symbolic sword of justice, the judge can chat easily to those in the witness-box, a few feet to his right; to the jury, a few more feet beyond the witness-box, to counsel in the well of the court to his left, and to the prisoner in the dock in front of him. Because judge, witnesses, counsel and prisoner are all part of this tight concentric circle, they do not have to raise their voices much to hear one another. This is as things should be; a conversational tone of voice helps to keep down the temperature: but it does mean that the only non-participants who are assured of hearing and seeing all are people who have least need to, those sitting on the benches of the City Lands Committee, and those in the Public Gallery. The first, who are directly behind counsel and thus almost part of the inner circle, are the friends and relations of the city aldermen and senior members of the bar. Today, as on all days of the trial, they were mostly women; and they sported a variety of fetching, and less fetching, hats. Above them, slung beneath the arches of the ceiling in a sort of oaken container, were the seats of the Public Gallery. Here twenty-five assorted citizens, some of whom had been on the pavement all night (and looked it), had already gathered to watch the proceedings. There were two policemen to watch them. Below privilege, above democracy : thus by a few justice would be seen to be done.

But not by the Press (or, as Mr. Justice Marshall was later inevitably to call it, "the fourth estate"). Or heard either. It is true that a few were lucky enough to find seats in a small area on either side of the dock but the majority of journalists were placed on benches *behind* the dock. Now the dock in Court No. 1 is huge. It is the size of a small room. It is as big as it is in order to hold up to a dozen prisoners simultaneously (before shipping them off to Botany Bay, said Wayland Young) and it is as high as it is to prevent any prisoner from jumping out (if, as Mr. Griffith-Jones would put it, he be so minded). The result is that those on the top bench behind the dock can see the judge, the bobbing heads of counsel when they are standing up, and part of the jury : those on the bottom bench can see nothing but the back wall of the dock : and *nobody* can hear *anything* for certain. The solution to this grotesque situation would be to lower the dock several feet so that it is more on a level with the well of the court. But the occasions when there are a hundred journalists to cope with are so rare that I daresay it has never occurred to them.

One had heard so much, one had read so much, it was difficult to remember where or when one had first read or heard it. Profumo, Keeler, Rachman, Rice-Davies, Astor, Edgecombe, Gordon, Ward—they were like stopping places on a London bus. Other names too had been bandied about, those of peers and cabinet ministers lurking on the periphery. There had been tales of unspeakable orgies, of a sort of General Post of unbuttoning of trousers and lifting of skirts. Tremendous whipping parties were said to go on at a house in Mayfair; at one, I was told, a small grocer had had a heart attack and died. A certain senile delinquent was understood to derive exquisite pleasure from waiting on tarts with nothing on but a little gingham apron : another's private joy was believed to be urinating on a piece of plate glass which some supine whore held obligingly above her head. Still others were said to find difficulty in getting off the mark without the aid of manual, oral or electrical stimulation.

No one, it seemed, was interested in, or indeed capable of, doing or having it straight. The players were new but the play was as old as civilisation. Would we be hearing from some of these players, and if not from them, then about them? It had been said for some time that if the good doctor's ship was going to go down, he would make a point of taking all the first-class passengers with him. (As events turned out it was the first-class passengers who abandoned ship first, quicker even than the proverbial rats.) Rumour abounded, and none knew where fact began and fiction ended.

One thing, though, was certain and that was that the events leading to this trial were almost unique of their kind. In most criminal cases a crime is committed, the police are informed of it and then, working backwards from it, they seek to discover the criminal. But in this case police action had been stimulated not from below but from above. They had started their investigations not after but before they were aware that any crime had been committed. They did not seek to discover the criminal because there was no criminal to discover; and their efforts were directed to finding out not whether Dr. Ward had done it, but what Dr. Ward had done.

But now surmise was at an end, and we were, we believed, about to hear the truth for ourselves. We were here, judge and jury, learned counsel and solicitors, police, witnesses and a hundred journalists—to discover one thing and one thing only: whether Stephen Thomas Ward, the prisoner at the bar, as well as being a deviationist, which we knew, was also a criminal. Sooner or later and it would probably be sooner, some wigged figure would tell the jury to dismiss from their minds everything they had ever read about the case and concern themselves only with the facts and the law as it was presented to them. This is somewhat harder to do than it sounds. But it was something that we on the Press benches could share in too, for what the jury were about to hear, we would hear ourselves. And at the end of it all we could, as it were, compare notes and see whether or not our verdict tallied with theirs. None of us on that first day, I am sure, had any idea how disparate the results would be.

And now there was a stirring in court and we all struggled to our feet, and a door at one end of the judge's bench opened, and a tall sheriff and a lean alderman came in, followed by a tiny, tubby judge. He came billowing in like a small Dutch *schuyt* under a full spread of canvas, grey and black and scarlet, and he came to anchor just beyond the sword of justice, slightly left of centre. And when he had settled himself in and sniffed the air around him, he looked, I thought, like nothing so much as a keen determined mole, all set for a good day's burrowing, a mole moreover whose beady eye signified that he was not going to brook any nonsense from anybody. This was Sir Archie Pellow Marshall, sixty-four years old, Cornwall Congregationalist and non-Conformist Liberal, reared and nurtured in the great English Puritan tradition. On a recent visit to Washington he was reported to have said, "Christian virtues, abstinence, discipline, unselfishness, patience and humility are at a discount in England now". (Abstinence and discipline, I reflected, were not exactly Ward's strong points.) He had been President of the Cambridge Union and a Liberal candidate three times. Most of his career had been spent as a criminal lawyer on the Midlands Circuit. Some of his colleagues referred to him endearingly as the Hen: I was told of one occasion when he returned to counsel's bench after the lunch interval to find, sitting among his nest of papers, a single boiled egg.

And facing him now, alone in that vast dock which until a moment ago was quite empty, was the accused himself; a man also born in the Puritan tradition, the son of a parson, but who from an early age had abandoned tradition and shaped his own course. There was no mistaking the now familiar figure, the roué of fifty who looked thirty-five, perceptive eyes set in a face rather too full to carry them, boyish hair swept back along the sides of the head to meet at the back like the wings of a partridge. Ageing men who look half their years are often fairies; and one wondered whether within this screaming hetero, a homo was not struggling wildly to be let out. But this was an afterthought. He was dressed in a sober heather-mixture suit, and one's first and most striking impression was that he was a man of intelligence and dignity.

And so, for a moment, the Puritan and the Libertine faced each other; and as one's thoughts were dwelling on this, a man in a black gown suddenly shouted out, as though his life depended on it: "All persons who have anything to do before my Lady the Queen's Justices of Oyer and Terminer and General Gaol Delivery for the Jurisdiction of the Central Criminal Court draw near and give your attention God Save the Queen." A French woman journalist next to me said, "It is strange that so gallant an affair should begin by asking God to save the Queen". And so we were off.

There were some legal arguments to begin with. Mr. James Burge, Ward's counsel, wanted Count 3 to be put on a separate indictment. The reasons for this were obscure at the time (we did not then know what Count 3 referred to) but became apparent later. The judge refused the request. Mr. Mervyn Griffith-Jones, for the Crown, then made a submission about the suppression of certain witnesses' names. The judge said he felt rather concerned about suppressing witnesses' names, which was what we had all felt at the Magistrate's Court. "I think I might tell you now," he said, "that you will have to make the case for each witness for the suppression of a name." Good for the judge! No favours to the defence, none to the prosecution. It augured a fair trial.

Then the counts were read. There were five altogether (two concerning abortion had been placed on a separate indictment). The first three were concerned with living wholly or in part on the earnings of prostitution at various dates between June 1st, 1961, and June 8th, 1963; the fourth was inciting Christine Keeler to procure a girl under twenty-one to have intercourse with a third person, and the fifth was *attempting* to procure a girl under twenty-one to have intercourse with a third person. The details of all this would no doubt be spelt out in good time. To each charge Ward answered firmly and clearly, "Not Guilty", and in doing so explained a little of his enormous success with women; for not even those two prosaic words could disguise the charm and resonance of his voice.

"William Tukes."

"Edward Edgeson."

"Janet Chapman."

The assistant clerk of the court read out the names, and the rude mechanicals, the long and the short and the tall, filed down the court towards the jury-box. From the commanding height of the dock Ward looked down on them as they went by. He examined them keenly, for he and Mr. Burge had the right to reject up to seven of them without giving any reason. The contrast between Ward's face, in which concern and contempt were unconsciously mingled, and those of the eleven men and one woman who were going to judge him was remarkable. For a moment their roles were reversed: Ward was the judge, they were on trial. He assumed the part as if born to it: it was like watching a platoon commander inspecting his men before Sunday Church Parade. Surprisingly, he passed them all; even a little black-haired pixie of a man who was not only unable to read the oath but had the greatest difficulty in repeating it after the clerk. Perhaps Ward and his counsel felt that such an underdog would be more likely to identify himself with the hunted than the hunters.

The last juryman said that he would give a true verdict in the issue between the prisoner and his sovereign lady, the Queen, and then the judge said that the court would sit until 4.30 every day instead of the usual 4 p.m. He asked counsel how long they thought the trial would last, and Mr. Burge said that as the prosecution kept pulling things out of the bag like serving additional evidence on him that very morning, it was hard to say; probably the rest of the week. Was there, one wondered, something more than just academic curiosity in the judge's inquiry? The question died in the air, for Mr. Griffith-Jones was on his feet: "May it please your lordship..." The trial of Stephen Thomas Ward had begun.

Mr. Mervyn Griffith-Jones was educated at Eton and served in the Brigade of Guards. During the trial his dapper figure was often to be seen entering and leaving the building, wearing a neat double-breasted suit and bowler, and carrying a rolled umbrella. He is a good-looking man in a chiselled, square sort of way. Square is a word that suits him. He is so ultra orthodox that some aspects of modern life have escaped him altogether. The most famous example of this occurred during the *Lady Chatterley's Lover* trial when, as prosecuting counsel, he solemnly asked the jury whether it was a book they would wish their servants to read. It simply had not occurred to him that the members of the jury might not have servants; or, if they did, that they might have minds of their own. His colleagues find this sort of naïvety quite endearing. As an advocate he has a reputation for perseverance and ruthlessness. "If, during a trial, a relevant document suddenly turns up in the Shetland Islands," one of his contemporaries said to me, "Mervyn will send a police officer there by special aeroplane to fetch it."

Mr. Griffith-Jones's opening speech lasted an hour and a half, but reading it afterwards gives one no idea of what it sounded like at the time. It reads moderately sensibly, but it sounded totally unreal. Somehow or other Mr. Griffith-Jones managed to make everything seem so very much worse than it could have been. One realised that however badly Ward had behaved, it could hardly have been as badly as this. I was reminded of what Mr. Burge had said at the Magistrate's Court, that his learned friend would make even a honeymoon sound obscene. I did not doubt it. He gave the strong impression that he thought that sexual intercourse was shocking.

The outraged tone of voice in which he delivered his strictures did nothing to increase their appeal. He seemed to be assuming a part, not merely as the state prosecutor of public criminals but as the state guardian of private morals, to be acting as a sort of Establishment front man for an ethos which few people besides himself any longer believed in. Nor was he helped by a use of language which at times wandered perilously near to Wonderland. Instead of "although" he said "albeit", a word which I didn't think anyone wrote any more, let alone said. For "it doesn't matter" he said "it matters not"; for "with each other" he said "the one with the other"; for "if in a mind to" he said "if so minded". When he wanted to tell the jury that Christine Keeler left home to look for work and found it as a dancer at Murray's Club, he said : "She then left home in search of employment, and she obtained employment at a club called Murray's Club as an *artiste*." When he wanted to tell us that Mandy Rice-Davies had gone off with a young Persian he said that she "went to live with a Persian boy friend whose acquaintance she had made". He over-reached himself in describing how Ward had seen a pretty girl in a shop. "The defendant", he said, "*cast his eye* through the window of the shop." One had a mental picture of Ward letting his one glass eye fall into his hand, and then as it were hurling it through the shop window. It was this weird mixture of the colloquial with the archaic that at certain moments made Mr. Griffith-Jones, to us on the Press benches, seem so curious a figure. But how were the jury, new to court procedure and with the burden of responsibility heavy upon them, reacting to him? To them, were not these very small pebbles indeed, and would they even see them in the flowing tide?

The first three counts, said Mr. Grffiith-Jones, concerned living on the earnings of prostitution; of Christine Keeler at Wimpole Mews during a fifteen month period between June 1961 and August 1962; of Mandy Rice-Davies at Wimpole Mews during a four month period between September and December 1962; and of "two women certainly" (though he did not at this juncture name them) at Bryanston Mews during a five month period between January and the beginning of June 1963. The prosecution's case, said Mr. Griffith-Jones, was that these women were prostitutes, not street walkers admittedly, but women who sold their bodies for money none the less; and the law was that if the jury were satisfied that they were prostitutes and that Ward was living with them or habitually in their company or exercising influence over them in any way, then it was up to him to prove that he was not living on their immoral earnings, either wholly or in part. When I heard this I thought that Mr. Griffith-Jones was going to have an uphill job: even if he did satisfy the jury that the women were prostitutes rather than good-time girls, surely Ward, with his earnings from his osteopathy and drawings, would have little difficulty in proving that he was not living on immoral earnings. That very morning an exhibition of his drawings had opened at a Bloomsbury gallery, and prices were being asked up to five hundred guineas. But then Mr. Griffith-Jones had this to say: "Whatever the extent of his earnings for this period may have been, *from the evidence that you will hear and indeed from what he himself has told the police, they were quite obviously not sufficient for what he was spending.*" This was the crux of the matter, the beginning and end of the prosecution's case: if it could be shown that

Ward was living beyond his income from all regular sources, then from any common-sense point of view the case against him had been proved.

Miss Christine Keeler, said Mr. Griffith-Jones, had first met Ward at Murray's Club in 1958. He had invited her down to his cottage at Cliveden, which he had rent-free from Lord Astor, and "*he introduced Christine Keeler to one Peter Rachman*, of whom you have read in the newspapers". We had indeed: he was the horrible Pole who had made millions out of London slum property, and it was common knowledge that he had kept Mandy Rice-Davies in jewels and mink for a couple of years. Now Mr. Griffith-Jones was telling us that Rachman had lived with Christine Keeler too, "*shortly after the defendant had introduced her to him*". If this was so, if Ward did count Rachman among his friends and had so to speak passed Christine Keeler on to him, then that too would count heavily against him. But since this had happened in 1958, and the first count against Ward was not until June 1961, one wondered why Mr. Griffith-Jones was allowed to introduce it.

Christine Keeler went to live with Rachman in a flat at Bryanston Mews, the same flat, oddly enough, which Ward took some time after Rachman's death four years later and which figured in the third count of the indictment. In 1959 she left Rachman to go and live with Ward in a flat in Orme Court, but there was not then, said Mr. Griffith-Jones, nor at any other time, any suggestion that she and Ward had been to bed together. Christine went back to work at Murray's Club where she met Mandy Rice-Davies who was also working there. Mandy too was invited down to Cliveden and, unlike Christine, went to bed with Ward.

In 1960, said Mr. Griffith-Jones, the two girls went to live together in a flat in Comeragh Road. "There they were frequently visited by the defendant, *he bringing on a number of occasions his men friends to see them*. Indeed he paid for half the rent on one occasion with a cheque he had received from Lord Astor." Mr. Griffith-Jones hastily went on to say that there was no evidence as to why the cheque was paid to Ward and *it had nothing really to do with the case*. Well, if it had nothing to do with the case (and the date was still well outside that of the first count) why did he mention it? One was left in a dilemma, not knowing quite what to think and in the end thinking this : that if there was something fishy in Ward's payment of the rent with Lord Astor's cheque, then it should have figured in a separate count and we could all have heard evidence on it; but if there was nothing in it it should never have been mentioned. It was the fact that it did not figure in the indictment that was largely responsible for all the subsequent rumours that the prosecution were protecting the establishment.

But leaving Lord Astor aside, the fact that, in Mr. Griffith-Jones' words, "Ward was paying for the girls' accommodation and bringing men round to see them" was obviously another point to be chalked up against him. Would evidence be brought to substantiate the claim, or was this not considered necessary because the date was outside the dates of the indictment? And as with Lord Astor, if the claim was not going to be confirmed by evidence, what right had the prosecution to introduce it?

The last thing that happened before the girls left Comeragh Road, said Mr. Griffith-Jones, was that Ward proposed to Mandy that they should marry and then live on her immoral earnings (or, as he put it in his own weird language : "The general tenor of the suggestion was that he would not take it amiss if she went with men and thereby earned their keep"). This suggestion was so unlikely—even the defendant could not keep back a smile—that it was difficult to believe that it was presented seriously.

In about March 1961 the girls left Comeragh Road, Mandy to take up residence at Bryanston Mews as Rachman's mistress, and Christine to live with the Persian boy friend. In June of that year, the opening date of Count 1 of the indictment, Christine went to Wimpole Mews to live with Ward.

Mr. Griffith-Jones summed up what he regarded as Ward's criminal activities there by saying that Christine *"was being used by him not only to make a little money from intercourse she was having from time to time with men who visited the flat, but also to procure girls for his own satisfaction"*. The second of these two allegations obviously referred to Count 4 of the indictment, which was that he incited Christine Keeler to procure a girl under twenty-one to have intercourse with him between May and June 1961. I must here confess that in my naïvety I did not know (and other journalists I met did not know) that if a man asks a friend to introduce him to a girl over the age of consent but under twenty-one, and he subsequently has a romp with her, that constitutes a criminal offence. If this is the law it seems not only ludicrous but outrageous; at the time it was further confirmation of a growing suspicion among many of us that the prosecution were hoping that by bringing enough charges, however absurd they might be, some were bound to stick.

Just how absurd this procuring charge was we now learnt. "Keeler went off modelling," said Mr. Griffith-Jones, "*and you may think that the object of that was in order that she should meet pretty girls and bring them back for the defendant.*" Could the jury believe anything so far-fetched? Then Mr. Griffith-Jones described a real Alice in Wonderland incident concerning a girl called Sally Norie. Sally Norie and her boy friend, he said, were having lunch in a restaurant. Christine and Ward were also having a meal in the same restaurant. "The boy friend was acquainted," said Mr. Griffith-Jones, again jumbling up the colloquial and the formal, "with Ward." He went on: "The defendant cast his eye around" (Ward's eye at this period was working overtime) "telling Christine Keeler that the girl was attractive and said, 'Try and do something', or words to that effect." Christine persuaded the boy friend to take her home in order that Ward might make himself known to Sally Norie. The upshot was, said Mr. Griffith-Jones, that the girl was invited to Cliveden and Wimpole Mews and in due time "went to bed with the defendant". This was the happy end to the story that we had all been expecting, and I felt like giving a small cheer. But it seemed that Mr. Griffith-Jones had not finished the sentence, for he then added in the most sinister fashion, "... *and was introduced to other men*". Not to make up a four at tennis presumably. No, the implication was obvious: the introductions to other men were so that they could enjoy her body too, and Ward would reap some benefit as go-between. Presumably there would be evidence on that too.

By way of winding up the chapter on procuring, Mr. Griffith-Jones then related an equally dotty incident concerning Miss R. It was through Miss R's shop window that Ward had cast his eye, and liking what he saw, said Mr. Griffith-Jones, told Christine Keeler: "Go in and get her. Say it is your brother and he thinks he has met you before." This was the girl whom Mr. Griffith-Jones said was respectable and did not want to go to bed with anyone. She must have changed her mind because she did in fact go to bed with Ward. This was all that Mr. Griffith-Jones had to say on the subject—nothing about introducing her to other men—and one realised with a sort of numb shock that he was asking us to consider this a criminal offence. The rumours one had heard about the prosecution scraping the bottom of the barrel seemed to be coming true.

Mr. Griffith-Jones now turned to the men whom Christine had brought back to the flat for intercourse, Profumo, Ivanov and others, and he had these damaging things to say about Ward: "Certainly in the case of some of them she was paid money and in one case paid some £20. She has said that over a period, roughly speaking, *she must have paid to the defendant about half of what her earnings were from that particular exercise.*" Mr. Griffith-Jones went on, "Sometimes Ward would be hard up, short of cash, and he would tell the girl to telephone one of the gentlemen who was seeing her fairly regularly and who was paying her £20 a time. *He would ask her to ring one of them up and go round to see him, earn her money and then bring it back.* Sometimes the man would go to the flat and *Ward would be there throughout*, though not actually nearby. On another occasion he told her to go out and see Charles. *She did so and was in fact paid £50.* When she came back she paid some of that to Ward by way of repaying him money he had lent her". Finally, just before Christine left the flat in August or September 1962, there was the matter of the Indian doctor,[*] which was to prove such a persistent thorn in the side of the defence. "Ward told her that an Indian doctor wanted to rent her room to take a girl there and he suggested that she should be the girl. He said that the man only wanted to take the girl there, and that *it might be that if she were to see him he would pay the rent of her room.*" Here again the inference was obvious: "if she were to see him" really meant "if she were to go to bed with him". Christine however left the flat before any

---

[*] Dr Emil Savundra, who later was sentenced to eight years' imprisonment and fined £50,000 for offences connected with his Fire, Auto and Marine Insurance Company.

arrangements could be made, and almost immediately afterwards Mandy Rice-Davies who "for some reason had left Peter
Rachman" (they had in fact quarrelled) moved in.

We were now on to Count 2 of the indictment and the Indian
doctor was, so to speak, carried forward from Count 1. "Almost
as soon as she got there she was introduced to the Indian doctor.
She was told thereafter by the defendant that the doctor wanted
to rent her room—the same proposition—in order to bring girls
there. The defendant said that the doctor had already paid £25
—he was holding it in his hand—and asked Davies if she would
mind the doctor using the room. Davies said she didn't mind
because she was out most of the day and these visits were taking
place in the morning.

"The next morning the Indian doctor called. Davies was there
and gave him coffee and they had a nice little chat and after the
Indian doctor had gone—nothing improper taking place—the
defendant came back. He asked about the Indian doctor and
said something like, 'Why let outsiders in? *Why don't you be the
person who goes to bed with him?*' Davies agreed.

"Thereafter on a number of occasions the Indian doctor visited
Miss Davies, leaving between £15 and £25 each time on the
dressing table, *out of which she said she paid Ward some £2 or
£3 a time. That was exclusive of the rent the doctor was paying
to Ward for the facilities.*"

Apart from another man who, said Mr. Griffith-Jones, was
also visiting the flat to have intercourse with Mandy, often when
Ward was there, that was the only evidence against Ward on
Count 2; for on December 14th one of Christine Keeler's West
Indian lovers, by the name of Edgecombe, turned up at Wim-
pole Mews while she was there and started shooting. As a result
Ward gave up the Wimpole Mews flat, and he and Mandy went
off to separate flats of their own.

Some time early in the New Year Ward moved into the flat
in Bryanston Mews where Mandy had lived with Rachman and
which had become vacant after Rachman's death at the end of
November. This brought us to Count 5 and to easily the dottiest
of all the prosecution's stories. "It happened," said Mr. Griffith-
Jones, "that in this flat there had been installed by Rachman
what is known as a two-way mirror." Anxious lest we found him

too familiar with the wilder shores of sex, Mr. Griffith-Jones said, "Precisely how it works I'm not sure"; and then showed that he knew how it worked by saying : "There was an aperture in the sitting room through which one could look into the bedroom; no one in the bedroom knew they were being watched." Mr. Griffith-Jones then made a splendid effort to disassociate himself from the mirror altogether. "This was useful, I suppose," he said, "for any man so minded", a statement which could mean almost anything or nothing. Mandy, said Mr. Griffith-Jones, had broken the mirror while she was there, but when Ward moved in "*it was proposed to have it put in order again*".

On December 15th Ward went to a party given by "a very respectable lady who had been one of his patients" and there he met her companion, Miss X, aged eighteen. "*Immediately afterwards,*" said Mr. Griffith-Jones, "he got in touch with her and asked her to go to his flat at Bryanston Mews." There seemed to be some contradiction here, for a moment earlier Mr. Griffith-Jones had said that Ward did not move into Bryanston Mews until January, but nobody commented on it. This appointment did not take place, but Ward did call on her early in January, presumably at the flat of her companion, the highly respectable lady. While we were imagining Ward among the tea-cups and buttered scones Mr. Griffith-Jones said this : "Ward said to Miss X that he had a new flat. He told her the flat had a two-way mirror through which you could see from the lounge into the bedroom, and he said he thought he could make a little money there from people who would pay to watch through the two-way mirror people performing on the bed." I had a vision here of Miss X dropping both tea-cup and scone, and saying quietly, "I *beg* your pardon" ! What she did say, according to Mr. Griffith-Jones, was that she was not the least interested in watching anything like that (as well she might), whereupon Ward said (slapping his thigh, no doubt), "I don't want you to *watch*, I want you to *perform* !" There was a sort of Mack Sennett touch to this whole dream-like episode; it was a conversation which had the same air of total implausibility as that between Mellors and Lady Chatterley's father (and which Mr. Griffith-Jones himself was only too familiar with). Who knows, perhaps Ward did mention a two-way mirror to Miss X; but not at this time, in this place, in this way. Totally unaware of the impression he was making, Mr. Griffith-Jones pushed on. "This is not a case of a boy trying to take up a girl perhaps hoping to go to bed with her. *You may think there are matters far more sinister.*" Happily none of us, not even the jury, thought anything of the kind.

Mr. Griffith-Jones had now almost completed his opening speech, and as the clock beneath the public gallery showed twenty past twelve, the thoughts of most of us began turning towards lunch. So far the prosecution had not produced any surprises. Nothing had happened to alter radically the picture of Ward which recent events, including the proceedings at the lower court, had already shaped for us; which was that of a libertine but not a criminal. Certainly Mr. Griffith-Jones had made some damaging statements about Ward which he would no doubt be having confirmed from the witness-box. But obviously much here would depend on the credibility of the witnesses, and if Christine and Mandy were to be the Crown's principal witnesses, as they were at the lower court, then their word would not necessarily carry much greater weight than that of the defendant. The case, at this moment, seemed very open.

Open, that is at twenty past twelve, and ten minutes later shut. For we had not reckoned with Count 3, which we had almost forgotten, but which Mr. Griffith-Jones had been saving until this moment and was now ready to produce, as it were, from his hat. "Lastly, members of the jury," he said, in the flat drawl with which he usually spoke and which gave no hint at all of what was to come, "we have the evidence on living on the earnings of prostitution at Bryanston Mews for the last period from January to June 1963."

"There are two persons involved," said Mr. Griffith-Jones. "Neither Keeler nor Davies were there. They seem to have dropped out of the picture but there are two more who enter— one a Miss Ricardo and another Miss Vickie Barrett." Ricardo we knew about: she had given evidence against Ward at the lower court but was since said to have retracted this in a further statement. But Vickie Barrett was a name we were then hearing for the first time.

"Vickie Barrett," said Mr. Griffith-Jones, "was picked up by

Ward on a night in January 1963. She was walking in Oxford Street. Ward, driving a white Jaguar, pulled up by the kerbside and asked her if she would like to go to a party."

One was suddenly aware that everyone in court was listening much more keenly.

"Miss Barrett got into the car and was driven to Bryanston Mews. She was told that he would get her clients and look after her interests, take the money for her and keep it for her so she would then save a little and be able to buy new clothes and a more luxurious apartment, and therefore charge higher fees."

The rustling and coughing which is always present in court had died away now altogether. People were leaning forward so as not to miss a word.

"On that occasion when they got back to the flat no one was there. There was no party and the defendant told her that there was a man already in the bedroom. He gave her a contraceptive and sent her into the bedroom where she had intercourse with the man."

Not a sound anywhere now. Everything quite, quite still.

"Afterwards they came out and the defendant was still there. The defendant gave them coffee and when she asked for payment, said he would save the money for her. He took her back to Oxford Street and arranged to meet her two days later at the tube station there."

Now one was asking oneself, *could* it be possible? *This?*

"Ward again brought her back and the same procedure happened. A man was already waiting in bed for her. Thereafter for the next two and a half months, according to the girl some two or three times a week, the same thing would happen. That is, in ordinary language, just brothel keeping. Finally the girl left, but she never received a penny of the money which she had earned and which had been paid to the defendant for him to save for her."

Mr. Griffith-Jones was droning on now about the police, but no one was listening to him. For what he had just said had added, as it were, a wholly new dimension to the case, had altogether changed its colour and texture.

There were many roles in which one had visualised Ward; as a successful osteopath and socialite, as a lover of low life and low company, as an amateur artist, but never in one's most imaginative moments had one seen him as this, a straightforward professional ponce. He had a reputation for meanness certainly, but this was meanness of a different order. Even now it was almost impossible to believe : it was the odd jigsaw piece that refused to fit : apart from anything else, one would have thought that for such an imaginative man, this was a role that would have unutterably bored him. And yet it was true. It was true because Mr. Griffith-Jones had said it was true, and he would not dare to say a thing like this unless he had powerful evidence to support it. And because it was true it existed not only as a thing in itself but as something which coloured the whole case.

For if this was true, then anything was true. Not Counts 4 and 5 of course for they were too patently absurd to consider. But the prosecution could well be right about Counts 1 and 2. Indeed it now seemed that they probably were right. In admitting this to myself I felt that my reluctance to accept Ward's guilt over Counts 1 and 2 had been mere wishful thinking; and I was depressed at my own lack of judgement, at the inability to distinguish between the true and the false.

One thing was certain; that from this moment the trial had taken on a different hue, that nothing in it would ever be quite the same again. Even the defendant seemed to have changed. Before he had appeared as a man for whom one could feel some sympathy : such is the power of persuasion that now, even as one looked at him, he seemed to change colour, to become an object of contempt. One was annoyed with him, less perhaps for what he had done than for changing the image one had had of him.

Mr. Griffith-Jones had finished talking about the police and what Ward had said to them, and at five minutes past one he sat down. For an hour and a half he had had the privilege of so blackening the defendant that, before a word of evidence had been heard, there seemed no longer any doubts about his guilt. Would it not serve the interests not only of the defendant but of justice much better if, after the indictment had been read, prosecuting counsel were to confine himself to a simple statement of background facts? Then let the witnesses be called and the jury hear, freshly and for the first time, details of the allegations against him.

As it was, when Mr. Griffith-Jones sat down that Monday lunch-time, Ward was already half condemned.

"Miss Christine Keeler," called the usher, and one heard the cry echoing in the hall outside. There was, among Press, public and bar alike, a sense of keen and pleasurable anticipation. For this was the nymph who had started it all: nearly everything we had read and heard about the affair could in the last analysis be traced back to her. Was it more than coincidence that so many of the people she had been in contact with had come to ruin? It was because of her, indirectly, that the two West Indians Edgecombe and Gordon had gone to prison; that the Russian naval attaché Ivanov had been banished to some dismal post in Siberia; that the British War Minister, Profumo, had had to resign and the Government itself been on the point of toppling; that Ward was now in the dock. Without her we would not have heard about Lord Astor and his friends, Peter Rachman and his slums, Mariella and her parties, Ivanov, Lord Normanbrook and M.I.5. One way and another she was responsible for quite a lot. The photographs of her which had filled the newspapers during the past few weeks showed her to be uncommonly attractive, and on her own admission she had a prodigious sexual appetite. The anticipation was understandable.

She came into court wearing an odd sort of mustard coloured cloak, shaped like a small tent, which reached to within a few inches of her skirt, which was made of the same material. It was the sort of dress that aims at being chic and looks rather vulgar. This was the first thing I noticed. The second was how small she was. In her photographs she had seemed quite tall, but in effect, and despite the tarty high-heeled shoes, she was tiny, a real little doll of a girl, and here of course was half the attraction. She walked superbly on long slender legs, her carriage was remarkable; one was struck too by the mass of copper hair that reached to her shoulders and framed within it, the small oval face with the high cheekbones and hint of Red Indian blood. She was in short like an animal, and one could see at once her appeal to the animal instincts of men.

But that was all; and even that was not for long. For two things happened to dispel any illusions. The first was a close-up view of her. While she was walking to the witness-box and even while she was in it, I could not see her features properly. But when she walked out at the lunch interval a quarter of an hour later, she passed within a foot of me. It was a terrifying little face, vacant yet knowing, and it belonged not to a girl of twenty-one but to an already ageing woman. The eyes were dead, like those of fish on a slab : the face itself was painted an inch thick, but round the chin one could detect the lunar blemishes, the ravages of the years. What would she look like at thirty?

And then there was her voice, which in itself was enough to kill any romantic notions that anyone might have of her. For it was not just that it was the voice of any little shop girl, lacking style and distinction, but that she—or perhaps Dr. Ward—had tried to do something with it, to lift it out of the rut. The result —when one could hear it, which was seldom—was both bizarre and pathetic. It was perhaps unfortunate for her that almost the first words we heard her utter—in reply to a question about her early life—was that she had lived at Staines until she had gone to Slough : there are perhaps no two towns in Britain less happily named.

This attempt at improvement also showed in certain gestures she made when speaking. When in a tight corner or embarrassed, she would shrug her shoulders uneasily and rotate her right hand, movements aimed at conveying a sense of poise and composure but which merely revealed how unsophisticated she really was : indeed in the crass mistiming of her gestures she was only ever equalled, in my experience, by Sir Anthony Eden. Occasionally, out of nervousness, she would turn her head to one side, raise her hand to her mouth, and give a little genteel cough. For here she was in an alien world, where her charms meant nothing. She might have had her little moment in the street, with the jealous women booing and the randy men pressing their faces against the window of her taxi and the photographers asking her to pull the edge of her skirt a little higher still, but here the air was clinical, the women detached and superior, the men immune. Even Mr. Griffith-Jones who was, so to speak, on the same side as herself, clearly made her ill at ease. Probably no man had ever spoken to her before with such lofty detachment, and she had no idea how to cope with it. Sometimes she made a feeble attempt at a joke, hoping to strike some spark of warmth and recognition from Mr. Griffith-Jones's flinty exterior. She would have been wiser not to have attempted it: the jokes died on the wind: Mr. Griffith-Jones was not amused.

Christine Keeler was in the witness-box for only a quarter of an hour before lunch, but it was a revealing quarter of an hour. The first question of any importance concerned Rachman. It will be remembered that in his opening speech Mr. Griffith-Jones had said that Ward had "*introduced Christine Keeler to one Peter Rachman*", and this was undeniably one of the most damaging charges he had made against him. We all knew Rachman as an evil man, an exploiter of other people's misery for his own gain. It was difficult to think of anything that he and Ward might have in common except an interest in sex. If therefore Ward knew him, and if he had introduced Keeler to him, as Mr. Griffith-Jones had said he did, then the prosecution were already half-way towards proving their case. But now, astonishingly, Mr. Griffith-Jones did not ask Christine a single question about how she had met Rachman. All he said was: "After you had met the defendant, did you meet a Peter Rachman?" Not a word about Ward introducing her, but a sort of deft suggestion that there was nevertheless some connection between the two: a difference of emphasis which the jury, with minds not trained to spot such refinements, very probably would not notice. I had a feeling, the first of many, that Mr. Griffith-Jones was batting in a different league to the rest of us.

After Mr. Griffith-Jones had established that Christine had gone to live at Rachman's flat in Bryanston Mews, where he visited her frequently for purposes of copulation, the judge made the first of many incisive interruptions, most of which were short-cuts to the truth. "Were you paid anything by way of money or presents by Rachman?" he asked, a question clearly aimed at seeking to establish whether or not Christine was a prostitute. "Yes," she said, "he kept me." Although she had answered the question unequivocally enough, it was not good enough for the judge who said somewhat testily, "Will you answer the question?

Did Rachman give you money?" She said that he had. The judge then said to Mr. Griffith-Jones: "There comes a stage when I ought to warn this witness, but I do not think that stage is yet reached." With this completely mystifying remark, the court rose for lunch.

Over the beer and brawn at the pub the Christine Keeler stories were going the rounds.

Q. "What newspapers does Christine Keeler take?"

A. "One *Mail*, two *Mirrors*, three *Observers*, a *New Statesman* every week and any number of *Times*."

The rude mechanicals filed in by one door, the tall sheriff, the lean alderman and the tubby judge by another, the defendant popped up from the cells like a Jack in the Box, and Miss Keeler returned to the witness-box. She had left the tent half of her mustard coloured dress behind, revealing bare arms and a minuscule waist. She looked like a tiny tarnished wasp.

Mr. Griffith-Jones rose to his feet. To obtain a conviction against Ward he had to prove three things; firstly that Ward was providing Christine (and on Count 2 Mandy Rice-Davies) with what the law called "goods and services" for carrying out the trade of prostitution; secondly, that the two girls were in fact prostitutes; and thirdly, and perhaps most important of all, obtain independent corroboration of their evidence from another witness or witnesses. This last stipulation was written into the Sexual Offences Act because where sexual offences are concerned women, for a variety of reasons (including malice) are often disposed to lay false charges against men. This proviso should have been the sheet anchor of Ward's defence, but as the trial progressed it became increasingly forgotten. If the jury were satisfied that the girls were prostitutes and that Ward was providing them with goods and services, then the burden shifted on to him to prove that he was not living on immoral earnings. All in all Mr. Griffith-Jones had a long road to travel.

He did not start off very auspiciously. He had, during his opening speech, it will be remembered, said that while the two girls were living at Comeragh Road, *"Ward was paying for the girls' accommodation and bringing men round to see them"*, about as definite a way as one could imagine of saying that Ward was their ponce. But when he came to examine Christine on this there emerged a very different picture.

"Did you and Miss Davies go together to a flat in Comeragh Road, West Kensington?"

"Yes."

"Was that your idea or hers?"

"I think it was by mutual agreement."

"Did the defendant visit you there frequently?"

"Yes."

After Christine had said that she and Mandy had paid some of the rent and Lord Astor the rest, Mr. Griffith-Jones asked: "While you were there, were you introduced to other people by the defendant?"

"Yes, a few of his friends."

"Did you have sexual intercourse with any of those persons while you were there?"

"I can't really remember." Was this hedging, a sudden desire not to incriminate? It didn't sound like it. After all, this girl had been a sort of bin for the world's refuse: Russians, West Indians, politicians, peers, all had been grist to her mill. Why should she remember where and when she had done it with this man or that? But the judge thought she was hedging.

"Well, think, Miss Keeler."

She thought in vain.

"I can't remember."

One believed her. It made sense.

Mr. Griffith-Jones plugged on. "People he introduced to you?"

She thought again. Of all the people one has met in one's life, of how many can one say who introduced them to one, and when? This was two years ago: how many dozens of affairs had she had since?

"Maybe a couple," she said, trying to be helpful.

"Were you paid for it?"

Whatever answer Mr. Griffith-Jones was expecting could not have been the one that she gave.

"No," she said.

So another of Mr. Griffith-Jones' earlier allegations against

Ward had crumbled into dust. But he was not going to give in easily.

"Did you," he asked, "receive money from *anybody* while you were living at Comeragh Road?"

"I think," said Miss Keeler, "that I met Mr. Eylan."

"Were you receiving money from him at that time?"

"Yes."

"And having intercourse with him?"

"Yes."

Mr. Griffith-Jones reached for the $64,000 question. "Who," he asked, "introduced him to you?"

We all waited for the words "Stephen Ward" to form on her lips.

"I met him myself," she said.

It was soon after this that Mr. Griffith-Jones departed from his prepared script. Miss Keeler had said that after leaving Comeragh Road she had gone to live with a Persian boy friend and she was "also receiving money from another man". But before that she had gone abroad.

"And who paid for the trip abroad?"

There was a slight pause.

"I really can't remember."

This was odd. One may not remember who has introduced one to whom, but one surely remembers who has paid for one's trips abroad. But this whole story of Miss Keeler's going abroad was something we were hearing for the first time: Mr. Griffith-Jones had made no mention of it in his opening speech. Mr. Burge rose to his feet.

"The defence," said Mr. Burge, more in sorrow than in anger (and Mr. Burge's dislike of anger can hardly be said to have helped the defence), "is entitled to know what the case is going to be. Every single stage of this trial has been simply and solely to give indulgence to the prosecution and retard the actions of the defence. There is not a word in the evidence about going abroad. There is no suggestion and no notification that this is relevant to the trial of the accused. And now we have the leading question, 'Did you go abroad and who paid for it?'"

The judge looked at Mr. Burge whom he knew. "Mr.—" he said, and then after a long pause and on a lower note,

"Burge." It was an odd thing to do and he did it several times during the trial. "It is rare that a witness entirely follows in every detail and no more the deposition or statement, and here the prosecution are seeking to get all this girl's life at this particular time which is vital on the issue whether in fact in this case this witness should be regarded as a prostitute."

But was it vital, and, more important, was it just? For we were still just outside the period covered by the indictment. Was it not a cardinal principle of English law that past misdemeanours were never introduced to prejudice present proceedings. Even if Christine Keeler was proved to be a prostitute at this time, did that mean she was to be considered a prostitute for ever? It seemed that she herself had something to say on the subject. "I would like to say," she said, "that I am not a prostitute and never have been." This was too much for the judge, who said rather sharply: "We'll come to that in a moment." This obsession of Christine Keeler's to be well thought of, her concern with what she called later "my reputation", was one of the more pathetic things about her. Nor did it make the task of Mr. Griffith-Jones, whose whole case rested on proving her a prostitute, any easier.

And so by way of Comeragh Road we came to Wimpole Mews, and at long last to the period of the first count on the indictment. She had, Miss Keeler agreed, given Ward some money towards the rent of her room, but not regularly. Where was she getting money from? Well, some had come from the man who had financed her trip abroad. She had miraculously remembered who he was now, for in answer to a further question she said she had not had intercourse with him.

"Did you," asked Mr. Griffith-Jones, "receive money from anyone else to pay for the rent of the room?"

It was a cleverly worded question, for it assumed that whatever other monies Christine had received had gone automatically towards the rent of the room, when in fact there must have been other demands on her purse such as food, clothes and cosmetics. So that when Christine answered the question by saying, "Mr. Eylan", it must have seemed to the jury that here was clear evidence of Ward living on her immoral earnings. Yet they were hearing only a part of the story. What other monies had she received? She had just told us herself that she had had a loan from a man with whom she had *not* had intercourse. What other similar loans had she had? What was she getting from the modelling that Mr. Griffith-Jones had mentioned earlier? What had Ward himself lent her? And how could Mr. Griffith-Jones be so definite about the money from Mr. Eylan going towards the rent? Could not one equally logically suggest that the money from modelling was going towards the rent, and that from Mr. Eylan towards clothes and food?

In answer to further questions about Mr. Eylan, Christine said that he had only visited her about half a dozen times and that Ward was never in the flat when she had intercourse with him, although he did know when he was coming. She did not say and was not asked whether she had told Ward that Eylan was paying her. In his opening speech Mr. Griffith-Jones had said : *"Ward would sometimes be hard up, short of cash, and he would tell the girl to telephone one of the gentlemen who was seeing her fairly regularly and was paying her £20 a time."* Now the only gentleman who was paying her this sort of money was Mr. Eylan, and in order to substantiate what he had said, Mr. Griffith-Jones now asked Christine : "Did Dr. Ward ever say anything to you about going to Mr. Eylan?" Again he could hardly have been prepared for her answer.

"No."

So Dr. Ward had nothing to do with Christine's arrangements with Eylan, and yet another of the prosecution's contentions about him had crumbled.

Mr. Griffith-Jones now turned to other men with whom Christine had associated, for in his opening speech he had made two other very damaging statements about Ward that needed confirming. One was that Ward used to tell Christine to ring up one of the men she was seeing regularly, *"earn her money and then bring it back"*. The other was that when men came to the flat, *"Ward would be there throughout, though not actually nearby"*. This last remark was an odd assertion in view of Ward never being in the flat when Eylan called, but no doubt evidence would now be brought to substantiate it.

Mr. Griffith-Jones first turned to Profumo, the Old Warrior himself. In one way he was responsible for all of us being there :

yet already he was far from the stage, heading back fast towards obscurity. She had had intercourse with him at the flat, said Miss Keeler, and on one occasion he had given her some money for her mother. She had also had intercourse once with the Russian, Ivanov.

"Did he give you anything?"

"No."

"Was that at the flat?"

"Yes, it was."

"Was the defendant in the flat at the time?"

"No, he wasn't."

Having made no sort of headway at all with either Profumo or Ivanov, Mr. Griffith-Jones now turned to the man called Charles; and here he had better luck.

Ward, said Miss Keeler, had introduced her to Charles. She had had intercourse with him and on one occasion he had given her £50.

"How did you come to have intercourse with Charles?"

"Dr. Ward suggested if I went to him he would give me money."

This was the plainest, most direct evidence we had yet had that Christine was a prostitute and Ward was aiding and abetting her. As yet, however, it was uncorroborated.

"Up to that time had you had intercourse with this man?"

"No."

"Was anything suggested as to how you should get in touch with this man for that purpose?"

"I can't remember."

"You'd been introduced to him, and a few days later, when you were hard up, Dr. Ward suggested that you should get in touch with him?"

"He said the man would give me money."

When she said this, Miss Keeler made a curious pseudo-sophisticated gesture, which I had noticed before, of straightening her hands and holding them palm downwards an inch or two above the edge of the witness-box.

"Who made the appointment for you to go and see him?" said Mr. Griffith-Jones, now, I thought, pressing his luck rather too far.

"I really don't remember."

"After intercourse and after you had received the £50, did you speak to Ward about it?"

"I can't remember."

"What did you do with the £50?"

This obviously was the *coup de grace* : the inevitable answer was that she had given it, or part of it, to Ward. But the actual wording of her reply was most interesting. "*I repaid a loan* with some of it to Dr. Ward," she said; and suddenly the whole episode of the man Charles took on a much less sinister complexion. This was the first time we had heard about Ward giving her loans and it was not the last. A few moments later, having finished with the man Charles, Mr. Griffith-Jones said : "Did you give any of the money you had from these men to the defendant?"

"Well, yes," said Miss Keeler, "*to pay my debts.*"

"Did you have intercourse with other men while you were living at Wimpole Mews?"

"No," said Miss Keeler, "I don't think so."

"Can you tell the jury," said Mr. Griffith-Jones, "roughly speaking, what proportion of the money you received from men you gave to the defendant while you were at Wimpole Mews?"

We all knew from Mr. Griffith-Jones' opening speech what answer he was expecting : one half. Christine Keeler's reply must have been like a thunderbolt.

"Well, *I usually owed him more than I ever made* : I only gave him half of *that.*"

Here was evidence, and from the mouth of one of the prosecution's principal witnesses that far from Ward living on Christine's immoral earnings, she, in fact, was living on him : and she had said it not once but three times. Mr. Griffith-Jones' case seemed to be coming to pieces in his hands. Furthermore, he had failed to substantiate the allegation in his opening speech that Ward used to tell Christine to ring up one of the men she was seeing regularly "earn her money, and then bring it back". As for his assertion that when men came to the flat, "Ward would be there throughout, though not actually nearby", we had not heard a single word about it.

Mr. Griffith-Jones now turned to the question of the Indian

doctor. Some time before she left the flat, said Miss Keeler, Dr. Ward had told her that he had let her room to an Indian doctor, but that would not stop her living in it.

"Was the suggestion that you should go back there with the doctor?"

"Yes. I was to see the doctor."

"Does that mean to have sexual intercourse with the doctor?"

"Yes."

"Did he say what the doctor would pay, if anything, for this?"

"No," said Miss Keeler, "but I thought the doctor was to pay rent for the room and give me some money as well."

As with the man Charles, this piece of evidence, if true, was another clear indication of Ward acting as a ponce. As also with Charles it was as yet uncorroborated. But what immediately diminished its value as evidence was Christine suddenly volunteering the information, that she had never had intercourse with the doctor: so that as far as he was concerned Ward could in no way be said to be living on Christine's immoral earnings.

It was soon after this that Christine said the first of three things which, for the first time, gave one reason to doubt her truthfulness as a witness. It will be remembered that after Mr. Griffith-Jones had questioned her about Profumo, Ivanov and Charles (put like that, they sound like a vaudeville act), he asked: "Did you have intercourse with other men while you were living at Wimpole Mews?"; and she had replied, "No, I don't think so". Admittedly, this was not a categorical denial, but if she was uncertain about it, she could have answered, as she had to so many questions, that she couldn't remember. Now she told Mr. Griffith-Jones that she sometimes used to take a boy friend back *and he would stay the night*. A little later she admitted to what she had earlier denied, having intercourse with the man who had paid for her to go abroad. Finally, she agreed that "while coming and going at Wimpole Mews" she had intercourse with the West Indian Edgecombe. Had she forgotten all of that? It hardly seemed possible.

Lastly Mr. Griffith-Jones turned to another matter.

"Did you," he said to Christine, "ever introduce girls to Dr. Ward?"

"Yes," she said, "I did."

The judge, who was mole-sharp and never missed a trick, looked at Mr. Griffith-Jones and said : "This is the stage." They were up to their mysterious legal games again, like before lunch. The judge then turned to Christine Keeler and said : "On this matter that counsel is now beginning to question you, you are not obliged to answer any question that might tend to incriminate you."

But Miss Keeler had a much clearer idea of what was going on than some of the rest of us. Perhaps she had been forewarned.

"I already answered," she said, "at the preliminary hearing."

The judge then turned to the jury and said that the prosecution had already given Miss Keeler an undertaking not to take action against her, but this did not absolve him from giving the warning. This caused Mr. Griffith-Jones to rise to his feet and say the prosecution had not given any such undertaking. "But," he added magnanimously, "I give the undertaking now."

The meaning of these weird rites slowly dawned on me. In law Miss Keeler had been an accessory to Ward's wicked actions in getting Miss R and Sally Norie to go to bed with him; and now the prosecution was solemnly telling her that they were prepared to overlook, for the sake of the bigger fish in the dock, her own crooked role in the proceedings. Now, just because these two girls were under twenty-one, were we to consider Ward and Miss Keeler as two conspiring criminals? It seemed so.

Mr. Griffith-Jones plunged into his unenviable task with enthusiasm and energy.

"You are telling us that it became the understood thing that you find girls for him?"

According to my notes Miss Keeler had not told us this, but who was she to deny it?

"Yes."

"When you got girls for him, what happened between you and the girls, what did you understand was the idea of getting the girls?"

"He used to impress them in some way and they would fall for him."

"What would be the result?"

"I presume they made love."

"Did he ever tell you they made love?"

"Sometimes."

Between them Mr. Griffith-Jones and Miss Keeler had created a picture of a whole regiment of girls marching endlessly through Wimpole Mews, and every now and then Ward saying to Keeler, like a man choosing *hors d'oeuvres* from a tray, that he would like this one but not that. And what did it all boil down to but Miss R in the shop into which Ward had cast his eye, and little Sally Norie in the Brush and Palette restaurant?

"While you were living at Wimpole Mews, did you start modelling?"

"Yes."

"Did you in fact meet girls modelling and bring them back?"

"On a few occasions, yes."

That was all Mr. Griffith-Jones said about the modelling, although in his opening speech he had suggested *that the real object of Christine taking up modelling was to bring back pretty girls for Ward*. If these girls existed anywhere outside Miss Keeler's imagination, and if their stories had any relevance to the charges against Ward, then why were they not mentioned by name, and why were they not called in evidence?

And so, as the long afternoon wore on, Miss Keeler told us, with infinite tedium how she had helped to winkle Miss R out of her shop and spirit Sally Norie's boy friend away from the restaurant. And soon after she had done that, Mr. Griffith-Jones sat down.

It was now the turn of Ward's defence counsel, Mr. James Burge. Mr. James Burge was not a Q.C., as might have been expected in a case of this importance, and I understood that that was because Ward had been so pleased with his handling of the case at the Magistrate's Court that he had decided to retain him for the trial. On the other hand Mr. Burge was of the same seniority as many Q.C.s and considered to be the leading junior criminal counsel at the Bar. He was a jovial, sunshiney, Pickwickian sort of a man, who always seemed to be smiling. It was not entirely coincidence, I thought, that some of his practice was devoted to licensing cases. Beer and Burgundy seemed to blend with his beaming face.

In short, Mr. Burge was a very nice man; indeed, as the trial
went on, I began to think that alongside Mr. Griffith-Jones, he
was almost *too* nice a man. He was a civilised being, a person of
wit and humour. I had been told by one of his colleagues that
he was one of the few men at the Bar who could laugh a case
out of court. The atmosphere here, as I think he realised, was
not conducive to this sort of approach, but I was told he had
tried it once or twice at the Magistrate's Court with some success. In addition to his quip about Mr. Griffith-Jones making a
honeymoon sound obscene, he had also said that he had no
objection to some of Mr Griffith-Jones's leading questions, as
they were not leading very far. Mr. Griffith-Jones himself would
have been incapable of either of these two remarks. But equally
Mr. Burge could not match Mr. Griffith-Jones's cold relentless
plodding, his battering away at the walls until, by sheer persistence, they began to crack. It was this, in the last analysis, that
made one admire Mr. Griffith-Jones as much as one deplored
him. Because his own attitude to the case was committed, one
became committed in one's attitude towards him. It was this out-
ward lack of commitment, not in matter but in manner, that at
times led one to feel that Mr. Burge was doing himself literally
less than justice. They say that the days of the committed lawyer
are over : yet one would have liked to see Ward's defence accompanied by some passion, with his counsel as contemptuous of the
charges laid against him as the prosecution were contemptuous
of Ward himself. As it was, while I had no doubts which of the
two counsel was the more intelligent, urbane and congenial,
equally I had no doubts, where the jury was concerned, which
was the more effective advocate.

To be fair to Mr. Burge he was labouring under certain
handicaps. The first was that the judge did not appear—I do
not say he wasn't—as sympathetic to the presentation of the case
for the defence as he was to the case for the prosecution. His odd
little trick, when addressing Mr. Burge, of allowing a noticeable
pause between "Mr." and "Burge" has already been noted.
There were other instances, and they increased as the trial went
on, when various remarks he made and the moment at which
he made them had the effect of taking the edge off what Mr.

Burge was saying. He did not do this, or he did not do it so often, with Mr. Griffith-Jones.

Mr. Burge's other great handicap was his inability to hear much of what the witnesses were saying. Miss Christine Keeler was only the first of many female witnesses who gave their evidence in a whisper. Again and again Mr. Burge found himself saying: "You went where?"—"What do you say he was doing?" —"You said what?" Often he repeated the witnesses' answers so as to be sure that he had heard right: often he heard wrong, so that the witnesses had to repeat themselves. But sometimes, while they were drawing breath to repeat themselves, the judge, who was halfway between Mr. Burge and the witness-box, saved them the trouble by relaying their answers for them. He did this, I thought, in a most unfortunate manner, raising his voice and enunciating each syllable, as though talking to a backward child. Psychologically, all of this combined to put Mr. Burge at a slight disadvantage. Nor was he helped by Ward's blow-by-blow comments on the trial which came tumbling over the dock wall in a seemingly endless stream of little pieces of paper.

Mr. Burge's object with Christine Keeler was to show that she was less a prostitute than what the Americans call a "party girl". Here he found himself in the odd position for a counsel of cross-examining a witness who was only too happy to agree with him; and his task in this respect was as easy as Mr. Griffith-Jones' had been difficult.

"You know the prosecution are endeavouring to prove that Ward had been living on the earnings of prostitution?"

"Yes, I do."

"When you were living at 17 Wimpole Mews, is it right to say you were frequently hard up for money?"

"Yes."

"And Ward gave you spending money?"

"Yes."

"It is quite obvious to anyone who has seen you, if you wished to earn money by selling your body you could have made very large sums of money?"

"Yes." Miss Keeler looked suitably flattered. Mr. Burge repeated "Yes" after her, and glanced round the court almost as if to say, "There, you see! This girl isn't a tart at all". This little trick of echoing the favourable reply of a prosecution witness was one that Mr. Burge practised often. To me it sounded somewhat naïve, but it may well have impressed the jury.

"But whilst living with him it was obvious to everybody that you were *not* making large sums of money?"

"Yes, that's right."

"Yes."

Mr. Burge elicited from Miss Keeler that she was living rent-free at Wimpole Mews and having use of telephone, lights and hot water; that many men took her out to restaurants and theatres without having intercourse with her; that among these men was Mr. Eylan who had been taking her out for two years and whose money presents to her were "purely incidental"; that the man who had paid for her trips to France and America was a Mr. Michael Lambton to whom she had been engaged; and that she had looked for work modelling and on television and had, in fact, appeared on one television quiz show. Dr. Ward, she agreed, had a normal working day in which he met men as well as women, and often in the evenings men used to come round for a game of bridge. ("Men!" commented Mr. Burge, sadly, "we had not heard about *them* from the prosecution!") She also agreed that Dr. Ward had telephoned the police on one of the occasions when the West Indian "Lucky" Gordon had attacked her (the inference being that Ward would never have done such a thing if he had been living on her immoral earnings), though she denied that Ward had ever taken her to Scotland Yard to talk to Chief Inspector Partridge of the Narcotics Squad about giving up smoking reefers.

These efforts of Mr. Burge to redress the balance were only partially successful. For one thing, the stench that the prosecution had laid could not be removed so quickly; for another, we had all read too much already, we had formed our own impressions before the trial began. And then, when all was said and done, it was not because of his drawings or his osteopathy or his bridge parties that Ward was here; it was because of sex.

Nor was Mr. Burge much more successful in his efforts to show that Christine could not be relied on as a truthful witness. She agreed with him that she must have made "about twelve" statements to the police since April (in fact she had made many more). This did strike one as a suspiciously large number, as though the police had gone on and on at her until they found something which would stick; but as Mr. Burge did not press Miss Keeler on the circumstances in which the statements were taken, this did not carry us much further. Later in his cross-examination he questioned her about the Gordon trial, where her evidence that Gordon had attacked her was instrumental in his receiving a three year prison sentence. Now Mr. Burge knew (though we and the jury did not), that a Mr. John Marshall had made a statement saying that it was he who had attacked Christine. Mr. Marshall and his sister, Paula, were old friends of Christine's: it was at, or near, her flat in Devonshire Street that the incident happened, and it was where Christine was staying now, during the trial. An odd thing about Marshall was that he had appeared briefly at the Magistrate's Court as a witness for the prosecution, but like Ronna Ricardo had subsequently shifted his ground and been treated by the prosecution as a hostile witness. Mr. Burge also knew that two witnesses whom Gordon had asked for his defence were said by the police to be not available; but that it had later transpired that one of them was on bail at the time, waiting for trial on a charge, oddly—or perhaps not oddly—enough, of living on immoral earnings.

In the light of this knowledge Mr. Burge now asked Christine:

"Did you take the oath on a previous occasion when you attended the trial of a man called Gordon?"

"Yes."

"Did you tell the whole truth about that?"

"Yes, I did."

"Did you say all your injuries were caused by Gordon?"

"Yes, and they were."

"Did you know that the man Gordon alleged that the injuries were not caused by him?"

"The man is mad. Of course they were."

"And that he wished to call two witnesses, one called Fenton and a man called Comacchio?"

"Yes."

"And did you say those two men were not present at the time of the incident?"

"Yes, I said they were not present because they were not present."

"Did you know that Sergeant Burrows, the officer in this case, was the officer in that case as well?"

"Yes."

"Did you hear him say, when Gordon asked for Fenton and Comacchio, that they were not available?"

"Yes."

After Miss Keeler had admitted to the judge that Gordon must be added to her already formidable list of scalps ("but not for money"), Mr. Burge asked her:

"Had he been pestering you and hammering on your door, and were the police called on a number of occasions?"

"Yes."

"Did you say anything about getting rid of Lucky Gordon or getting him deported?"

"No, never."

We know now what we did not know at the time; that in this part of her cross-examination Christine was lying. She was lying when she said that she had told the whole truth at Gordon's trial and lying when she said that Fenton and Comacchio were not present. She was moreover lying about these matters on oath for the second time; for, like Profumo, once she had started to lie, she had to keep up with it.

But at this moment in time her lying could not be proved. The jury could assume from Mr. Burge's questions that he had reasons to believe she was lying, but not knowing what the reasons were, they had nothing on which to form a judgement. If Christine's evidence at Gordon's trial was true, she would naturally reject Mr. Burge's assertions; but if it was false, she would also reject them, for not to do so would mean an admission of perjury and the prospect of imprisonment. Of course Mr. Burge was right to test Christine on the point, for an admission of perjury on her part would have virtually destroyed the case against Ward altogether. As it was, nothing was proved one way or the other.

This was on the debit side. Where Mr. Burge succeeded was in his cross-examination about Christine's relationships with various men. It will be remembered that in his opening speech

Mr. Griffith-Jones had stated categorically that it was Ward who had introduced Christine to Rachman, but that when he had examined her he had not bothered to substantiate the assertion: he had let the jury assume it to be true. But now we were given the truth of the matter.

"The circumstances of being introduced to Rachman were that Ward was looking for a flat to go and live with you?"

"Yes."

"And one of the flats the agents had given you was the one at Bryanston Mews?"

"Yes."

"And without any question of meeting Rachman, you went with Ward?"

"Yes," said Miss Keeler, "*and Rachman was there.*"

So that was what had happened. Mr. Griffith-Jones' damaging statements in his opening speech had turned out to be completely without foundation. No doubt he had grounds for making them but it was most unfortunate that they had ever come to be made.

Of the rest of Miss Keeler's evidence to Mr. Griffith-Jones, it will be recalled that the only sections that had been really damaging to Ward had been her references to the man Charles. She had been asked by Mr. Griffith-Jones: "How did you come to have intercourse with Charles?" and she had replied: "Dr. Ward suggested if I went to him he would give me money."

Mr. Burge now took this up by saying: "Are you saying really that it's true that the accused asked you to go and get £50 from..."

Before he could finish the question, Miss Keeler said: "*He never asked me.* He suggested that I could get some money from Charles *because I was hard up.*" This was not quite the same thing as Mr. Griffith-Jones' assertions that Christine *was being used by Ward to make a little money from intercourse.* Then Mr. Burge asked:

"Who is Charles?"

"I don't know." What did she mean, she didn't know?

"Where did he live?"

"He lived off Park Lane." That was vague enough!

"Was it a flat or a house?"

"A house."

Here the judge intervened to ask: "Are you telling the jury you had intercourse with men whose names you don't know?" This was a good question, a challenge to Christine either to supply the name or else admit the judge's not very flattering suggestion.

"I *did* know his name."

"You have remembered Charles," said the judge, "and you have remembered he lived in a house off Park Lane, and you have told me that you did know his name. Take your time. What was his name?"

But Christine, without taking her time, said: "I really can't remember what it was."

There were only two explanations of this. Either Charles was an invention, a mythical figure who had grown out of Christine's numerous conversations with the police and whom perhaps she herself had come to believe in: in view of her vagueness about who he was and where he lived, this on the whole seemed the most likely explanation. Or else he did exist and for some reason best known to herself she was refusing to implicate him; but this, in the light of the judge's pressure on her, seemed less likely. What was impossible to believe was that he did exist and she had forgotten his name, his profession and his address.*

Finally Mr. Burge touched on the subject of the Indian doctor.

"Did Mandy Rice-Davies receive the Indian gentleman at the flat at Great Cumberland Place?"

"Yes."

"Was the idea to shift the Indian doctor's relationship with Mandy Rice-Davies from Great Cumberland Place to Wimpole Mews?"

"No."

"Did Ward tell you the police had inquired about the Indian gentleman and he had said he had never been to Wimpole Mews?"

If Mr. Burge was asking this question on Ward's instructions, as he must have been, then Christine gave him a surprising answer.

"It's wrong."

Yet when all was said and done about the Indian doctor and

* We now know that "Charles" was the financier Charles Clore.

Charles and Tom and Dick and Harry, the crucial question that remained was : had any money passed from her to Ward, and if so, how much? She admitted to Mr. Burge that when Ward was hard up she sometimes gave him "small payments of money", but almost in the same breath she added that Ward used to give her "quite a lot of spending money". Finally she repeated what she had already told Mr. Griffith-Jones about owing Ward more than she ever made.

"You never returned to the accused," asked Mr. Burge, "as much as you got from him?"

Her answer was quite definite.

"No."

How could anybody continue to assert, unless the English language had lost its meaning, that Ward was *living* on Christine Keeler's *earnings*?

PART II

IF THE MAIN interest on the first day of the trial had been centred on the show's leading lady, that on the second day was supplied by the female bit players. There were five of them, and they were as different as they possibly could be. Their lowest, and indeed only, common denominator was that at one time or another Ward had made to each of them some sort of sexual proposal.

The first to be called was Sally Norie at whom Ward had cast his eye in the Brush and Palette restaurant. She was dressed in a sort of black, sleeveless outfit with a string of pearls round her neck, as though she were just off to some cocktail party. Yet it was clear, even before she opened her mouth, that she was quite a different type to, say, Christine Keeler; what Mr. Griffith-Jones would call "respectable". Her hair was stacked in a pile on top of her head. She looked very sad and rather strikingly, quietly beautiful.

It was not Mr. Griffith-Jones who rose to examine her but his junior, Mr. Michael Corkery. Determined to stick to the rules of the game by avoiding leading questions, he asked:

"Have you seen Ward before?"

This was clearly beyond Miss Norie, who assumed that as she wouldn't have been brought here unless she had seen Ward before, and as Mr. Corkery looked too intelligent to ask a question to which everyone in court knew the answer, the question must mean something other than what it appeared to mean.

"No," she said.

It is not the custom of lawyers to start apologising to laymen for confusion caused by their own rules.

"Just think carefully," said Mr. Corkery, shifting the onus of stupidity away from the rules and back on to Miss Norie, "I mean Dr. Ward."

Miss Norie thought carefully, and the truth slowly dawned on her.

"I met him in 1961," she said.

Miss Norie spoke in even more of a whisper than Miss Keeler, but an educated whisper. Her story, as told to Mr. Corkery and Mr. Burge, was ordinary beyond belief. She had met the defendant in the Brush and Palette restaurant as had been originally outlined by Mr. Griffith-Jones. She had gone out with him a number of times. She had been down to the cottage at Cliveden a number of times. Intercourse had not taken place the first time she had been down to the cottage, and she could not say for certain when it had taken place nor how many times.

With his first question Mr. Burge voiced what we were all thinking.

"I do not suppose you thought you were participating in criminal activities during this time?"

"No, I didn't."

Later Mr. Burge said: "As you got to know Dr. Ward you got to like him?"

"Yes."

"And he liked you?"

"I think so."

"And the affair developed until eventually you were intimate with him?"

"Yes."

"It was free and voluntary on your part?"

"Yes."

"It was not the first affair you have had or the last, was it?"

"No."

And that was all there was to it. Except, of course, that yet another assertion made by Mr. Griffith-Jones in his opening speech had not been substantiated. Long ago, it seemed now, somewhere in the far reaches of yesterday morning, out of sight and out of mind, Mr. Griffith-Jones had said of Sally Norie: "In due time the girl went to bed with the defendant *and was introduced to other men*"; and there had not been the slightest doubt in our minds that Mr. Griffith-Jones had meant by this, for the purpose of sexual intercourse. Indeed to make the charge of procuring stick, he *had* to mean this. Yet we had not heard a word about it. Once again the prosecution's promise had been belied by its performance.

Sally Norie came out of the witness-box and sat down on the front row of the Press benches behind the dock. The next witness was Miss R, who was an Austrian. She was extremely pretty and extremely well built: one could understand Ward casting his eye at her ample bosoms through the window of the shop. She had a wealth of light auburn hair, and she was accompanied into court by another woman with light auburn hair whom I took to be her sister but who turned out to be her mother. She was dressed in a blue jacket and skirt with white sweater, and she had pink fingernails. She was allowed to remain anonymous because, according to Mr. Griffith-Jones, she was "respectable" and "of no public interest".

Mr. Griffith-Jones asked her how old she was, and in a voice which had only the suggestion of an Austrian accent she said she had been born in May 1941 (which made her twenty-two). Mr. Griffith-Jones then asked:

"What is your father's occupation?"

It was an odd sort of question and it deserved, and got, an odd sort of answer.

"My father," said Miss R, "lives in Berlin."

Mr. Burge was on his feet. "I really do not see the point of that question," he said.

Mr. Griffith-Jones's reply threw little light on the trial but was revealing of himself. "I simply wanted to find out," he said, *"the type of family she came from"*—and the inference here presumably was that if her dad was an architect or doctor or perhaps even a barrister, she would be less likely to succumb to Dr. Ward's charms than if he were a plumber or a dustman. We were back once more in the Is-this-a-book-you-would-want-your-servants-to-read country.

Miss R's story was only a little less dull than Miss Norie's. She told how Ward had come to know her through Christine Keeler being a customer in the shop. He had invited her out to lunch several times and also down to the cottage. When Mr. Griffith-Jones asked whether Ward had tried to make love to her at Wimpole Mews there was a very long pause before she said, in a much quieter voice: "Yes, he did."

The significance of this pause did not become apparent until later. "Was that," said Mr. Griffith-Jones, "before you had gone down to the cottage?" (Mr. Griffith-Jones pronounced "gone" to rhyme with "lawn".) "Yes," said Miss R. She added that she had "repulsed" him then but admitted to going to bed with him on her first visit to the cottage.

Mr. Griffith-Jones kept returning to the cottage, and in a series of leading questions, showed some of his terrier-like qualities.

"Did you agree to go down to the cottage in advance?"

"I must have done."

"Were you asked several days beforehand?"

"Yes."

"Had you been out to a party?"

"Yes, outside London."

"Who had taken you to the party?"

"Ward."

"Had you gone to the party alone with him, or with other people?"

"With other people."

"What did you do at the cottage?"

"We went for a swim and had coffee."

"Did the others go home afterwards?"

"One couple stayed."

"Had you up to that time had sexual intercourse with the defendant?"

"No."

"When you found the others gone back to London, did you say anything about going back yourself?"

"Yes. He said 'Why don't you stay here at the cottage with me?' "

One could see the picture emerging from Mr. Griffith-Jones's canvas at last. *Scene:* The Cottage in the Woods. *Dramatis Personae:* Little Red Riding Hood and the Wolf. But it was a picture whose details were soon to become blurred.

"What did you say about that?"

"I accepted." *Accepted?* Wasn't that rather out of character?

"Was there anyone else staying the night?"

"Only two, a couple."

"Was that the first occasion that intercourse took place between you?"

"I think so, yes." What did she mean, *think so*? Old men may forget, but respectable girls of twenty-two remember where and when they allowed their lovers first to take them. Later Mr. Burge blurred the image still further, so that Little Red Riding Hood became almost unrecognisable.

"The reason you were intimate with him, as you said at the magistrate's court, was because you liked him and he liked you?"

It was the same line of approach as he had used with Sally Norie, and it could hardly fail; for what self-respecting woman is going to admit publicly that she has been so weak as to go to bed with a man against her will?

"Yes."

"And this, I think, was not the first occasion on which you had been intimate with a man?"

"No."

"You had had affairs with men before?"

"Yes, before I came to England."

Now Mr. Burge turned, not to the cottage but to Wimpole Mews.

"You did say *you thought* it was at Cliveden that you first slept together, but in fact you had slept with him at Wimpole Mews before you ever went to Cliveden?"

Now Mr. Burge would never have said this unless he had instructions to; and the meaning of a scribbled note which Ward had handed down to him a few moments before became apparent. So did Miss R's vagueness about when and where she had first slept with Ward, and her long pause before even admitting to Mr. Griffith-Jones that Ward had tried to make love to her in the flat.

"I stayed there," she said, "but no sexual intercourse took place." *Stayed* there? Why, if not for sexual intercourse? And where had she slept? Chaste in Ward's bed, or on the sitting-room sofa?

"I think," said Mr. Burge, pressing her a little, "on three occasions."

But Miss R was not prepared to contest the matter any further.

"I don't remember," she said.

It did not ring true. Having intercourse three times with a

man at his flat is one of the things in life a young girl remembers. As Miss R made her way across the court to join Sally
Norie on the front bench behind the dock, I felt that she had
been trying to give the court the impression that she was a harder
girl to get than in fact was the case. It wasn't succumbing to
Ward that she minded, but having succumbed to him so soon.
Perhaps like little Christine, she was thinking of her reputation.

"Miss X!" called the assistant clerk of the court. We waited
what seemed a very long time and nothing happened. "What has
happened to your witnesses, Mr. Griffith-Jones?" said the judge
at the very moment that Mr. Griffith-Jones must have been asking
himself the same question. Miss X swam into our ken and out
of it. "Miss Marilyn Rice-Davies," shouted the assistant clerk.

Until the proceedings at the lower court Miss Rice-Davies had
been just a name. Rather a grand name, it is true, and one—
like others in the case—which conjured up visions of informal
week-ends in comfortable country houses. ("Cynthia and I are
popping down to the Rice-Davies's on Saturday. John and Paula
Hamilton-Marshall are going to be there. Why don't you come
too?") I wondered at what moment in history the house of Rice
had decided to merge with the family of Davies, and why? Her
family lived in Birmingham, in what she later called the "exclusive suburb of Solihull"; and her father worked in a local
factory. She was clearly a cut above Christine socially, and
indeed her object from the beginning seemed to have been to
outshine her at every stage of the game. A mixture of demure-
ness and sauciness had marked her appearance at the magistrate's
court. When asked by counsel if she was aware that Lord Astor
had denied her statement that she had been to bed with him
she said : "Well he would, wouldn't he?"*

It was the same here. Unlike Christine, who photographed
better than she looked, Mandy Rice-Davies looked much better
than her photographs. She was still only eighteen and had not
yet lost, as Christine had, the bloom of youth. It was a
hard, cat-like little face but a very pretty one. After two years
as Rachman's mistress she still looked fresh as a milkmaid, and
that was quite a feat. Astride her golden head sat a little rose-
petalled hat, such as debutantes wear at garden parties. Her

* A much quoted phrase which has since passed into common English usage.

shoes, unlike Christine's, were quite lady-like. Her simple grey sleeveless dress accentuated the impression of modesty—until one looked at it closely. Then one saw that the slit down the front was only held together by a loose knot at the middle. When she walked one could see quite a long way up her leg.

As with her appearance, so with her performance in the witness-box. It was a marriage of the brazen and the bashful. She was in turns pert, cool, innocent, tearful, giggly. Unlike Christine she was never pathetic; unlike her too she was not in the least abashed either by the company or her surroundings. She was one of the very few female witnesses one was able to hear. She smiled at Ward, at Mr. Griffith-Jones, at the judge. When counsel was thinking out the next question she pouted at friends in court, gazed at the ceiling, fingered the pearl bracelet on her left wrist, or stroked one fleshy arm with the other. At one moment she was calling counsel "Sir" from behind lowered lids, the next she was trying to split a joke with the judge. She was in short wholly unpredictable, and what made most of her evidence a matinée of suspense was that no one, not even she, had any idea what new revelations she was about to spring on us.

She opened startlingly enough when Mr. Griffith-Jones questioned her about Comeragh Road.

"How did you pay for the rent of the flat at Comeragh Road?"

"I didn't pay for it."

"Do you know who did?"

"Yes, sir."

"How was it paid?"

"By cheque."

"Whose cheque?"

"Lord Astor's cheque."

"Had you met Lord Astor?"

"Yes, sir."

"Who introduced him to you?"

"Stephen—the defendant."

"Did you have intercourse with him?"

"Not when he paid the money—two years later."

"Were you having intercourse with any other man or men at Comeragh Road?"

"Peter Rachman."

"Anyone else?"

"Douglas Fairbanks."*

"Anyone else?"

"A boy friend of mine."

Her hands, one on top of the other, rested on the edge of the witness-box in an attitude of complete composure.

"Were you paid by anyone?"

"No, except Peter Rachman. He kept me. I had a weekly allowance."

"Who actually arranged for the payment of the rent with this cheque?"

"Lord Astor and Stephen."

"Did you speak to either of them about it?"

"Yes, to both."

The judge asked her where she had met Lord Astor.

"At Cliveden."

"Did you ever see him at the flat?"

"No, but I know Stephen brought Bill—Lord Astor—round to the flat."

The judge wanted to be sure about this. "Stephen Ward had taken Lord Astor round to Comeragh Road when you were out?"

"Yes, sir."

It was perfectly obvious to all of us what Mr. Griffith-Jones was driving at. But what was the point of it? Why try and establish the existence of an offence with which Ward was not charged, involving someone who had not been called as a witness? Why make such a fuss about Lord Astor's cheque if, as had been said earlier, Lord Astor's cheque had nothing to do with the case?

For the next three-quarters of an hour Mr. Griffith-Jones examined Mandy Rice-Davies closely; and with one exception he fared no better with her than he had with Christine Keeler. It will be remembered that in his opening speech Mr. Griffith-Jones had said that before the girls had left Comeragh Road Ward had asked Mandy to marry him ("The general tenor of the suggestion was that he would not take it amiss if she went with

* Douglas Fairbanks has publicly denied this allegation by Mandy.

men and thereby earned their keep.") The following dialogue
shows what a grinding job Mr. Griffith-Jones had in his efforts
to substantiate this claim.

"Did the defendant ever say anything about marriage?"

"Yes, sir."

"What did he say?"

"He said we ought to get married sometime."

"Did he say how you would live and where you would get the
money from?"

This was an odd question to ask about a man who was earning
several thousand a year—unless of course it was leading somewhere.

"Well," she said, "he had a good practice and said he had
friends everywhere." This was a fair enough answer. After a
quite noticeable pause she added, almost as if for the prosecution's benefit: "I don't know whether he meant he wouldn't
mind my going out with other men if we were married."

"Why should that occur to you?" said Mr. Griffith-Jones. "If
a man asks a girl to marry him, that is not generally what she
understands."

"It just went on in the conversation," said Mandy, "I can't
remember that part of it exactly."

"What were the friends going to do?" asked Mr. Griffith-
Jones. "You must help us as much as you can."

"Because they're always useful, aren't they? They could be
financially useful."

True enough, and harmless enough; but this was getting us
nowhere. Now the judge intervened.

"Why should a friend be financially helpful to him?"

"Because they were very influential people."

Very influential people is a phrase used by social climbers to
denote a sort of super-Establishment—people whom they wrongly
imagine can fix anything for anyone at any time.

"That may be the case," said Mr. Griffith-Jones, "but because
a man is influential, it does not necessarily help you financially?"

"At that time I was trying to model and do film work and
Stephen helped many top models. One of the top models in
America was Stephen's girl friend."

We were a long way now from Ward's alleged proposal of

marriage. More and more I had the impression that Mandy was answering the questions spontaneously, that she had quite forgotten what she had put in her statements many weeks before. It was left to the judge to unearth it.

"If you were to receive financial help from such a person, what was to be the *quid pro quo*?"

This was a strange question. Mandy had just made it clear that the financial help was to come indirectly from influential people who were able to arrange such things as modelling and film work. What financial help was the judge talking about? And what on earth did the last three words mean? She looked utterly blank.

"Do you," said the judge, when the titter had died away, "understand that?"

"No."

The judge reached for his cold chisel.

"What were you to give for what you were getting financially?"

It had been a long journey, but we had arrived at last.

"Oh," she said, "sex, I suppose."

In Mandy's world that was what girls often gave in return for what they got financially. Yet I doubt when she said it that she had any idea that she was still being questioned about Ward's alleged proposal of marriage.

Nor were Mr. Griffith-Jones's other efforts with her much more successful. He tried to find out if there had been a pattern of prostitution during her stay at Wimpole Mews.

"While you were there at Wimpole Mews did you have intercourse with other men in the flat?"

"Yes, I had a boy friend."

"Any others?"

She looked up at the ceiling, trying to remember.

"Oh yes. That was the first time I had intercourse with Lord Astor."

"Was that at the flat?"

"Yes."

"Was Ward at the flat on that occasion?"

"Once."

"When you had intercourse with Lord Astor?"

"It was quite normal for him to be in the flat."

A gasp of surprise came from beneath the Ascot hats on the City Lands Committee benches.

The judge said: "It was normal for Ward to be in the flat when you were having sexual intercourse with other men, was it?"

"Oh yes," said Mandy gaily, and then, "it's quite normal, isn't it? There's nothing wrong with it?"

But both manner and matter were too much for the judge.

"This is the third time you have gone on talking without reason for so doing. Now answer the question. Do I understand that it was normal that when you were having intercourse in the bedroom Stephen Ward was in the flat?"

She looked demure as could be and milkmaid fresh.

"Yes, sir," she said.

And in her world, where old-fashioned morality did not exist, it was of course perfectly normal.

Mr. Griffith-Jones took up the cudgels again.

"These people you were having intercourse with—did they pay you any money?"

"Oh no, sir." She sounded quite shocked.

"Lord Astor?"

"Oh, no."

"Did the defendant ever ask you to introduce girls to him?"

"No, sir."

"Did you?"

"No, sir."

Mr. Griffith-Jones tried another tack.

"Were you ever shown any books in the flat?"

"There were Russian books. There were lots of books."

"Any in connection with sex?"

"No, sir."

"Did you ever see anybody looking at books in connection with sex?"

"No, sir."

Later the judge asked her: "While you were there, did other girls visit the flat?"

"Yes, sir."

"Were you ever in the flat with any other people who used either your room or his bedroom for sexual intercourse?"

"No, only Stephen."

"Were you there when Stephen Ward used his own room for intercourse?"

"Yes, sir."

"How many girls did he go to bed with while you were in the mews?"

"Two."

"Do you know who they were?"

"No, sir. They haven't been in this case."

"Did you see men other than Ward having intercourse in the flat?"

"No, sir."

"Did you introduce anybody to the defendant yourself, girls I mean?"

Mr. Griffith-Jones had already asked this question a few minutes before. He got much the same answer now as he had then.

"No, I don't think so as far as I can remember."

The conversation then turned to modelling and Mr Griffith-Jones asked: "Whose suggestion was it that you should take up modelling?" Here was an echo of his earlier suggestion to Christine that she had taken up modelling so as to bring back pretty young girls for Ward.

"It was my suggestion."

"Did you meet other girls there?"

"Yes, sir."

"Did you bring them back to the flat?"

"No, sir."

I had the same feeling about this line of questioning as I did about the whole case; not that Ward had committed a single obvious crime which cried out for justice, but rather that the prosecution were trying very hard to elicit facts which would bring Ward's activities into the compass of a recognised crime.

Mr. Griffith-Jones was a little more successful in his questions about a man whom Mandy had tried to borrow money from.

"Did you know anything about the rent he had to pay for the flat?"

"It was a bit behind."

"Did he ask you to do anything about it?"

"He asked me if I could borrow £250."

"Who could you borrow £250 from?"

"Somebody he introduced me to."

"Who was that?"

She turned to the judge and said: "Have I got to mention the name?"

The judge said "Yes" and we all waited breathlessly for another peer or film star or Cabinet Minister to hit the dust.

"Mr. Ropner," said Mandy, and for all the light it shed she might as well have said Hopkins or Brown or Cartwright.

"Ropner," said the judge, as though by saying the word out loud it might tell him something.

"Ropner," repeated Mr. Griffith-Jones, so there should be no doubt about it. "Did you borrow money from him?"

Mandy's reply was very curious: "I didn't go to bed with him," she said. Nobody had asked her whether she had.

"Was the idea that you should go to bed with him and then borrow the £250?"

"I suppose so really."

"Who mentioned that?"

"No one mentioned the going to bed."

"I only want to know what the idea was. Was the idea to have sexual intercourse?"

"Yes."

"Did you ask Mr. Ropner for the £250?"

"No, sir." She added about Mr. Ropner: "I liked him, but I didn't fancy him"—meaning presumably that she liked talking to him but not the idea of going to bed with him.

Since no money had passed and since Mandy had not been to bed with Ropner, this was not evidence of Ward's living on immoral earnings. On the other hand, if the story was true, it showed an *intention* of doing so which, when it came to the push, would make the jury disinclined to give Ward the benefit of the doubt. But was it true? Some of Mandy's answers had been so strange. Why say "somebody he introduced me to" when asked whom she was to borrow the money from? She must have known that the prosecution's case rested largely on whom Ward had introduced to whom. Would it not have been more natural to say "a friend of his"? Again, what was the object of the little drama about not mentioning Ropner's name when she had shown no such inhibitions about the names of Lord Astor and Douglas Fairbanks? And finally why say that she hadn't been to bed with Mr. Ropner before she was asked about it?

There remained the Indian doctor, the mysterious shadowy figure whom we never saw or heard but whose activities, if true, proved more damaging to the defence than almost any other single individual. She had first met him, she said, with Ward at a coffee bar in the Marylebone High Street. The next day, when Ward was out, the Indian doctor called round. She added that many of Ward's friends called round for coffee. She gave him coffee and talked to him.

"Did anything take place on that occasion?"

"No, not then. Not on that occasion."

Later Ward had mentioned the Indian doctor to her again. He had asked whether she liked him. She said she had and Ward had said: "He is a very rich man and wants to have your room because he has got a girl friend and it's difficult for him to take her anywhere." He had added that the doctor had already given him £25 for the rent of the room. The money was in notes and he had shown it to her.

"Did Ward say anything more to you about the Indian doctor?"

"He said: 'If you like the doctor, why let his girl friend go out with him? Why don't you go out with him?' I said I'd like to see him again and he came round the next day."

"Did you ask him round or tell Doctor Ward you would like to see him?"

"I think he just turned up."

"Did you have sexual intercourse with the Indian doctor?"

"Yes, sir."

"At the flat during the day?"

"Yes, one time during the late afternoon."

"How often did that happen?"

"Only about five times."

"Once or twice a week?"

Here Mandy said "Oh," and looked again at the ceiling. It had seemed a simple enough question.

"How often?" said Mr. Griffith-Jones.

"It lasted about one and a half weeks and then I was fed up."

Fed up? Yet only yesterday Christine had said that Mandy was "receiving" the Indian gentleman at the flat at Great Cumberland Place a few weeks later. It looked as though somebody wasn't telling the truth somewhere.

"He was coming round to the flat about every second or third day?"

"Every third day sometimes." What did she mean *sometimes*?

"Was he paying you?"

"Well, yes."

"How much did he give you?"

"It depended. He asked me what I wanted. He bought me a tape recorder which was £25."

The judge, mole-sharp as usual, asked the only questions we really wanted to hear.

"What was the smallest amount he gave you after sexual intercourse?"

"£15."

"And the largest?"

"£25."

Mr. Griffith-Jones said: "How did he use to give it? Did he hand it to you or leave it for you?"

"He left it anywhere, on the dressing table or somewhere." She added: "He came round once or twice and we didn't have sexual intercourse but he still gave me money."

"How much altogether?"

"Over £100."

This was clearest evidence we had yet had that Mandy was a tart and that Ward was assisting her in her activities; and if what we had heard was true then the assumption must be that Ward was partly living on her earnings. *But was it true?* The Indian doctor had already issued a statement denying it was true. Would he come and take the stand and deny it in person? What was Ward's version of it all?

The answer to these questions lay in the future. Yet there was another set of questions to which Mr. Griffith-Jones received some quite revealing answers now.

"When you were at the flat," said the judge, "were there any other occasions when you were handed money?"

Mandy's answer was as surprising as it was irrelevant.

"Several times," she said, referring to Ward, "I gave him money. Just a couple of pounds or something like that." This was a far cry from Mr. Griffith-Jones's assertion in his opening speech that the Indian doctor had left between £15 and £25 on the dressing table *"out of which she said she paid Ward some £2 or £3 a time"*. She may have said something of the kind elsewhere but she had said nothing of the kind in this court.

Mandy's answer to the next question was even more surprising.

"Apart from the £20 or so from modelling and what the Indian doctor was paying you and what I gather Mr. Ropner gave you" (*according to my notes Mandy had not said that Mr. Ropner had given her anything*) "had you any other money coming in?"

*"What Stephen gave me."**

So Ward had given her money too, just as he had given it to Christine. How much, one wondered? But no one, now or later, ever asked.

The judge intervened again.

"Will you tell us all how much you gave the defendant?"

"Apart from rent?"

"Yes, apart from rent?"

"In all about £25. I paid for the food as well, you see."

"I was coming to that. Actual amount about £25?"

"Yes, sir."

"And in addition you paid for the food?"

"Yes, sir."

Subtract from the £25 whatever money it was Ward had given her, and there could not have been much in it either way. Was this another of the reasons why we were here? For a five pound note and a packet of Frosties? It seemed so.

If contempt of court were to mean contempt for the proceedings of the court, then half the journalists I spoke to in the pub

* In January, 1964, Mandy admitted that while living at Wimpole Mews she was still receiving from Rachman £100 a week allowance. (See page 247.)

that lunch-time would have been in the dock too. Their remarks on the triviality of most of the morning's evidence, especially that of Sally Norie and Miss R, would have shaken even Mr. Griffith-Jones's sang-froid.

And there was another Christine Keeler story going the rounds. *Q.* What did Christine Keeler's doctor say to her? *A.* A few days on your feet and we'll soon have you back in bed.

Mr. Burge opened his cross-examination by tidying up a few loose ends. No, she had not received any money from Mr. Ropner until she had left Wimpole Mews and gone with Christine to live at Great Cumberland Place. No, she did not know that before she ever came on the scene Lord Astor used to lend Ward substantial sums of money through his solicitor. Yes, she agreed that £6 a week was a reasonable rent for the flat and that Ward had complained of her excessive use of the telephone. Yes, it was true that Ward had had her parents down from Birmingham to stay at the flat when she was in hospital after having tried to commit suicide when she learnt of Rachman's death.

Then Mr. Burge turned to a question that had been troubling Press and Parliament for some time.

"Is it right you were going abroad on the night of June 16th?"

"Yes, sir."

"Were you stopped at the airport by police officers in charge of this case?"

"The second time."

"They'd stopped you before?"

"Yes, on a motoring offence, and they said they'd issue a warrant for my arrest."

"Were you taken to Marylebone Lane Police Station by Chief Inspector Herbert and Detective Sergeant Burrows, the officers in this case?"

"Yes, sir."

"Was it suggested there might be a charge of stealing against you in relation to a television set?"

"Yes, sir."

"Were you allowed to go when you had entered into bail?"

"Yes, sir."

"How much was the bail for?"

"£1,000."

"Did they give you any reason why the date June 28th had been selected for you to answer your bail?"

"No, sir. It was quite obvious."

"That was the day on which you gave evidence at the Magistrate's Court?"

"Yes, sir."

"And you gave evidence under the pressure that you had this possible charge being made against you?"

The smile which for most of her evidence had been on Mandy's face had now left it.

"Yes, sir. I had already seen the television company and told them I was settling the question of the television set."

"Did you point that out to the police officers on June 16th?"

"Yes, sir."

There were no doubts at all about what Mr. Burge was trying to do. He was suggesting that the police had brought pressure to bear on Mandy so that she would be where they wanted her at the time they wanted her. It was moreover, to those who knew anything about police methods in this country, a perfectly reasonable suggestion. It is by no means unknown for the police when they wish to take someone into custody for some purpose or other, to use as the pretext for doing so some trivial offence. In 1949 for instance when the Notting Hill police wished to bring back Timothy Evans from South Wales to question him about the disappearance of his wife and daughter, they brought a charge against him of stealing a briefcase in order that they might do so. To stop Mandy from leaving the country because of a suspected charge of stealing a television set, and to ask her to enter into bail of £1,000 for an object which could not be worth more than £100 at most was clearly nonsensical. The thing had been done to ensure that one of the two vital witnesses in Ward's committal proceedings would turn up as planned.

The judge, however, took a different view of Mr. Burge's approach.

"Whatever happened then," he said to Mandy, "have you told the truth in the witness-box?"

"Yes, sir."

"Anything you said about the Indian doctor you still hold out as being true?"

"Yes, sir."

The judge turned to Mr. Burge.

"Mr.—Burge. I'm beginning to wonder whether it's really worth your while going on asking the questions you have been in view of the last two questions and answers?"

I was beginning to wonder something too—whether the judge had any idea of the effect of this intervention on the minds of the jury, and whether he would have made it if he had. For his remarks to Mr. Burge implied that he believed that Mandy was telling the truth in the witness-box today, and if he believed it, then the jury, who like many juries look on their judge as a sort of immaculate conception, would follow his example and believe it too. Indeed the judge's ready acceptance of Mandy's word prevented the jury from considering the alternative, which was that she might be giving false evidence as a result of police pressure; and that if she was she was unlikely in a million light years to admit it. In which case her answers to the judge proved nothing one way or the other. Mr Burge, however, was not going to be deflected so easily. He answered the judge with candour and courage.

"It would be a waste of time," he said, "to attempt to defend Dr. Ward if I cannot cross-examine witnesses concerning pressure that may have been put on people. I am instructed to appear for my client and to endeavour"—here he paused— "*whatever the atmosphere of this trial*—to present his defence."

He turned again to the witness-box.

"Is it correct on June 28th you went into the witness-box at Marylebone and gave evidence about the Indian doctor?"

"Yes, sir."

"While still under oath at the witness-box were you seen in a room at Marylebone Police Station by Chief Inspector Herbert and Detective Sergeant Burrows?"

"Yes, sir."

"What happened there?"

"A man arrived from the television company and I paid him some money."

"That was when you were actually under oath in the witness-box?"

"Yes, but it was only about the television."

Of course it was only about the television. But this did not affect Mr. Burge's argument, which was that Mandy had found herself in a position where she was vulnerable to pressure, and therefore to telling lies. With great skill he then followed this up by examining the reliability of Mandy as a truthful witness.

"I am suggesting," he said, still referring to the Indian doctor, "that you are not telling the truth. You do understand that, don't you?"

"Yes, sir" (much quieter this time).

"Are you a truthful person?"

"Yes, sir."

"Has anybody in a position of authority ever said to you you are a liar?"

"Yes."

"Is it right on May 1st, 1963, you appeared at West London Magistrate's Court?"

"Yes, sir."

"And did the learned magistrate, Mr. Seymour Collins, say to you that if you wanted to get something and get it by a lie, you would lie?"

"Yes."

"Was it true?"

"No, sir."

"He was wrong?"

"He was talking about the motoring offence."

"I don't want to embarrass you, but the motoring offences were not just parking offences. They were making a false statement, obtaining an insurance certificate and possessing a forged licence and making a false entry in the registration book?"

"Yes, sir."

She said this quite boldly, smiling a little, not a bit abashed, if anything perhaps a little proud. One realised that she had absolutely no sense of morality, as most of us understand the word, at all.

"When the police interviewed you, you knew that you had already been convicted of a criminal offence?"

"Yes, sir."

"And they pointed out to you that there was a possibility of another criminal offence, namely stealing a wireless set or television?"

"Yes, sir."

"Was it clear that they were out to obtain evidence against the accused, Stephen Ward?"

"Yes, sir."

"Was pressure placed upon you that these matters which I have mentioned might make it difficult for you unless you gave evidence against Stephen Ward?"

"Yes, sir."

Later Mr. Burge established that one of Mandy's earlier interviews with Mr. Herbert and Mr. Burrows took place in Holloway Prison where she had been taken in connection with the motoring offences. It did not require much imagination to picture the scene. "You didn't want to go back there, did you?" asked Mr. Burge, and Mandy replied, "No."

"In those circumstances you have given this account of the Indian doctor?"

"Yes, sir."

Mr. Burge could hardly have been more explicit if he had tried. He had got Mandy to admit that she was being pressurised by the police to say what they wanted her to say, and he had also got her to admit, with a wealth of evidence to support it, that she was a liar. What he was not able to get her to say— and it would have been surprising if he had—was that she had never seen the Indian doctor at Wimpole Mews. And yet, because this was his client's case he had to put it.

"Is it true that the only times you saw the Indian doctor were at 63 Great Cumberland Place after you had left Wimpole Mews?"

"No, sir."

"Would that again be quite wrong?"

"Yes, sir."

It may have been quite wrong, but then again it may not. For the first time Mandy's evidence was open to doubt. Before some of it had seemed true but trivial. Now there were at least reasons for thinking that the more damaging parts of it were false.

Mr. Burge had established that Mandy was given to lying and, because of alleged pressure put on her by the police, that she had a motive for lying. Now, before he finished with her he sought to find another motive.

"There is something you want very much as a result of this case, don't you?"

Mandy smiled. "Yes, sir."

"Money?"

"Oh, yes."

"Big money?"

She smiled again. "If it's possible, yes."

"For your story?"

"No, sir, I'm not selling my story."

"Is it true you have been negotiating with a number of news-papers for selling your story?"

"I did, yes."

"Would they have given you enough?"

"I am still under contract with a daily paper."

"The value of your story depends on the conviction of this man?"

"No, sir."

"Do you realise that because of the laws of libel your story would not have the same value if he was acquitted than if he was convicted?"

"I hope he is acquitted."

This was all right as far as it went, but it did not go very far. Mr. Burge turned to Rachman.

"Of course you have reason to have malice against the accused?"

"I have no malice against the accused."

"Let me remind you. First of all when you attempted to kill yourself that was because you were so distressed that the man you lived with had died?"

"Yes, sir."

"Did you think he had left you a substantial sum of money?"

"No, sir."

"Did you go to Somerset House in order to find out whether or not there was money available to you?"

"No, I wanted to find out what date he married."

"You were very annoyed because the accused had said to your parents when they were staying there that this was a demonstration by you because you were disappointed at not getting any money?"

"No, sir. That wasn't what was said."

Mr. Burge pressed her. "Were you disappointed over the money question?" It was too much for Mandy. For two years she had been kept in luxury : she had been given diamonds, furs, a motor car and a weekly allowance. She had left the man in the hope that he would marry her and a month later he had died, leaving her nothing. The disappointment must have been colossal. Her self-confidence left her, and the tears welled up. She dabbed at her eyes with a finger and one of her false eye-lashes got loosened and had to be adjusted. It was not, as one newspaper tried to make out, a pathetic, but a slightly comic sight.

She said, holding back the sobs, that she did not know about not getting any money until three months later when Christine told her. She denied that the reason for her trying to commit suicide was disappointment over the money. "I thought I didn't have any friends," she said. She denied also that she had said she had enough jewellery and mink to get by over the next few years.

"Were you also extremely annoyed," asked Mr. Burge, "that the defendant had a lease of the flat at Bryanston Mews which yóu thought ought to be yours by rights because of your relationship with Mr. Rachman?"

One could see that she well might be very annoyed by this; to appear as a guest at a flat where for the last two years she had been the undisputed mistress.

"I didn't like him living there," she said, "because I didn't like the thought of other men being there."

Perhaps what she meant was that she did not like the thought of men other than Rachman making love there. But whatever it was was too much for Mr. Burge.

"That," he said witheringly, "must have shocked you."

It was soon after this that Mr. Burge's cross-examination of Mandy ended. He had been less successful when trying to show that Mandy was actuated by greed or malice than when trying to show that she had been actuated by fear. This was partly because of Mandy's replies, partly also because of his own unforceful manner: his questions seem more aggressive and searching in retrospect than they sounded at the time. To end on a dying note was particularly unfortunate as Mr. Griffith-Jones was now ready to repair whatever damage had been done.

"Just look at that document and tell me if that is your signature at the bottom of each page?"

She looked at the document and said it was.

"On April 25th, when you made a statement to the police, did you tell the police without going into details too much, what you have told the court today?"

"Yes, sir."

"To go to one particular detail that has been mentioned by my learned friend in which he suggested that you are not telling the truth, did you tell the police about the Indian doctor?"

Mr. Burge rose and said: "I must register a formal objection to this line of re-examination." I wondered why. The judge said, "I rule that the prosecution is entitled to proceed".

Mr. Griffith-Jones said: "On that occasion did you tell the police in effect what you have told the court today in connection with the Indian doctor?"

"Yes, sir."

If it is true that in any argument people are influenced by the last word they have heard, then the jury by now must have forgotten what Mandy had said about the police putting pressure on her. Mr. Griffith-Jones then dealt with the question of malice.

"Did I hear you right when you were answering Mr. Burge? Did you say that you hoped Dr. Ward would be acquitted?"

"Yes, sir."

"Is that your hope?"

"Yes, sir."

"Are you still friendly with him?"

"No, but I know what it's like in jail." She paused, then

added: "He doesn't deserve it. Why, you might as well arrest every bachelor in London!"

This not only resulted in a sympathetic ripple of laughter round the court but echoed precisely what many of us were thinking. The whole tone of her reply suggested sympathy, even affection for Ward. And this from a prosecution witness. Mr. Griffith-Jones could not have hoped for a more satisfactory answer had he written it himself. Now with a few deft flicks, he dusted the remaining bits of fluff from his sleeve.

"The suggestion has been made," he said, "that pressure has been put upon you. If in fact any pressure has been put on you, as has been suggested, has that caused you to say anything that is not true today?"

"No, sir. As I say there is a great deal behind it. You write down a thing on a piece of paper and you can look upon it any way you like but it doesn't mean it will be untrue and that is why I am here today."

While we were puzzling out just what this meant, the judge said: "Do the words given under oath in the witness-box reveal the truth in your case?"

"Yes, sir."

"That is what I wanted," said Mr. Griffith-Jones, with all the authority of the state behind him, "to be quite sure that what you have told the court today is the truth."

"Absolutely."

After this, could any jury have doubts as to what and what not to believe?

Mandy went to join Sally Norie and Miss R and Miss R's mother on the bench behind the dock where, with the spotlight no longer on her, she soon became fidgety and unhappy. The clerk of the court called the name of the next witness, Miss X. This was the girl to whom Ward was supposed to have made indecent proposals about a two-way mirror, which meant we were on to Count 5. She was a tall girl with very black hair and Anglo-Indian features. She was wearing a pink linen dress and high-heeled shoes and she had rather nice legs. She was quite pretty in a rather puddingy sort of way. She looked about twenty-five but said she was nineteen and had come to live in

London last year. She was a colourless sort of person, and unlike Christine and Mandy who used their hands frequently to express themselves she kept her arms soldier-like at her sides. Between answering questions she appeared to be doing some sort of deep breathing exercise, but this may well have been due to nerves.

She told Mr. Griffith-Jones how and where she had met Ward, how she had gone out with him, and how he had called on her by arrangement on the afternoon of January 3rd, 1963. He had told her, she said, that he had got a new flat.

"Did he say anything curious about that new flat?"

"He said there was a two-way mirror in that flat."

"And did you understand what that was?"

"Yes."

"What did Ward say about the two-way mirror?"

"He said he intended watching people through it and joked that if there was a funny incident he could make a bit of spare money by people sitting round and watching."

"Watching what?"

"Watching who was in the bedroom."

"Yes?"

"He said it was a big joke to him that people could sit around and watch, and that we could arrange seats round and make a little money on it."

"What did you say to that?"

"I told him I was not interested in watching other people in bedrooms and he said to me: 'I don't think I want you to watch—I think you will be at the other side'—or something like that."

"What did you say to that?"

"I thought it was all rather disgusting. I said I wasn't interested in the least."

Mr. Burge got up.

"Would it be true to say that Dr. Ward was never a friend of yours but an acquaintance?"

"I suppose that towards the end he became a friend."

"How many times did you see him altogether?"

"On about three or four occasions."

"You say this man who was an acquaintance who had never made any advances to you suddenly made a proposition that you should perform behind a two-way mirror? Is that what you are saying?"

"Yes, I am."

"Did he suddenly mention the two-way mirror at two o'clock in the afternoon in the flat?"

"He mentioned that he had moved to a new flat and then started talking about what was in the flat."

"Whatever it was, whether it was in bad or tolerable taste, it was quite clearly a joke and was not seriously meant?"

"Yes, he thought it was a joke."

The judge intervened to say: "You mean that the two-way mirror was a joke?"

"Yes."

"The question I put to you," said Mr. Burge, "was that the proposition about your performing was a bad joke in bad taste?"

"I thought it was."

"It was not a serious proposal at all?"

"No."

Mr. Burge sat down, for he had nothing further to say. He had made clear to all of us what should have been obvious to the meanest intelligence from the beginning; that so farcical a piece of evidence should never have been allowed to reach the Central Criminal Court.

There was little Mr. Griffith-Jones could do in the way of re-examination other than suggest that Miss X did not know whether Ward's suggestion was made as a joke or seriously. And then rather a curious thing happened. The judge suddenly intervened.

"That was the last time you met him?"

"Yes."

"You decided not to meet him again?"

"Yes."

"Can you tell the jury why?"

"Because I had been advised by the person I was staying with not to see Dr. Ward any more."

I felt that I would rather have heard these questions asked by Mr. Griffith-Jones than by the judge; for the effect of them was very slightly to take the edge off Mr. Burge's small victory.

Miss X was ushered out of the witness-box; and as she went I wondered in what circumstances she had been persuaded to come here to tell her snivelling little tale. Like a displaced person she was put alongside the other displaced persons sitting on the bench behind the dock : Sally Norie, Miss R, Miss R's mother and fidgety Mandy. I reflected that if things went on at this rate the whole bench would soon be filled with Ward's girl friends. These ones made a curious quartet. The only thing they had in common was Ward's sex drives : three of them had shared his bed and the fourth, by sheer stoutness of heart, had managed to escape a fate worse than intercourse.

What made the evidence of the prosecution at Ward's trial of such unflagging interest was the variety of the women who had been associated with him. The four on the bench could hardly have been more different : now a new star came to grace this milky cluster in the night sky. Her name was Margaret (Ronna) Ricardo and unlike Christine and Mandy she made no pretensions about not being a tart. It would be untrue to say she was not ashamed to admit it, for clearly she was ashamed or at least unhappy about it, but admit it she did. This honesty made a welcome change. She had red hair and a pink jumper and a total lack of any sort of finesse; but after the genteel caperings of Christine and Mandy and the deadly respectability of Miss R, this also was welcome.

We had heard of Miss Ricardo before. She had given evidence at the Magistrate's Court proceedings three weeks earlier. There, among other things, she had said that she had visited Ward two or three times at his Bryanston Mews flat (we were on to Count 3 now) and on each occasion she was asked to stay behind to meet somebody. Men had arrived and she had gone to bed with them. Since then, however, she had gone to Scotland Yard to make a statement denying this. At the moment nobody knew for certain what she was going to say.

She took the oath and in answer to Mr. Griffith-Jones said that she had visited Ward at his flat in Bryanston Mews earlier this year. This, of course, was the flat where Rachman and Mandy had lived for two years. Ward had shown her the hole in the wall where the two-way mirror used to be and which Mandy in her evidence admitted to having broken. Miss Ricardo had said to Ward that she had had a two-way mirror herself. Ward had told her, she said, that he would "either cover the hole up or else get a new mirror", and she had said she had got an ordinary piece of mirror at home that would cover the gap. Now Mr. Griffith-Jones had said of the two-way mirror in his opening speech that when Ward moved into the Bryanston Mews flat "*it was proposed to have it put in order again*". This reply of Miss Ricardo's was the nearest he ever got to substantiating the assertion. The reader will have noticed that far from a categorical assertion of proposing to repair the mirror, Ward was *undecided* as to *whether* to cover the hole up *or* get *a new mirror—a new mirror*, note, nothing about a new *two-way* mirror. But how could the jury be expected to notice this?

In answer to further questions by Mr. Griffith-Jones, Miss Ricardo said that she had visited Ward in Bryanston Mews with two other people, a man and a girl.

"Did you have intercourse with anybody on that occasion?"

There was suddenly a hush in the courtroom, as if we knew, as a pointer knows when he sniffs the wind, that something interesting lay ahead.

"Yes, I did."

"Who did you have intercourse with?"

"With my boy friend."

Miss Ricardo took a long time to answer each question and when she did, it was very quietly.

The judge said: "What did your girl friend do?"

There was another pause, and then she said: "She was with Stephen."

This time it was Mr. Griffith-Jones' turn to pause. Perhaps he knew what was coming. He said: "In the other bedroom?"

Now there was a very long pause indeed. Miss Ricardo looked miserable. She tried to speak, but nothing came out. Eventually she shook her head.

"In the same room?"

No answer.

"All four of you together?"

She nodded.

"Were you all taking part together?"

Another long pause while Miss Ricardo screwed up her face and bit her lip. She nodded again.

So that was it. A foursome. Who had done what to whom? A hundred imaginations ran riot. The permutations were endless. One looked at Ricardo standing so miserably in the witness-box, and at Ward sitting with dignity in the dock, and saw them naked and unashamed, like animals.

The judge said: "I want to hear what happened in that room, the four of you together?" Good God, were we not going to be spared the awesome details? Perhaps the judge realised what he was asking, for he said quickly: "Was there anything beyond sexual intercourse?" What did he mean *beyond* sexual intercourse? What is there beyond sexual intercourse except more sexual intercourse and variations on sexual intercourse? But Miss Ricardo shook her head.

"How many times," asked Mr. Griffith-Jones, "did you go to the Bryanston Mews flat?"

At the Magistrate's Court Miss Ricardo had said two or three times, but now she said, "Once".

"Miss Ricardo," said the judge, "I want to be quite certain about this. How many times did you go to Ward's flat?"

"Once," she said, "never more than once."

Mr. Griffith-Jones turned to the judge and said: "I desire to draw your attention to statements this witness has made on her deposition and my application is for permission to treat her as hostile."

A hostile witness! It was only three weeks ago at the Magistrate's Court that Mr. Griffith-Jones had used the same phrase about another prosecution witness who had wanted to change his evidence—not Ronna Ricardo but John Hamilton-Marshall, the brother of Paula with whom Christine was now staying. At this court Marshall had said that a statement he had given the police on April 10th was not correct, and there was no truth in a paragraph which said that Ward had asked him to go and see a girl who had just had an abortion. Asked by the magistrate why he had signed the statement he had said: *"I was there for six hours. I skimmed through because I was glad to get out."* Whether these words were true or not, they had the possibility of truth. To keep people waiting for a long time in order to get them to say what one wants is one of the oldest police techniques in the world.

Mr. Griffith-Jones handed the judge some papers and he studied them for a minute or two. A court official brought Miss Ricardo a chair and she sat down in the witness-box. Suddenly she lurched forward on it, her head disappearing below the ledge of the witness-box. For a moment I thought she had fainted, but equally abruptly she popped up again. The judge said to her: "Miss Ricardo, you know you have taken an oath to tell the truth and the full truth?"

She said, quite firmly: "That is what I want to do."

"Tell me again, how many times have you visited Bryanston Mews?"

"Once."

The judge nodded at Mr. Griffith-Jones, who directed Miss Ricardo's three statements to the police to be handed to her. As he was asking her to look at one of the statements, the judge said: "Before you look at the statement, you know people do not go into a lounge four in hand and have sexual intercourse unless there is some special relationship between them?" I had a feeling here that the judge was trying to convey to the court something above and beyond his actual words. The special relationship that Ward and Ricardo had presumably was that they inhabited the same far-off country, belonged to the same way-out set: one where intercourse was exchanged as freely and informally as drinks. "We at the Bar are men of the world," the judge said, echoing what judges have always said and wishfully thought; for theirs is one of the most cloistered of all the professions. "Just think out," he continued, "what previous relations you had before these events happened?"

Speaking so quietly that one could hardly hear her, Miss Ricardo said: "Well, I had my boy friend because I was fond of him and the girl friend of mine and Stephen were friends. We never set out to have sexual intercourse..." Her voice trailed away. It was a not unbelievable reply. Such citizens do not always set out to have intercourse. They take a few drinks and it happens. That is the sort of way they live.

Mr. Griffith-Jones now embarked on the cross-examination of a woman who until a few days earlier had been one of the prosecution's chief witnesses. It was a tussle between an advocate well known for his persistence and ruthlessness, for his refusal to take no for an answer; and on the other side a self-confessed prostitute who in her own way was equally stubborn, equally enduring, yet whose nervousness and misery were plain for all to see. One had to admire both; the one for his tenacity, the other for her courage.

"Do you see a paragraph in that statement beginning : 'About a week later Stephen telephoned me and came round to the flat.' Is that what he did?"

"Yes."

"Did you say in your statement : 'He asked me to go down to the country to a house party on Bill Astor's estate where he lived'?"

"Yes."

"And did you say in your statement : 'Stephen told me it would be worth my while'?"

"No."

"And did you say in the statement : 'And that his friends were wanting to meet the girls. It was not on a whore basis.' Did Stephen say that to you?"

"No."

"If he did not, how on earth did you come to tell the police that?"

"I wouldn't say anything like that."

"That statement was read over to you before you signed it?"

"If I signed it, I must have read it."

"How did you come to read over and sign that statement if you say now that he did not say it?"

"I don't know."

"Are you trying to help the court today?"

"I'm trying as much as I can."

"Were you trying to help the police?"

"Yes."

"By telling an untrue statement? What was the point?"

There was no reply. Mr. Griffith-Jones put the question again. Again there was no reply. Was it because the first statement was true, or because she did not have the intellect or the vocabulary or perhaps the nerve to explain how she had come to make a false statement?

Mr. Griffith-Jones read out more of the statement. "After Christmas I went to a flat in Grosvenor Square with Stephen. He introduced me to a man, but I can't remember his name.' Did he do that?"

"No."

" 'I had sex with this man in the flat. He gave me a "pony".' Did you say that?"

"No."

"You told the police that you were introduced to the man. How did the last part of the sentence come to be in the statement you signed unless you said it?"

There was no reply. Miss Ricardo bit her lip and screwed up the corner of her dress with her hand. She looked a picture of misery.

The judge said : "It was true, wasn't it?"

"No."

"Will you tell the jury why you said it?"

"I wanted to keep my flat, I think."

"Are you suggesting that the police just put these words into your mouth?"

"Yes."

Yes, this is precisely what she was suggesting, though it had needed the intervention of the judge to get her to admit it. But was it true? If it was true, then fear of reprisals, fear of the police who were everywhere in the Old Bailey, went some way to explaining her nervousness and hesitancy in answering. If on the other hand it was false, and her original statement was true, why risk a charge of perjury and the taunts of Mr. Griffith-Jones by coming to the Old Bailey to deny it? Because of pressure put on her by Ward's friends? But who were they?

"You must realise," said Mr. Griffith-Jones, "that to have these words put into your mouth and have this written down as yours is a very wicked thing to do." Perhaps : but it would by no means be the first time that such a thing had happened; and some people would say that the wickedness of it was debatable. "Did you never complain?"

"Who could I complain to?" asked Miss Ricardo. It was not a bad question, if she was speaking the truth. If a convicted prostitute wants to complain of the police, who *does* she complain to? Not, surely, to the police?

"The jury will want to know," said Mr. Griffith-Jones, not loosening his hold for a moment, "how it ever came that you were able to see that in writing, read it through and sign it as true when it is all invention put in by the police. How did you ever come to do it?"

Mr. Griffith-Jones was only the last of a long line of Senior Treasury Counsel who had been asking this question of witnesses and defendants down the long years. Yet Miss Ricardo's reply was none the less interesting for that.

"I think, at the police station," she said, "I was kept so long I was ready to sign anything."

Somewhere, not so long ago, one had heard these words before. Was Miss Ricardo slavishly copying what John Hamilton-Marshall had said, or had there happened to her precisely what he alleged had happened to him?

Mr. Griffith-Jones picked up Miss Ricardo's statement again, and referred to a passage where she said she had visited the defendant at Bryanston Mews. He read out: "'This left me alone with Stephen, and although I wanted to leave he wanted me to stay and meet his friend Tom.'" Mr. Griffith-Jones broke off and said to no one in particular, "Unless His Lordship directs, I will not read the surname". While we were figuring out all the Toms we knew, Mr. Griffith-Jones went on: "'Tom finally came with a girl who passed out. I went into a bedroom to have sex with Tom, but he was too drunk. He paid me in dollars and pounds.'" These three short sentences spoke of worlds elsewhere, way beyond our ken. "Did you say that to the police?" asked Mr. Griffith-Jones.

There was no answer, only an agonised expression and more biting of the lower lip. "It's an easy enough question to answer," said Mr. Griffith-Jones, "did you say that to the police?"

"I did."

"Is it true?"

"No."

"Why did you say it?"

This time Miss Ricardo answered readily and with vehemence: "I told you why I said it once before."

A little later, when the judge was speaking to her, she said : "A lot of people have been speaking to me on this matter recently."

Mr. Griffith-Jones, quick as a lizard, said : "Persuading you to change your evidence?"

"A lot of people," said Miss Ricardo, "have been trying to persuade me to change my evidence."

Had they now? Because the original evidence was true or because it was false?

Mr. Griffith-Jones picked up another of Miss Ricardo's earlier statements in which she said she had intercourse with various men who gave her between £10 and £20 a time : Ward was there on some occasions and on other occasions he would go out. She had never given Ward any of the money she had earned in this way and she did not know if the men she went with gave him money.

"Did you say that?"

She made a long, rambling reply which was almost entirely inaudible. At the end of it she said with passion : "I didn't want to sign that statement. I didn't want to have anything to do with it."

"You read the statement before you signed it, didn't you?"

"No, I didn't. It was read out to me."

"You must have realised if it was untrue?"

"That's why I didn't want to sign it."

"Why did you sign it?"

"I wanted the police to leave me alone."

"If that was so, didn't you complain and tell Stephen the police had been behaving so disgracefully?"

At this point Mr. Burge got up and said : "At this time Dr. Ward was in custody."

Mr. Griffith-Jones said : "You are perfectly right. I apologise." He turned back to Miss Ricardo. "Did you not complain to anyone else?" We had been over this ground once already. There was no answer.

"At some stage you were asked or told you would be required to give evidence?"

She answered this one immediately, definitely : "No, I was

told I would *not* have to give evidence." This seemed to her a very important point.

"In the end you had to give evidence at the Magistrate's Court?"

"Yes."

Mr. Griffith-Jones picked up another document and read out more passages. " 'By occupation I am a dancer and I also earn money by visiting men and being paid by them. I went to bed with men at the flat. When I went to bed with the men we had intercourse.' Did you say that?"

She nodded.

" 'On the occasions when this did happen at the flat, I had been invited to go there by Stephen.' Did you say that?"

She nodded again.

"Miss Ricardo, why did you say that?"

"Well, at the time I was scared."

Scared of whom? The police? We were nearing the end of a long day. The judge said : "You are telling the jury you deliberately went into the witness-box and said those things were true when they were not?"

"Yes."

The judge paused a moment and then said to her : "I will consider your case later." This sounded like a threat, but a threat of what? The impression was reinforced a moment later, after Mr. Griffith-Jones had indicated that this might be a convenient moment to adjourn. "I would advise you very seriously," said the judge to Miss Ricardo, "to consider your position overnight." What did he mean by this? It looked much as though he disbelieved her evidence today and was advising her to consider going back to her original evidence tomorrow. If her evidence today had been a pack of lies, well and good. But if it had been the truth—and she had struck many of us as being a truthful witness—was there then not a danger of encouraging her to commit perjury a second time?

"I have considered..." said Miss Ricardo, with the failing strength of a swimmer about to go down for the third time. But the judge raised his hand.

"Don't say anything now," he said.

And she didn't. And that was the evening of the second day.

PART III

AND ON THE morning of the third day Mr. Griffith-Jones and
Miss Ricardo took up the cudgels again; and she at once made
clear what the judge had called her overnight position.

"Yesterday I put to you two statements you had made to the
police, and the deposition you gave on oath to the magistrate.
You told the court that was untrue. Are you still saying that?"

"Yes," she said quietly, "I'm afraid so."

"You have said you made these statements to the police
because you were under various pressures from the police. Are
you saying that is right?"

She nodded.

"You made your first statement to the police and that statement you have told us contained really in effect the evidence you
have given to the magistrate, and that was on April 5th?"

"Yes."

"You say that was untrue?"

She glanced at the statement and said: "There is a lot in that
statement that is true."

"And a lot that is not?"

"Yes."

Mr. Griffith-Jones turned over a page of the document.

"You have a young sister about thirteen?"

"Yes."

"Her name is Dorothy?"

"Yes."

"After you had made that statement on April 5th did the
police interview your young sister on April 10th?"

"They interviewed both."

"I am only dealing with Dorothy at the moment. Did they
interview Dorothy? I think you were present?"

"Some of the time."

"And Dorothy made a statement?"

"Yes."

"After Dorothy had made a statement, did you tell the police about another girl, a girl called Diane?"

"Yes."

"And you volunteered that information, didn't you?"

"Yes."

"That was a girl whom the defendant Dr. Ward knew?"

"Yes."

"That statement is about Dr. Ward as well as about the girl?"

"Yes."

"Was that true?"

"It's all true."

I was wondering—many of us were wondering—who Diane was. I remembered that at the lower court Miss Ricardo had said that Ward had asked her if she knew anybody who could do an abortion, because a girl he knew was pregnant. Perhaps this was Diane?

"If in fact," Mr. Griffith-Jones went on, "the police were forcing you to say false statements and putting pressure on you when you made your statement on April 5th, how does it come that on April 10th you are actually volunteering fresh information about the defendant to the police?"

"I didn't want my sister to go to remand home."

"In spite of what the police had done and the pressure brought to bear on you, five days later you were volunteering fresh information?"

"My sister was on the point of going to remand home."

Mr. Griffith-Jones voiced what many of us were thinking. "How would this stop your sister going to remand home?"

Miss Ricardo's answer was as dramatic as it was surprising.

"I thought if I helped them, they'd help me."

It made sense. That is what people called along to police stations often do. Indeed the very words are ones which police officers are habitually supposed to use. "You help us and we'll help you." What the judge would call a *quid pro quo*.

Mr. Griffith-Jones put down the documents he was holding, picked up some other ones and handed them to the judge. Miss Ricardo, who had been standing until now, was allowed to sit down. We were about half way through this heavyweight contest, and if anything Miss Ricardo was just a shade ahead on points.

"Thereafter," said Mr. Griffith-Jones, coming out of his corner once again, "you never made any complaint to anybody, did you, about the fact that it was the police? You just let the matter go on?"

"Who could I complain to?" said Miss Ricardo angrily. "Who could I go to in authority?"

Mr. Griffith-Jones turned to Miss Ricardo's statement of June 18th and asked if that was right. Miss Ricardo said: "I told you about that statement yesterday."

"After making that statement you never complained to anyone else that it was untrue?"

"I didn't know who to complain to."

"On July 3rd you gave evidence at the Magistrate's Court and never complained then about what you said in April and June was untrue?"

"When I came out of the Magistrate's Court I was very upset. A policeman came up and said that I should not worry, and that Mr. Herbert wanted to see me."

Mr. Griffith-Jones then read out the statement that Miss Ricardo had made at Scotland Yard a few days earlier, and in which she had retracted much of what she had previously said.

I have come here this evening to make a statement about the Ward case. I want to say that most of the evidence I gave at Marylebone Court was untrue. I want to say I never met a man in Stephen Ward's flat except my friend 'Silky' Hawkins. He is the only man I have ever had intercourse with in Ward's flat.

It is true that I never paid Ward any money received from men with whom I have had intercourse. I have only been in Ward's flat once and that was with 'Silky'. Ward was there and Michelle. The statements which I have made to the police were untrue.

I made them because I did not want my young sister to go to a remand home or my baby taken away from me. Mr. Herbert told me they would take my sister away and take my baby if I didn't make the statements.

Mr. Griffith-Jones added that the statement also said that there was a threat that her brother would be nicked for poncing, and two days later he was in fact nicked for poncing.

> I believed what Mr. Herbert said and so I made the statements—three or four of them—and gave my evidence. I don't want to give false evidence again, particularly at the Old Bailey. I told my solicitor on Monday about this and he advised me to tell someone about it. This afternoon I went to the office of *The People* newspaper and made a statement to them.

Mr. Griffith-Jones said that the statement ended: "That is my signature on it. I just want everyone to know why I committed perjury. I do not want to do it again."

Mr. Griffith-Jones asked Miss Ricardo if she had made that statement and when she said she had, he then read a second statement, one she had brought along with her to Scotland Yard at the time of making the first statement.

> I wish to make a statement to Scotland Yard that the evidence I gave at the Stephen Ward hearing at Marylebone earlier this month was largely untrue. I visited Ward at his flat at Bryanston Mews on one occasion only and not several as I previously stated.
>
> This visit was made in company with my boy friend 'Silky' Hawkins with whom I had intercourse in the flat. No one received any money. At no time have I received money on Ward's premises, or given money to him.
>
> On this occasion there was no one else in the flat. Stephen was a friend of mine and made several visits to my apartment at Ladbroke Grove, and also to me in a friend's flat in Vauxhall Bridge Road, Victoria.
>
> The reason the earlier statement was divergent from the truth was my apprehension that my baby daughter and young sister might be taken out of my care following certain statements made to me by Chief Inspector Samuel Herbert.

Mr. Griffith-Jones asked if that was the statement she made to *The People* and she nodded. There then ensued a long bout of questioning in which Mr. Griffith-Jones endeavoured to get Miss

Ricardo to admit that she had changed her evidence in order to sell her story to *The People*. This was much the same line that Mr. Burge had pursued with Mandy the day before, and the fact that both counsel could adopt the same tactics for opposite ends made things somewhat confusing. Some of Miss Ricardo's replies were highly unsatisfactory and it took all of Mr. Griffith-Jones' persistence and singlemindedness to get her to admit that on July 18th she had informed *The People* that she was going to make an affidavit that her previous evidence was untrue.

"How does it come about," said Mr. Griffith-Jones, "that it was not until July 18th that you told *The People* your previous story was untrue when you had approached them to sell your story some three or four days before?"

This assumption of Mr. Griffith-Jones that she had tried to sell her story to *The People* a few days before was not entirely beyond dispute. She had, she told Mr. Griffith-Jones, said to many people that she intended to go back on her previous evidence; and it was not at all clear whether the first approach to *The People* had been initiated by her or the newspaper. Also some of her replies might have been more satisfactory if there had not been several misunderstandings, which were never cleared, between Mr. Griffith-Jones and herself as to whether they were talking about "people" or "The People". (*Q.* Did you tell *The People* you were going to make an affidavit to the effect that your previous story was untrue? *A.* I told a lot of *people* that.)

Later when Mr. Griffith-Jones again pressed her to say why she had waited until July 18th before telling *The People* that her previous story was untrue, she said: "I got sick of the whole business. I had asked a reporter a couple of days previously what I should do."

"Did it not occur to you the most appropriate person to tell would be someone at Scotland Yard rather than *The People* newspaper?"

"No."

This answer one could understand. Policemen are loyal to one another. Sentiment apart, they have to be in order to survive. If I was a convicted prostitute I'm sure I would not go to Scotland Yard to make a statement complaining of the behaviour of another policeman. With *The People* there would be no danger of such a statement being shelved and forgotten.

"Did you think of going to a solicitor?"

"I did."

"Why go to *The People* newspaper?"

"*I* didn't choose *The People*. *I* chose the reporter."

"Let me make my suggestion perfectly clear. My suggestion is that it was only because *The People* had refused to pay you the money that you thought of altering it?"

"No."

"Were *The People* newspaper so kind as to move you from your Bayswater Hotel to somewhere else for a few days?"

"Yes."

"Where did they put you up?"

"In Kent."

"Did they keep you at an hotel in Kent?"

"It was a house."

"The reporter's house?"

"I don't know." That didn't sound very convincing. Later she said : "I *think* it was the reporter's house." She said she had stayed there two or three days and the name of the reporter was Ted Wilson. But why be so cagey about it?

"The object of taking you down to Kent was because now you had told them that your previous evidence was untrue it was headline news, and *The People*, being a newspaper that was published on Sunday, perhaps naturally enough did not want any other newspapers to collar the story, so they took you down to this house so that no other newspaper could get hold of you. Is that the position?"

It was half the position and none the worse for that. Miss Ricardo supplied the other half. "The police were hunting me. I was very frightened." As well she might be; she was one of the prosecution's star witnesses.

On the whole Mr. Griffith-Jones had been no more successful in his efforts to show that Miss Ricardo had altered her evidence in order to sell her story to the papers than Mr. Burge had been with Mandy the day before; there was after all no evidence that any newspaper had given either of them a penny piece. On the balance of probabilities it seemed to me that Miss Ricardo was speaking the truth. There were two reasons for this. One was a negative reason, the difficulty of believing the opposite, i.e. that she was speaking the truth at the Magistrate's Court but was lying in her teeth now. It would have taken, in my view, a woman of much greater intellect, nerve and sense of loyalty to Dr. Ward than ever Ronna Ricardo possessed to have gone through the ordeal first of going to *The People* newspaper to make one false statement, then of going to Scotland Yard to make another, and finally of standing in the Old Bailey witness-box, with the eyes of all England (not to mention the judge and Mr. Griffith-Jones) upon her, and lie and lie and lie. And the second reason for giving her the benefit of the doubt was the quality of many of her answers. *"Who could I complain to?"* *"I thought if I helped them they'd help me."* *"I told you why I said it once before."* *"I think at the police station I was kept so long I was ready to sign anything."* *"I was told I would not have to give evidence."* There was a third reason too which made one regard her evidence favourably, and that was she had not tried to deny *everything* she had previously said: she had admitted that the story about Ward and Diane was still true and she had also admitted—bravely because she minded admitting it—what the judge so appositely described as "the four in hand". Taken all in all both the manner and the matter of her answers made more sense in the context of truth than of fiction.

This impression was strengthened by one of the answers she gave in her very brief cross-examination by Mr. Burge. He began by asking her if it was true that she had made false statements and given false evidence because of the strong pressure she was under from Mr. Herbert and Sergeant Burrows.

"Yes."

"Yes." Pause. "You have a young sister who lives with you?"

"Yes."

"And I think you have a child?"

"Yes."

"Yes. Was it put to you that if you didn't provide some evidence against the accused Ward that those two would be taken away from you as being in need of care and attention?"

"Yes."

Mr. Burge then referred to her statement of April 5th **and** a sentence which ran: "There was a two-way mirror in the flat". Before Mr. Burge could question her on this she said, shaking her head: "I never said this". And indeed, unless she had invented the thought, it would have been impossible for her to have said it. For the evidence we had heard so far on the two-way mirror was that it had been broken by Mandy during Rachman's tenancy, and that when Ward arrived in the flat there was only a hole in the wall where the mirror had been.

"If you didn't say there was a two-way mirror in Ward's flat," said Mr. Burge, "how do you suppose it came to be in the statement?"

"I didn't see the statement," said Miss Ricardo, "before going into court." She added, almost in tears: "I definitely *wouldn't* have said this if I knew there wasn't a mirror there."

I would have liked to see Mr. Burge press this point a little further. For there could be only two explanations of it. Either Miss Ricardo had made a statement about the two-way mirror which she knew to be untrue, *or* the police officer who had taken her statement down had written something she had not said. As it was, Miss Ricardo seemed to be wilting under her long ordeal, and so, when her only answers to further questions about the four in hand were nods and sobs and shakes of the head, Mr. Burge, on a somewhat anti-climactical note, brought his short cross-examination to an end.

The next witness was Mr. James Eylan, the man whom Christine said she first met while at Comeragh Road and who had had intercourse with her for money there and at Wimpole Mews. Mr. Eylan's appearance in the witness-box did not last more than ten minutes, and yet he was someone whose image remained vividly in the mind long after those of more exotic witnesses had faded. In one way this was curious because there was nothing remarkable about him as a person, and his story was dull in the extreme. In appearance he looked typically English, a cross between Enoch Powell and the man from the Pru, a sort of poor man's David Niven. He wore a carefully pressed grey suit, white shirt and old school tie. He was as dapper in his own way as Mr. Griffith-Jones was in his. He looked about forty and his hair was thinning on top. His voice was as clipped as his neat little moustache; and he gave firm precise replies to the questions put to him. What made him memorable in the context of the trial was not what he looked like, not even what he said, but rather that he was there at all. For he was the only prosecution witness to confirm what Christine had said; that she had slept with men for money. He spoke not only for himself but in a sense for all the men who had had Christine Keeler and paid her for it. And by the time he had finished one thing was certain beyond dispute: in the legal sense of the word Christine Keeler was a whore.

"Did you visit Miss Keeler at Wimpole Mews?"

"Yes."

"Did you have intercourse with her there?"

"I did."

"How often?"

"I should say about three times there, and on several occasions elsewhere."

"Did you pay her money on each occasion?"

"Yes."

"Generally speaking what amount?"

"Mostly £15 and on one occasion £10."

"Was there anyone else in the flat?"

"No."

"Did you also lend her money?"

"On one occasion, yes."

"Was it at her request?"

"Yes."

"Were you paid back?"

"No."

"How did she make the request?"

"She was always hard up financially and used to ask for money for her mother and others things."

"Did you ever meet the defendant Ward?"

"Briefly on one occasion in 1961."

"Where was that?"

"At the Wimpole Mews flat when I called there."

"Can you tell us about how much money in all you must have paid her, excluding the loan?"

"It would be a total of £100 to £120."

Mr. Griffith-Jones sat down and Mr. Burge got up.

"It is quite clear that the accused did not introduce you to Miss Keeler?"

"Yes."

"Had you met her before you went to Wimpole Mews?"

"Six or nine months before. I called at Wimpole Mews to take her out and she introduced me to him."

"Is it right that you took her out to restaurants and places of entertainment and that quite apart from the question of intercourse she was an amusing and attractive companion."

"Yes."

"Is it also right that the only occasions when you had intercourse with her at Wimpole Mews was in the middle of the day during lunch time?"

"Yes."

"When it was known that Dr. Ward would be at his surgery?"

"That is correct."

Mr. Burge had established that Ward was no friend of Mr. Eylan's, though he had not yet succeeded in proving that Ward did not know of Eylan's lunch-time visits when he was at his surgery. Much more interesting though was his attempt to persuade the jury that Christine Keeler, by going out with Mr. Eylan to restaurants and other places of entertainment was not a tart in the conventional sense of the word (i.e. a woman who has indiscriminate and joyless sexual relations with strangers). Would the jury be prepared to accept such a distinction and, as a matter of law, would the judge let them?

Mr. Burge sat down and Mr. Eylan was shown out of the witness-box. He had come from nowhere and now he was going back to nowhere. He was like someone whose face one glimpses in a fog, who is never seen again yet always remembered. One knew nothing about him: where he lived, what his job was, if he was married, what his wife thought about it all if he was married, where he went for his holidays, if he liked animals. He was utterly anonymous. One knew one thing about him and one thing only; that he had given Christine Keeler money for her favours. And on this thing, to a very large extent, would the verdict of the jury depend.

Up to this moment in the trial the general feeling in court had been that although there could be little doubt that Ward was a habitual associate of prostitutes there had been little in the way of evidence to justify the charges of living on their immoral earnings, which, when all was said and done, was why we were here; and the impression on the Press benches that this was really a political trial, an instrument of revenge by the Establishment for the scandal caused by the exposure of Profumo, was growing all the time.

But with the calling of the name of Vickie Barrett this changed. For she was the witness for whom we had been waiting, the girl whom Mr. Griffith-Jones had said in his opening speech had visited Ward's flat for a period of over two months to give sexual comfort and stimulation to a variety of men for money which she had never received. Would her performance in the witness-box bear out the promises that Mr. Griffith-Jones had made of her? If it did, then as surely as the coming of night the jury would find, and rightly find, Ward guilty.

She came into the witness-box, a little whey-faced blonde, wearing a sort of green raincoat with a white scarf round her neck; and when she turned to face the court and while she was giving the oath, one's impression was one of shock; shock that Ward, whom one had believed to be a man of some fastidiousness in his tastes, had sunk so low. For of all the whores the prosecution had paraded or were still to parade before us this one was the bottom of the barrel. Christine and Mandy and even Ronna Ricardo had had a certain style, a kind of robustness, which compensated for their other deficiencies, but this little waif had nothing. She was like a little sad, sick elf, a photograph, as Rebecca West later put it, from a famine relief fund appeal. Clearly no improving influences had come to grace her life, no Professor Higgins had taken her under his wing: she was, in officers' mess parlance, a ten bob knock in the Bayswater Road. I looked at her standing so awkwardly in the witness-box, and then I looked at Ward, intelligent and sophisticated, in the dock, and I found it difficult to reconcile the two.

Just before Mr. Griffith-Jones rose to start his examination, Mr. Burge said that he wanted to object to the admissibility of all of Vickie Barrett's evidence. The reasons for this were that her evidence was additional to that presented at the lower court and had been put in by the prosecution to corroborate Miss Ricardo's evidence. But as Miss Ricardo had now gone back on her original evidence, there was nothing for Miss Barrett to corroborate. After listening to what Mr. Griffith-Jones had to say the judge ruled that the evidence was admissible.

Mr. Griffith-Jones said that her evidence was going to take some time, and a chair was brought for her. She began her evidence in a thin small voice: before she had gone far it was clear that of all the witnesses so far she was going to be the most inaudible. She remained quite still in her chair, even while she was speaking: her face was totally without expression, her hands devoid of movement. She looked sick and stupid and sad: yet she hardly ever hesitated for an answer.

"Your home is in Birmingham? Did you come to London first in the summer of 1961?"

"Yes."

"Did you stay with a friend and, I think, work in a café?"

"Yes."

"In August 1961 were you arrested in Bayswater for soliciting for the purposes of prostitution, and did you appear at the Magistrate's Court?"

There was no audible answer.

"And after that did you go and spend two days in Holloway Prison?"

"Yes."

"And after that did you go back to Birmingham to your parents' home?"

"Yes."

"And you remained and did a job in Birmingham for some two years?"

"Yes."

"Did you return to London in about the second week of January this year?"

"Yes."

"And did you go and stay with a friend of yours called Brenda O'Neil?"

"Yes."

"Where?"

"In Leighton Road."

"Where do you say?"

"Leighton Road. It's off Kentish Road. N.W."

"And what does Brenda O'Neil do?"

"She's a prostitute."

"Was she a girl you had met when you were previously in London?"

"Yes."

"Had you been acting as a prostitute while you were in Birmingham?"

"No."

"Since your conviction in London in 1961, have you done any prostitution?"

"No."

This seemed a rather curious answer in view of what we had already heard. Mr. Griffith-Jones pointed to Ward.

"Do you know the defendant?"

"Yes."

"Will you tell the court how it came about you met him?"

The overture was over, and now the curtain was about to rise. Although the audience had been hushed ever since Vickie Barrett had entered the box, they now became quite rigid, as wax-like as she was, fearful that some small sound should come between them and her words.

"I met him in Oxford Street. I was going down to the club. I was walking in Oxford Street about 12.30. I was just by Oxford Circus Tube station and about to turn the corner to go towards the London Palladium when he drove up in a white Jaguar."

One could picture the scene vividly.

"Yes."

"Well, he stopped the car and got out. Then he came up to me and asked me if I'd like to go to a party. I said, 'No'."

"What did you say then?"

"I said: 'I don't like parties'."

"Yes."

"Well, then he said it wasn't actually a party. It was just a few friends with wives and girl friends. He wanted a girl himself to have a conversation with."

"What else did he say?"

"That he hadn't got a girl friend for himself for the party and wanted me to accompany him. He said he would give me some money if I stayed for two hours. I told him I wasn't a prostitute and he said he didn't want anything to do with me except to have conversation. We got into the car and drove to his flat. On the way he told me what he wanted me to do."

A novelist, looking for words to end a chapter, could not have hit on a more effective last sentence. Mr. Griffith-Jones picked up the cue.

"What was that?"

"He said he had a man in the flat who wanted to go with a girl and he said the man would give him the money."

The judge said: "Who was to be paid the money?" and Vickie Barrett said: "Stephen Ward."

I glanced at Ward. He was looking down towards his knees. There was a slightly quizzical expression on his face, and he seemed to be listening as intently as the rest of us.

"What was he going to do with it?" said Mr. Griffith-Jones, meaning the money.

"He said if I visited him two or three times a week he would save the money and I could live in a flat."

"Did he say what, if any, advantage there was in a flat with clothes and so on?"

"He told me—with clothes and that in the flat—he could introduce me to the best clients."

"Did he say anything else on the way to the flat?"

"No."

It was only afterwards, reading Vickie Barrett's evidence that one was suspicious of the too eager readiness to say what she was expected to say. "On the way he told me what he wanted me to do." "He said the man would give him the money." And the inconsistencies too. "I haven't done any prostitution since August 1961." "I told him I wasn't a prostitute." But at the time she sounded quietly convincing.

"And you arrived at the flat?" said Mr. Griffith-Jones. Now we were going into the sordid details and you really could have heard a pin drop.

"Yes, in Bryanston Mews."

"On arrival did he take you into the flat?"

"Yes."

"Was there anybody in the living room?"

"No."

"What did he say to you?"

"I asked him where the man was."

"What did he say?"

"He said he was waiting in the bedroom."

"Yes."

"Well then he gave me a contraceptive and told me to go to the room and strip and he said he would make coffee."

"Did you go into the bedroom?"

"Yes."

This was Ward's bedroom; it was the only one in the flat.

"Was there anyone in the bedroom?"

"Yes, a man."

"Where was he?"

"In bed."

"Dressed in anything?"

"No."

"Did you go to bed with him?"

"Yes."

"Did you have sexual intercourse with him?"

"Yes."

After intercourse, said Vickie Barrett, she returned to the sitting room alone, leaving the man in bed, and Stephen Ward came in with the coffee.

"Was anything more said, while you had coffee, about money?"

"Yes, Ward said it was all right. He had already received the money."

"Did he say how much he had received?"

"No."

"Did you agree to him keeping it for you?"

"Yes."

Later Ward had driven her back to Oxford Street. On the way he told her he would pick her up at Oxford Circus Tube station on the following Wednesday. This meeting duly took place and she went back with him to Bryanston Mews.

"What happened when you got there?"

"Exactly the same thing as before. There was a different man in the bedroom in bed. I had been given a contraceptive again by Ward and I had normal sexual intercourse with the man."

"Did you go back into the living-room?"

"Yes."

"Did the man come with you?"

"Yes."

"And you had some coffee? Ward being there?"

"Yes."

"Was anything said about money?"

"I asked him again. He said he'd received the money."

"Was there ever anything said about a 'monkey' to be paid for each visit?"

"No."

She said that Ward had again taken her back to Oxford Street. On the way he had given her his telephone number and she had written it down in her diary. The diary was now produced for Vickie Barrett to identify and then passed on to the judge. The judge said to the jury: "What is written here is Stephen Ward PAD 8625," and he handed the diary to Mr. Griffith-Jones. Mr. Griffith-Jones said to Vickie Barrett: "On this page 'Stephen Ward' is the first of six names to appear..." whereupon Mr. Burge got up and said to the judge: "One wonders how an entry made by a witness in a diary can be evidence. I haven't seen it yet." The judge said: "Look at it Mr. Burge. Then perhaps you will cease to wonder."

Continuing his examination, Mr. Griffith-Jones said: "The name and the telephone number are the first of six names and numbers written down there. Are the names of the other people your clients?"

"Yes."

"For the purposes of prostitution?"

"Yes."

But hadn't she *twice* said earlier in her evidence that she hadn't done any prostitution since 1961?

"Did you meet any of those persons through Ward, or are they quite independent?"

"I met one."

"Are the names Vasco, Jimmy, Carlo, Jupiter, Bwana?" Mr. Griffith-Jones made them sound like entries at a dog-show.

"Yes."

"Which one did you meet through Ward?"

Her reply was inaudible.

On the following Friday, she said, she telephoned Ward after midnight, and he came and picked her up at Leighton Road where she was living with Brenda O'Neil. They went back to Bryanston Mews.

"Was there a man there?"

"Yes."

"Was he in bed or in the sitting room?"

"He was in the bedroom in bed."

"Were you given a contraceptive?"

"No."

"Were you given anything else by Ward?"

She said no, but when she went into the bedroom there was a cane on the bed.

"Did you use it?"

"Yes."

"At whose request?"

"At the man's request."

"Did you have ordinary sexual intercourse?"

"No."

The judge asked: "During this time how were you dressed?" She answered at once: "In underwear and high-heeled shoes."

"Where did you find the high-heeled shoes?" asked Mr. Griffith-Jones.

"They were my own."

"Was the man naked?"

"Yes."

"After you had finished that performance, did you go back into the sitting room?"

"Yes."

"Did the man go back?"

"No."

"Was Ward still in the sitting room when you returned?"

"Yes, with the coffee."

"Was anything said about money on that occasion?"

"Yes, Ward said he had received the money from the man."

"Was anything said about the money to be paid for whipping the man?"

"No."

"Did Ward say whether or not he got the money on other occasions?"

"Yes, he said he had the money off the men."

"I don't know about these three times, but by this time you had returned to a life of prostitution generally, apart from these visits to the flat?"

"No."

No?

"Were you offering yourself to anybody else at this stage apart from the men you met in the flat?"

"No."

Well what about Vasco and Jimmy and Carlo? Not to mention Jupiter and Bwana?

Vickie Barrett said that after the third visit there was a standing arrangement for her to telephone Ward after midnight; and that for the next two and a half months she had visited the flat two or three times a week.

"You told us of the third occasion when you were asked to whip one of the men with the cane. Were you asked to whip other men?"

"Yes."

"Was it always with a cane?"

"Not always."

"On one occasion you used a whip?"

"A horse-whip."

"Who handed you that?"

"It was in the bedroom."

"Did you whip only one man with the horse-whip, or more?"

"Two or three men with the horse-whip."

"Was it the same horse-whip each time?"

"No."

"There were two different men with the same whip?"

"Yes."

She was word perfect. One could not fault her.

"Did you beat other men with the cane?"

"Yes."

"Was it the same cane?"

"Yes."

Later Mr. Griffith-Jones asked her about the names in the diary. Had she met any of them at Ward's flat?

"Yes."

"Who did you meet?"

"Vasco." She added: "I met him before."

"As a prostitute?"

"Yes."

Before when? If she was speaking the truth when she said earlier that she hadn't been a prostitute since 1961, she couldn't have seen him for nearly two years.

"It happened you had known him before," said Mr. Griffith-Jones, "and here he was in bed waiting for you at the flat?"

"Yes."

It must have seemed quite like old times. Yet so convincing was Vickie Barrett in her evidence that the preposterousness of this coincidence, and indeed the implausibility of the whole thing did not strike one till later.

"What sort of age were these men who you found waiting in bed at the flat?"

"They were middle aged or elderly."

"Did you ever ask Ward how the savings were getting on?"

"Yes."

"What did he say?"

"He said he had nearly enough."

"Did he tell you how much he had?"

"No."

"Did he ever say anything again about the flat and the clothes he had proposed to give you?"

"He didn't say anything about the flat."

"Did he say anything about clothes?"

"He bought me some clothes."

"He bought you some clothes, did he? What sort of clothes did he buy?"

"Well, there was a dress and a costume and two pairs of high-heeled shoes."

Mr. Griffith-Jones had almost finished now. He could afford to relax a little.

"With your knowledge of the trade, Miss Barrett—or rather profession—what would be the normal payment for services such as you rendered? How much a time?"

"£5 in the flat."

Looking at her I thought she'd have been lucky to see £1.

"And for the whipping, what is the market price?"

If Mr. Griffith-Jones was at all conscious of the delicacy of his phrasing, he did not by so much as the flicker of an eyelid let us know it.

"£1 a stroke."

Did she tell Ward after each beating how many strokes she had given? Or did Ward get the men to tell him and trust them not to cheat? Or did he leave the coffee to simmer on the boil while he went to the keyhole and listened? This was a field we had not even entered.

"You remained in London and carried on with prostitution?"

"Yes."

Mr. Griffith-Jones sat down, and for the first time in nearly half an hour the court was able to relax. One could almost hear the exhalation of breath, though it was not an expression of relief. For what we had just heard had fully confirmed what Mr. Griffith-Jones had said in his opening speech. There had been flaws in Vickie Barrett's evidence certainly, inconsistencies and contradictions, but against the solid oak of most of it, they were quickly forgotten. She had seemed, in her soft pathetic little way, so certain: she had rarely hesitated. Somewhere deep down perhaps one felt that such a relationship as she had described was utterly out of keeping with all one had ever heard or read about Ward, that her story was a tissue of lies, a total invention. Then one dismissed such thoughts as wishful thinking. One did not like to face the truth about Ward because that meant one had been wrong in one's judgement of him. Yet one had to face it. Ward was a ponce, a pimp, a professional brothel-keeper. And by far the nastiest thing of all about him was the bit about taking the money from the men and not giving any of it to Vickie: this was meanness of an order that made one want to vomit. Surely

something so detailed, so huge as this could not have been contrived. And if it was true, then the sooner he was sent down
the better.

Although Mr. Burge knocked some large dents in Vickie
Barrett's armour, he did not, at this time, succeed in piercing it.
One reason for this was that his questioning seemed somewhat
fragmented: he would pursue what looked like a profitable line
of inquiry up to a certain point and then, just as it seemed he
was about to strike gold, he would switch the search elsewhere.
He cannot have been helped in what he was doing either by
Ward's constant offers of advice coming down to him from one
side, or the judge's translations of what the inaudible Vickie
Barrett was saying from the other. As a result Vickie Barrett
managed to maintain her composure throughout, and the ten-
sion, the silence in court that had marked Mr. Griffith-Jones's
examination of her, continued until she stood down.

One of the first things that Mr. Burge wanted to question her
about was her assertion that she had done no prostitution
between 1961 and early 1963.

"You came back from Birmingham to stay with Brenda
O'Neil when she came out of Holloway Prison?"

"Yes."

"Do you know how long she had been in Holloway Prison?"

"Well she was sentenced to three months and she got a
month's remission."

"You joined her just after she came out?"

"Yes."

"Was it directly she came out?"

"She wrote after coming out and asked me to come down."

A little later Mr. Burge asked her: "Did you appear in court
for soliciting on April 23rd?"

"Yes."

The judge said: "Where were you taking your clients at
about the time you were convicted in April?"

"Nowhere."

"You were soliciting and had nowhere to go?"

"In the streets."

Mr. Burge said: "That clearly isn't true, is it? In fact you were living at that time with Miss O'Neil?"

"Yes."

"Where was she taking the men?"

"Anywhere."

"You were living together and both carrying on the business of prostitutes in the West End of London. You have said you would have sexual intercourse for £5 and give a beating for £1 a stroke." Mr. Burge paused. "Would that be in the streets?"

It was a nice conceit: I had a vision of the traffic piling up as Vickie Barrett, in underwear and high heels, laid into innumerable bare bottoms in the middle of Church Street, Kensington. But, as always, she was ready for it.

"Sometimes the men wanted to go to their flats. After April 23rd I got a flat."

"Miss Barrett," said Mr. Burge a little later, "if you had no money coming in, and Ward never gave you any, how did you live?"

"We lived in a flat," said Vickie Barrett, "it was a man's flat, and he gave us money and food and everything."

"Who was the man?"

"Mr. D."

"And what does Mr. D do?"

"He's an electrician."

A kind of Happy Families figure began to form in my mind: Mr. D, the electrician; not a young man certainly, not a ponce at all; about fifty, with spectacles and a bit of a stoop, a man whose life was dedicated to filaments and electrodes and cells, and who out of the sheer goodness of his heart managed to keep two wayward young girls supplied with money and food. Gladstone would surely have approved of him.

"Did you know where your friend Brenda was taking her clients?"

"In the car."

"Whose car?"

"The client's car."

Later again Mr. Burge tried to get Vickie Barrett to reconcile her previous contradictions.

"What you are saying to the jury is that during the time you were going to Stephen Ward's, you were not soliciting and had no money except what the electrician gave you. Is that correct?"

"Yes."

"Are you saying that during that time we are inquiring about in February and March, you were not soliciting in the streets?"

"Yes, that's true."

"And not getting any money by means of prostitution?"

"I got it once."

Just as I was thinking that she must have admitted the once in order to fit in with some further point in her evidence, Mr. Burge said: "Were you picked up by Mr. Lazzolo in Shaftesbury Avenue?" (Mr. Lazzolo was the Vasco of her diary and, apparently, a well-known painter.)

"Yes."

"Did you go to his studio and have intercourse with him, and were you paid £4?"

"Yes."

"When was that?"

"That was after I met Ward."

This meant, though one did not have time to realise it then, two fantastic coincidences; that when she found Vasco waiting in bed for her at Ward's flat, it was pure chance that she happened to know him already; and secondly, that a little while later it was also pure chance that he happened to pick her up in Shaftesbury Avenue.

"Now that you have remembered you were in Shaftesbury Avenue and were picked up by Mr. Lazzolo during this time, isn't it true that you were picked up by other people as well?"

"No."

I couldn't understand these persistent denials of prostitution: they seemed so pointless. Then it occurred to me with a cold shudder that the prosecution were trying to show, not merely that Ward had been living off Vickie Barrett's immoral earnings, but that if it hadn't been for him she would not have gone back to a life of prostitution at all. Could they be thinking, or hoping to prove, anything so patently idiotic?

"So your sole source of income, you say, was the money given to you by the electrician?"

"Yes."

Another point that Mr. Burge had to investigate was the peculiar circumstances in which Vickie Barrett had been brought forward as an additional prosecution witness. She had been arrested for soliciting on the night of July 3rd and taken to Marylebone Lane Police station. That very day the Marylebone magistrate had committed Ward for trial at the Old Bailey.

"Were you bailed out that night?"

"No."

"You were kept in custody?"

"Yes."

"Did you know that Ward had been in court there the day before, facing committal proceedings?"

"No."

No? How could she have *avoided* knowing? It was on the front page of every newspaper, and almost the sole topic of conversation. Moreover she herself had a direct connection with it.

"Do you say that you don't read the newspapers?"

"I do."

"Are you saying that you didn't know that on July 3rd Ward was committed for trial?"

"I didn't want to read about it."

Why not for heaven's sake?

"Do you mean that you did not want to be associated or exhibited in the papers or in any way connected with something like that?"

"Yes."

And that didn't ring very true either. Had she not heard, asked Mr. Burge, about the large sums of money Christine and Mandy had expected to be paid as a result of giving evidence? She said she had. Later Mr. Burge said: "Did you hear about the arrest of Stephen Ward?"

Her reply was extraordinary. "I heard," she said, "that a *Dr.* Stephen Ward was arrested."

"And you had no idea who this was?"

"No. I didn't know he was a doctor."

"You thought it was some other Stephen Ward?"

"Yes."

"Then did you read in the papers about him and other persons—Christine Keeler and so on?"

"Yes."

"You still thought it must be another doctor?"

"I think I saw his photograph in the newspapers."

"When did you first see the photograph and say: 'There is the man, the same Stephen Ward that I know'?"

But she avoided answering the question. "Brenda showed it to me," she said.

Lastly—or rather lastly before the luncheon interval, Mr. Burge explored the same line of country about selling material to the newspapers as he had earlier tried with Mandy and Mr. Griffith-Jones had tried with Ronna Ricardo. Having got Vickie Barrett to admit that she did not want in any way to be exhibited in the newspapers, he asked her: "Didn't you in fact know that Christine Keeler and Mandy Rice-Davies had referred to the very large sums of money which they had been paid or expected to be paid as a result of giving evidence in the case?"

"I'd heard about it, yes."

Mr. Burge picked up a newspaper dated July 23rd which carried a photograph of Vickie Barrett, and asked her to look at it.

"When was the photograph in those garments taken?"

"A few months ago."

"By whom?"

"By a man doing different photographs."

"Did you sell it to the newspaper?"

"No, I didn't."

"Did you receive money for it from the newspaper?"

"No."

"Did you give it to the newspaper?"

"No."

"There are other photographs that have appeared of you in the Press, aren't there?"

"Yes."

The judge said: "Do you happen to know how the newspaper got hold of it?"

"No, I don't."

Although he pressed her with further questions on this subject, at this time Mr. Burge was unable to shake her: that lay in the future. It was now almost lunch time and Mr. Burge wanted temporarily to wrap things up.

"I suggest Ward picked you up near Oxford Street and paid you for your services twice?"

"No, that's untrue."

"Do you know whether or not he had done the same for Brenda?"

"We had some discussion and she said she'd done business with Stephen Ward."

Had she? Was this yet another coincidence?

"And all this story you've told at the last moment on July 4th, is absolutely untrue?"

"That's not true."

"Did they say to you what a godsend you were?"

"No."

"Sent at the last moment to give copy-book evidence about a man living on immoral earnings?"

"No."

Mr. Burge looked at the clock and said he had several more questions to put and asked permission to ask them after the adjournment. It seemed an odd thing to have to ask permission for. The judge said that he would have liked to have finished with Miss Barrett's evidence before lunch, and I wondered why: what was the rush? Suddenly Ward was on his feet, leaning over the edge of the dock and talking agitatedly to Mr. Burge. They conferred for a few moments and then Mr. Burge said to the judge: "In view of what I have been told, I understand there might be a disturbance in court if I..." Presumably he was going to say "am not allowed to ask further questions". Ward must have been feeling very strongly about Vickie Barrett. The judge said: "I don't want anyone to feel there has been any injustice." He said this with quite a smile, and then he added, in a quite different sort of voice: "I cannot shut my eyes to the way witnesses such as this are being approached."

With this remark the pendulum which during the greater part of Mr. Burge's cross-examination had been swinging away from Vickie Barrett and towards Ward, now abruptly stopped. Indeed it began to move back the other way. For if the judge was not objecting to Mr. Burge suggesting that Vickie Barrett was a little liar, then one did not know what he was objecting to; and if he *was* objecting to that, then, as before, what he thought, the jury would be inclined to think too. But what if Vickie Barrett *was* a little liar? What then?

It was after lunch. The tall sheriff and the lean alderman had barely disappeared and the judge hardly settled himself in his seat when Ward got up and said: "I apologise for my outburst this morning." It was the first time he had spoken since he had said Not Guilty a million years ago, and the strength and resonance of his voice again commanded attention. The judge said, generously: "I accept it," and then Mr. Burge got up again.

"You have given the name of Vickie Barrett?"

"Yes."

"What is your correct name?"

Mr. Burge could not hear her mumbled reply, and neither could I: the judge had to relay it for both of us: Janet Parker.

"Do you use another name?"

"Carol Bolton."

"Any others?"

"No."

Mr. Burge turned to the morning's unfinished business.

"You know a gentleman called Mr. Douglas Burns. Is he a photographic agent?"

"Yes."

"Where did you meet him?"

"It was through the housekeeper at 37 Clanricarde Gardens." (Earlier she had given this as her present address.)

"When did you last see him?"

"About three weeks ago."

"Before July 3rd?"

"Yes."

"As a photographic agent did he arrange for photographs to be taken of you?"

"No."

"How did you know he was a photographic agent?"

"From what the housekeeper told me."

I wondered what possible professional interest a photographic agent could have had in Vickie Barrett before July 3rd.

Mr. Burge held up another newspaper carrying a photograph of Vickie Barrett.

"Can you tell me when this was taken?"

"It was a few months ago."

"Where?"

"In somebody's flat."

"Whose flat?"

"I don't know his name."

"Where was the flat?"

"It was in Paddington, but I don't know the road."

Mr. Burge was having some difficulty in hearing. "It was where, do you say?" The judge said, enunciating each word: "It was in Paddington, but I don't know the road."

"Who took you there?"

"A client."

"Who was the client?"

"I don't know."

"Did he take the photograph?"

"Yes."

"Did he give you a copy?"

"No."

It was clear that Mr. Burge had some inside information about Mr. Douglas Burns, for he now returned to him again.

"Is it not true that you and Mr. Douglas Burns have an agreement on a fifty-fifty basis for the sale of photographs to the Press?"

"No."

"When did you last see Mr. Burns?"

"Last week sometime."

"Did you see him yesterday?"

"I think he was here. I think he was talking to some men."

"Did you speak to him yesterday?"

"No."

Mr. Burge tried another tack.

"How did you come to court today from your London address?"

"By bus and taxi."

"Who was in the taxi with you?"

"The man my mother asked to look after me."

"Who was that?"

"The man over there."

She pointed just below Mr. Burge, in the general direction of the bulky figure of Mr. Wheatley, Ward's solicitor. It seemed unlikely that *he* had been her taxi companion. Yet the immediacy with which she had answered and the certainty with which she had pointed may well have put Mr. Burge off his stroke, for he did not press her as to the man's name. However he was to have a second bite at the cherry later.

Lastly Mr. Burge returned to the mysterious Bunbury-like electrician, Mr. D; and with a few short questions and answers he succeeded not only in drastically altering our previous image of him but in so widening the cracks he had already made in Vickie Barrett's evidence as to ensure its eventual disintegration.

"When you were at Leighton Road, had you been living with Mr. D?"

"Yes."

"And had the other girl Brenda been living with him too?"

"Yes."

"And while you were living there, had you not both been soliciting?"

"Yes."

"Was there any possibility of Mr. D getting into trouble as a result of the activities of yourself and Brenda?"

"I don't know."

So here at last was an admission by Vickie Barrett that her previous statement about not having been a prostitute since 1961 were untrue; that at the time when, according to her, she was visiting Ward's flat to meet men, she was also living with Mr. D, getting money and food from Mr. D and soliciting elsewhere. Here in brief was evidence that she was a bare-faced liar.

Nor was it to be the only evidence, for the next witness was Vickie Barrett's friend and stablemate Brenda O'Neil. There was not much to choose between them, for whereas Vickie looked fair and undernourished and sad, Brenda looked dark and undernourished and sad : she had her hair done in a beehive and wore a tattoo mark on her right arm. Her most surprising piece of evidence was that she too had had intercourse with Ward, and once again one experienced a sense of shock that his tastes were so unselective. Perhaps it was because of this that the prosecution had brought her forward. She said that she had been to bed with Ward twice and on each occasion been paid for it. The first time he had picked her up in Oxford Street, but quite independently of Vickie Barrett. "He asked me back to his flat and I went and had intercourse with him. He also sketched me" (I wondered whether the sketching had been done before intercourse and as a stimulant to it or afterwards as a relaxation from it). Vickie Barrett's story was bedevilled with fantastic coincidences and here was yet another. It was quite by chance apparently that, of all the prostitutes operating in London, Ward had happened to pick up the girl with whom Vickie Barrett was sharing lodgings, at the very time when, according to Vickie Barrett, she herself was visiting his flat three times a week to whip and sleep with men. Had Ward had Brenda on the same nights that Vickie had been there? Had he nipped out before Vickie's arrival for, so to speak, a quick one? And if that was so, then presumably there was not much time between Brenda being bundled out of his bed and through the front door and an elderly man arriving and being bundled into it?

So far Mr. Griffith-Jones's questions had only established more evidence as to the extent and variety of Ward's sexual proclivities, which perhaps was their only object. But as the examination proceeded it transpired—I don't know whether Mr. Griffith-Jones had bargained for this—that Brenda and Vickie had often discussed Ward.

Ward, said Brenda, had told her his first name and she had recognised him from Vickie's description. She had mentioned Vickie to him because Vickie had mentioned him to her. She thought that Vickie had done business with him in the same way as she had.

"Did he say," asked Mr. Griffith-Jones, "whether he had asked her anything or to do anything?"

"No."

"What else did he say about her?"

"Only that he had sketched her."

Later she told Mr. Burge that Vickie had said to her that she *had not seen Ward* after the one visit when she had done business with him.

"And by doing business you understood her to mean exactly what you did?"

"Yes."

In his re-examination Mr. Griffith-Jones succeeded only in shaking Vickie Barrett's evidence even further.

"You said that Vickie Barrett did the same business as you did?"

"Yes."

"Did you understand that she did that business with Ward?"

"Yes, so far as I know she did."

"Did she give you details of what happened when she got to his flat?"

"So far as I know he sketched her and she had a drink and had her business with him and she left."

"Did she tell you she had done that more than once?"

"No, when I spoke to her she had been there only once."

Now there was something here which was quite inconceivable. This was that if the story that Vickie Barrett had told Mr. Griffith-Jones about her first visit to Bryanston Mews was true (Ward handing her a contraceptive, finding the naked man in bed) it is inconceivable that she would not have related it to Brenda O'Neil. Brenda O'Neil was one of her closest friends. It was Brenda who had written to ask her to come and live at the electrician's establishment, and they were seeing each other every day. One could just understand Vickie Barrett not mentioning her visits to Ward at all, but what was impossible to believe was her letting Brenda assume that she had had normal business with him if in fact she had had nothing of the kind. It was equally inconceivable, that if Vickie's accounts of all her other visits to Bryanston Mews was true, that she would not have told Brenda about them either. After all Brenda had been picked up by Ward *after* Vickie's first visit to the flat; so that when Brenda told Vickie about it, Vickie either had just been there again or was contemplating going there again in the near future. Are we to suppose then that while Brenda was prattling away to Vickie about her own visit that Vickie remained totally mute; that she did not say a word about the future visits to the flat that she herself had made or was about to make?

The suspension of one's belief in Vickie's story was accumulative, not immediate. Two things decided it beyond any shadow of doubt. The first was the combined evidence of certain defence witnesses who testified that they had been in Ward's flat at the time Vickie alleged that she was there but they had never seen her. The second was her own evidence when recalled to the witness-box by the defence two days later. As this evidence is closely connected with the evidence she had already given, it would be as well to deal with it now.

It will be remembered that Mr. Burge had asked Vickie a great many questions about a photographic agent called Douglas Burns. She had admitted knowing him but said she had not seen him since the previous week. She had strenuously denied that he had ever taken any pictures of her. She had said that the pictures that had been published of her had been taken in a room in Paddington by a client whose name she didn't know and she could not say how these pictures had appeared in the Press. She had side-stepped Mr. Burge's questions as to who had accompanied her to court that day.

Between the occasion of Vickie Barrett first giving evidence and her being recalled by the defence two days later, Mr. Burge had been shown a Press photograph of Vickie Barrett arriving at the Old Bailey on the very morning he had cross-examined her, in the company of Mr. Douglas Burns. Her face was completely hidden under some sort of covering. The object of this was that other photographers would not be tempted to take pictures of her and so bring down the value of the pictures which Mr. Burns had taken and which he was already hawking to the Press with some success.

When she was recalled she was reminded that she was still under oath, and then Mr. Burge said: "You will remember that I asked you questions about your coming to court when you gave your evidence?"

"Yes."

"The point was as to whether or not you were in association with a Press photographer called Burns and you denied it?"

"Yes. That was because I thought I might get him into trouble."

One wondered what conceivable trouble Mr. Burns might

get into merely for performing his somewhat distasteful job.

"Did you mean therefore that you are prepared, if you think you are justified, to tell an untruth on oath in the witness-box?"

"I only told that one untruth."

That in itself was as big a lie as she had yet told.

"You said you had not seen this man Burns for a long time. Have you modified your answer because you know the defence had a photograph of you and Burns arriving at court together?"

"No. Burns said to me if I told the truth everything would be all right."

"But you didn't tell the truth?"

She had an answer for everything.

"He said that *after* I had been in court."

I was just wondering who she was expected to go and tell the truth to, when suddenly the judge said: "You learned after you gave your evidence that if you did admit that you did come with Burns, in fact he would not get into trouble and everything would be all right. Is that the position?"

"Yes."

Vickie appeared relieved, as well she might, by clarification from this somewhat unexpected quarter. I myself had been hoping, when I saw the judge about to intervene that he would say, as he had said to Ronna Ricardo: "I will deal with your case later." It would have been rather more apposite; for while Ronna Ricardo gave the semblance of telling the truth, Vickie Barrett, by any yardstick, was lying.

Mr. Griffith-Jones did nothing to retrieve the position in his brief re-examination.

"Why did you think that it would get Mr. Burns into trouble?"

"Because I didn't want photographs to get in the paper at all."

Here Vickie Barrett was practising, as she had done so often before, the old trick of avoiding the question she had been asked by answering another one.

"Is Mr. Burns a friend of yours? How did he come to be with you?"

"An agreement was being negotiated between Douglas Burns and myself and my mother."

"An agreement was being negotiated ..." She said it as though it were a million dollar contract, and at that moment I do believe the poor little thing saw herself on the wing to Hollywood. Yet she was admitting now what two days earlier to Mr. Burge she had vigorously denied.

"What sort of agreement?"

"He had taken photographs and had said that in some way he would distribute them in the Press."

Here was an admission of yet another lie; but the judge intervened with a little more fatherly clarification. "You are under age and your mother has stepped in?"

"Yes."

Mr. Griffith-Jones tried to salve something by asking if her account of her visits to Dr. Ward was still true, and she said it was. But by this time there were few people left in court—the jury perhaps least of all—disposed to believe her.

Reading Vickie Barrett's evidence later, I wondered how I could have suspended disbelief for so long. I think the answer was the bigger the lies she told, the more she hoped to get away with them. At the time one was so bemused by what Vickie Barrett had to say and the quiet certainty with which she said it that I believe that if she had added that she had found Mr. Kruschev waiting to have his bottom tanned, I would have whole-heartedly believed her. For someone so stupid she was an extremely skilful liar. She lied and lied without batting an eye-lid; and it was this that had made one swallow so uncritically all the things she had said : not merely the factual lies about not being a prostitute, Douglas Burns and the photographs, etc., but her whole preposterous story.

Just how preposterous her story was, one realised the more one considered it. For a start, who was the man waiting naked in bed for her the first time she ever went to Ward's flat? Had he been having dinner with Ward, or did he come round for a drink afterwards and say : "I rather feel like having a tart this evening, old man. I wonder if you'd pop out and get me one?" And did Ward reply : "Why certainly, my dear fellow, and why don't you use my bed while you're at it? Take off your things and hop in, and before you can say Jack the Ripper I'll be back with whatever I can find going along Oxford Street."

Who were these men anyway who were quite happy to roger or be caned by some little whore they'd never even seen? How long were they left naked in Ward's bed before Vickie Barrett arrived? (It would seem quite a long time.) Why did they not pick up their own tarts and take them to their own flats? According to Vickie, one of them, Mr. Vasco Lazzolo, had done this: he had had Vickie previously in his studio. Well, if he had done, what on earth was an established portrait painter like him, a man of some will and selection, doing trundling round to Ward's flat after midnight in the freezing dead of winter, clambering into Ward's bed and waiting there shivering for some girl he'd never seen? The thing didn't begin to make sense; and the reason it didn't make sense was because it was not true: there were no men waiting for Vickie Barrett in Ward's flat: there never had been.

There were other questions too which could not be answered satisfactorily. Were we expected to believe that Ward had proposed and Vickie had accepted the whole bizarre arrangement within minutes of his first picking her up in Oxford Street and her telling him she was not a prostitute? Were we expected to believe that Ward had doled out contraceptives to her, like soup to refugees? Of course this fitted in with the picture she was trying to convey of Ward as a professional ponce, but it is a fact that tarts carry contraceptives in their handbags: they are as much a part of their stock-in-trade as tools to a plumber. And most preposterous of all, were we expected to believe that Vickie had gone back there week after week for two and a half months, caning men and whipping men and having intercourse with them, and not being paid a penny piece for it? Were we expected to believe her story about Ward's promises of a flat and clothes and better customers? Were we to believe that Ward had actually gone out and *bought* clothes for her. (How did he know if they would fit?) Of course ponces arrange such matters for their whores; but they also have some sort of relationship with them which it was clear that Vickie and Ward had never had.

The trouble was that Vickie Barrett was trying to paint a picture of Ward as a professional, and the image would not stick. She had overdone it. If she had told only one small lie about Ward, if she had said there was just one occasion when she had slept with a man in Ward's flat for money, then not only would her evidence have sounded truer but she would have been saved all the factual lies which in the end betrayed her. She had aimed too high; for the whole point about Ward's relationships with women was that he was *not* a professional but an amateur : it was to friends, not strangers, that he introduced the pretty girls he knew, and it was for fun, not money that he did it. To have done what Vickie Barrett had alleged he had done would have unutterably bored him.

Two questions remained. Had Vickie Barrett invented everything she had said and said with such conviction? I do not think that even so fluent a liar as she could have managed that. I believe that she had done what she said she had done, but not in Ward's flat and not in Ward's presence. Certainly she had been to his flat, and if his story was true he had had intercourse with her (or what for him passed as intercourse) twice. But there must have been many other flats which she visited for normal and abnormal sexual relations: that was her daily business. It would not have required much effort or imagination to apply the familiar details to a new location.

And finally there was the biggest, most vital question of all. *Why* had she lied? What benefit would she gain from it, and who had persuaded her to do it? We were not to be given an answer to this question until after the trial.*

The last witness of the day was a man of whom we had already heard much, whose spirit had seemed to hover, as it were, over many witnesses, yet who so far had not graced us in the flesh. This was Detective Chief Inspector Samuel Herbert. He looked like so many of his kind that it is difficult in retrospect to describe him. He was clean shaven, square built, wearing a greeny suit, and aged, I should say, between forty and fifty : in short a good family man. He looked the sort it would be useful to have in a tight corner. He did not need and was not offered any assistance in taking the oath. He picked up the Bible with the ease and familiarity of a country parson and rattled off the tautological absurdities in a voice which wearily told us that

* For Ward's letter to Vickie Barrett and subsequent interview with her by R. Barry O'Brien, see page 235.

he had been this way before. He gave his evidence in the flat text-book tones in which all police officers are encouraged to give, and do give their evidence, venturing and gaining nothing, revealing nothing either. He had not grasped the first principles of spoken communication: he preferred the abstract to the concrete, the passive to the active, circumlocution to directness. Long before he lumbered into sight one knew the questions or sort of questions he would be asked and the answers or sort of answers he would give: they were as predictable as Mandy's had been unpredictable; and it was this that made his occupation of the witness-box seem like a fragment from eternity.

After he had outlined to Mr. Griffith-Jones the circumstances in which Vickie Barrett had come to give evidence, he was asked:

"The defendant was seen on February 5th?"

He replied: "That would be by Sergeant Burrows." (Note *would be*, not *was*.)

"Was he again seen on March 22nd, April 3rd, April 9th and April 26th?"

"That is correct" (Note three words instead of one).

Mr. Griffith-Jones then ran through in chronological order the various dealings that Mr. Herbert had had with Ward. He referred particularly to a letter which Ward had written to Commander Townsend of Scotland Yard on May 26th and which he now read out:

Dear Commander Townsend,

Thank you for the interview that you gave me. I'm sure you can understand my feelings on this matter. From my point of view there is a situation where I am entitled to feel that the allegations made are false.

Although I have no knowledge of the precise charges I have a pretty good idea, from the questions reported back to me, what they add up to, and yet the questioning goes on.

This implies either one or two things—that you shall be 100% certain that no influence or interference or pressure can be laid against the police, or that someone is really out to get me at any cost even on a charge that would later be found to have no substance. The making of such a charge would, as you know, be utterly ruinous to me. How I have survived up to now I do not know, and it is probably due to the extreme loyalty of my friends.

I am also entitled to feel that malice has been at work. Otherwise how could this thing have started?

There is also a great danger that newspapers offer money for specific information or for a certain type of story to irresponsible people. This was clear in the case of the Vassall landlady. I know that Mandy Rice-Davies has been offered money for a call-girl story and that she had offered such a story to *Time Magazine* and other newspapers. I also know that this was after the inquiries had started and was only to substantiate a story already in existence. . . .

Everyone wanted me because he said he thought information would be useful. In the case of the Labour Party it was to shop Mr. Profumo and in the case of the Press to avenge the imprisoned journalists. They accepted information in both cases. In both cases they failed to evaluate [if] the source was leaked for malice. This I now know you will not fail to do.

I am completely satisfied after I saw you that I am in no danger from the police in this respect, since I know the truth myself. You will realise from my point of view that I also welcome the completion of the inquiry, which I would like to be as full as possible.

Ward had gone on to say, said Mr. Griffith-Jones, that he would like Commander Townsend to examine his finances and his records, ask his secretary any questions and talk to his solicitor who was looking after his money.

There are innumerable friends and acquaintances whom you haven't yet got in touch with, whose names I can give you. You may search my flat. More than this I cannot suggest but in return I do beg you to look for the malice behind all this and expose it for what it is.

There is just one other possibility that struck me. It is the danger concerning unintentional false evidence.

Ward then added some details he had heard about a man

who was looking for a girl to swear a false affidavit against him in relation to a call-girl story in a foreign paper. He said he wanted to find out who had made the charges, and he would get his member of Parliament to look after his interests. He ended by saying he had no complaint against the police and mentioned their "tactful conduct".

The letter is interesting as showing something of the fearful strain that Ward must have been experiencing after nearly three months' intense police investigation of him, in which most of his friends had been interviewed about him—many of them several times—in which he himself had been interviewed at least five times, and in spite of which no charges had yet been made. Mr. Herbert said that as a result of Ward's letter he had called on him at Bryanston Mews and told Ward that he wished to take up his offer of examining his accounts and records and would like a letter to his secretary and solicitor authorising him to do so.

Reading from his notebook Mr. Herbert said that Ward had replied:

"Certainly I am prepared to give you a letter and I entreat you to deal with the matter as quickly as possible, as the strain is bringing me to the verge of a nervous breakdown.

"What exactly has been alleged against me? I believe it has been said that I procure young girls for men in high places?"

Mr. Herbert said that his answer to this was that procuration was among the allegations, and that Ward had replied:

"It is ridiculous to say I have received money for introducing girls to men. Of course I always had pretty girls around me and took them to parties, but if this was followed up by the men and the men gave them presents, surely there is no complaint against me, and in any case I don't see anything wrong in it."

Not only did this reply of Ward's sound as though it were something he might well have said, but it was in capsule form the whole of the case for the defence.

Mr. Herbert mentioned other details of the conversation and then Mr. Griffith-Jones brought him to the time of Ward's arrest.

"You saw him at 12.05 p.m. on Saturday June 8th at an address at Watford?"

"It was in a road at Watford. He was standing on the door-step. Sergeant Burrows was with me. I said: 'You know who I am and you also know I have been making inquiries about you for the past few weeks. As a result I now arrest you for living wholly or in part on the immoral earnings of prostitution on various dates from January 1961. You will be taken to Marylebone Lane Police station'."

"He said: 'Oh my God, how dreadful. I shall deny it. Nobody will come forward to say it is true'." This was just the sort of phraseology one could imagine Ward using.

They got into the car and eventually arrived at the police station. Mr. Griffith-Jones was going to ask about further con-versations that took place there when Mr. Burge rose to contest the admissibility of the evidence. He made two points. The first was that the police had not only asked Ward many questions but had also cross-examined him, although the Judges' Rules quite specifically laid down that a person in custody should not be cross-examined. Asked his opinion Mr. Griffith-Jones said that again and again Ward was reminded he was under caution, yet he had gone on pressing the police to ask him questions, saying he wanted to help them all he could. This sounded very probable. I had only met Ward once myself, on the evening of the first day of the trial when he must have been under a similar sort of strain, and he was almost unbearably loquacious: he simply could not stop talking. Nor is there anything odd about this: except in hardened criminals (who have the sense to keep quiet) the shock of sudden arrest inevitably brings on logorrhoea. In the Chinese Communist handbook on the indoctrination of newly captured prisoners there is a section which is rather charmingly headed: *Great Need to Talk, Utter Dependence on Anyone Who Befriends, and Great Need for Approval of Interrogator*; and this weakness has been exploited by inquisitors the world over, ever since interrogation techniques began. One of the dangers though of allowing the admission of statements made in such circumstances is that the person in custody may succumb to the temptation to say things that are not true: he feels his own loneliness and society's hostility so acutely and his urge to lessen them is so great, that he often hears himself saying things *which he thinks the interrogator wants to hear.* This is why interrogators invariably start off by trying a sympathetic rather than an aggressive approach: On the whole it works better. Commander Burt of Scotland Yard has written of this in his memoirs, of "the power that loneliness wields". "Men become desperate in its clutches" he goes on, "they snatch at any bond, even if that bond is a shackle".

The judge gave his ruling. "The Judges' Rules" he said "were never intended to put the police in this dilemma, that even when they are being pressed by a person who is being interviewed to go on asking whatever questions they like they still have to remain completely silent and say nothing." This struck me as being perfectly fair and reasonable, for if Ward was as guilty as the police believed him to be, they would be foolish to deny themselves an opportunity of reaching what they believed to be the truth. But what struck me as being unfair and unreasonable—and this was Mr. Burge's second point— was that although the Judges' Rules state that whenever possible a statement by an accused person should be written down and signed at the *time*, and although Herbert and Burrows had admitted that they had interviewed Ward *for one and a half hours*, no written statement was taken. Presumably this was because Mr. Herbert thought, and rightly thought, that Ward would speak more freely if he did not see pen and ink recording his every word. On these grounds Mr. Burge again asked for the evidence to be ruled as inadmissible. But again the judge ruled against him. "I agree" he said "that it would be more satisfactory if the statement *had* been put into writing and signed, but I do not think Mr. Burge, that the Judges' Rules are laying down that if this is not done then *ipso facto* the evidence is excluded." He added: "I have to satisfy myself that the circumstances were not unfair". But the circumstances (*ipso facto*) are *always* unfair: the police *always* have a position of advantage. The fact of the matter is that if the accused is guilty, which he often is, we tend to forget about the unfairness. But the possibility that the accused may be innocent, and indeed that his appearance of guilt may stem from the results of such unfairness, is one that seldom occurs to us.

This argument is not an *apologia* in advance for any self-incriminating things that Ward may have said. We heard in great detail what he was alleged to have told the police after his arrival at Marylebone Lane, but in the context of the whole trial I doubt if it made much difference to his case one way or the other. There were only two passages which, if true, seemed at all damaging to him. The first was about Mandy Rice-Davies.

I said to him "Do you recall the time that Mandy Rice-Davies was living with you" and he replied "Yes". I said "Did she pay you any money?" and he said "Well, she used to give me £6 a week towards the rent".
Sergeant Burrows said: "Where was she working at the time?" and he replied "She didn't work, she never worked". (*This was not quite true: Mandy herself had admitted to doing some modelling and getting paid for it*.) I asked "Where did she get the money?" and he said "She seemed to have plenty of boy friends. I cannot help it if they gave her money".
I said "Did you know she had sexual intercourse with different men at your flat and received money?" (*This seemed a strangely worded question: the only man that Mandy said had paid her for intercourse at Wimpole Mews was the Indian doctor*.) He said "I thought she might have done but it was nothing to do with me. I was not always there".

The other passage concerned Christine Keeler. Sergeant Burrows asked Ward if she paid him any money, and Ward replied "Occasionally, but she used to buy the food". Burrows had then asked Ward where she got the money from to pay for the food and Ward had said: "She never did very much work, but at one time she did work for the B.B.C. television." Ward had added that she had male visitors to the flat, that she had a lot of friends, that he knew she used to go into the bedroom, and that she would be sometimes there when he returned. (The phrase *male visitors* did not strike me as one that Ward would have ever used, and indeed the whole passage sounded somewhat unlikely.) At this stage, said Mr. Herbert, he said to Ward: "I don't think we should discuss this matter any further. I have cautioned you time and time again."
Later Ward was to deny and deny strenuously the police account of this interview with him. Apart from the inconsis-

tencies in it already pointed out, one cannot help being slightly astonished by the detail of it, especially concerning Christine Keeler. Although the conversation had lasted an hour and a half, during which time neither police officer had written a word, they had yet managed to remember not only the phrasing of each question and answer, but which officer had put which question and the precise order in which they had occurred.

What did strike me as being potentially far more damaging to Ward was an incident which Mr. Griffith-Jones did not subsequently choose to exploit. This was Mr. Herbert's description of the conversation he had with Ward about Mr. Eylan. "I asked Ward : 'Do you know a man called Eylan?' and he replied 'Do I know him?' I said 'You should, because you introduced him to Mr. Profumo' and Ward said 'Oh yes, Jim Eylan. A good chap. I know him well'." Later Ward denied that he had ever said this on the excellent grounds, corroborated by Mr. Eylan in his cross-examination, that he had met Eylan only once, and that was for four minutes; and we were left with the thought, as no doubt we were meant to, that the police had put things into Ward's mouth which he had not in fact said. But if Ward had known that Christine was sleeping with Mr. Eylan and that he was giving her money, what more natural than to pause to collect his thoughts ("Do I know him?") and then to *pretend* he was an old friend in order to put the whole thing on a cosy, family basis?

Finally Mr. Griffith-Jones turned to Ronna Ricardo.

"It has been suggested that great pressure has been put upon this girl by you and Burrows, something in the nature of threats that her baby and sister would be taken away from her and that she would be charged with larceny and so on. Have either of you ever brought any pressure of that kind upon that girl?"

Mr. Herbert did not answer the question directly. "No threats or pressure," he said, "have been put on that girl or any other witness."

Mr. Burge established that Ward was a man of previously good character, a successful osteopath and a talented artist. He took Mr. Herbert to the time that he had started his inquiries into the case on April 2nd, and then he asked a real bombshell of a question:

"Is it right that between April 2nd and June 8th, that when the accused was arrested you interviewed no less than 125 to 140 prospective witnesses?"

"Yes."

My God, I thought, 140 possible witnesses and this trivia was all they could produce as the result of it. They really had been hard pushed to find anything that would stick.

"Is it right that you interviewed Miss Keeler on twenty-four occasions?"

"Yes."

Twenty-four occasions? It hardly seemed possible. Why?

"And she had been interviewed on fourteen other occasions by Sergeant Burrows and other persons about the other cases of Gordon and Edgecombe?"

"Yes."

"Were you concerned with the case of Gordon?"

"Only inasmuch as I was present when he was arrested."

One could see the drift of Mr. Burge's questioning. We all knew about the rumours concerning the false evidence that was alleged to have been given at Gordon's trial, and the fact that two witnesses he had asked for were said not to be available. Mr. Burge wanted to know how far Mr. Herbert was involved in the case.

"You were not in charge of those investigations?"

"No, sir. Sergeant Burrows was in charge of that matter."

"And were you present at the trial?"

"Only part of the time."

Mr. Burge pushed on. Who took the decision, he asked Mr. Herbert, about the availability of people whom Gordon wanted at his trial? Mr. Herbert said that he had taken charge of inquiries for those people.

"Was the court informed that two witnesses were not available although Gordon wanted them?" (These were the two men Fenton and Comacchio.)

Mr. Herbert's reply was inaudible.

"In fact one of them was in custody?"

"No, he was remanded on bail."

Mr. Burge's next object was to destroy any unfavourable impression the jury might have had as a result of Mr. Herbert's account of what Ward had said to him at Marylebone Lane about Christine and Mandy. His questions and Mr. Herbert's answers are not without interest.

"Did you inform Miss Keeler at one of the twenty-four interviews that if she assisted you in giving evidence against Ward, no proceedings would be taken against her?"

"I never informed her of that."

"It is quite clear that there were matters upon which proceedings could be taken?"

"Yes."

"Are you saying you never mentioned to her the possibility of any proceedings against her?"

"*It may have been mentioned* but I cannot recall the incident."

"Can't you be a little franker about this?"

"*Perhaps so far as my memory serves I may have mentioned to her* the question of proceedings being taken against her."

"Did you intimate that there were matters upon which she could be charged?"

"*I cannot recall* so doing."

"You think you might have done?"

"*I might have done*, and I will go no further than that."

"It would be remarkable if you had not?"

"*I cannot recall it.*"

It would have been astonishing if he had not told Christine that there were matters on which she could be charged. She was in fact an accessory to the alleged procuring of Miss R, and Mr. Griffith-Jones had stated in court on the first day that she would not be proceeded against. Why then was Mr. Herbert so equivocal in his replies?

Mr. Burge turned to two aspects of Mandy's evidence. First he tried to probe deeper into her assertion the day before that the police had threatened to make things difficult for her unless she gave evidence against Stephen Ward.

"Did you interview Miss Rice-Davies on April 23rd at Holloway Prison?"

"I did."

"And had you seen her previously to that occasion?"

"I saw her at West London Court the day before and I told her: 'I believe you can help me in the case of Stephen Ward'."

In answer to further questions Mr. Herbert said that he saw Mandy before the car charges at West London Court on April 24th.

"You saw her on the 24th, and was it then that the police asked for the remand?"

"Yes, sir." He added: "I first asked on the 24th if she would be willing to make a statement and she said she would be."

Now Mr. Burge put the question which all this time he had been leading up to.

"The whole matter in her mind was clearly connected, and in fact pressure was put upon her. Is that correct?"

"No, sir."

It may or may not have been correct; but Mr. Burge had established that Mr. Herbert had approached Mandy for help on two occasions when she was most vulnerable to influence: in Holloway Prison when she was awaiting trial and at West London Court before the hearing of the charges—both occasions when she must have been extremely worried about what was going to happen to her. Even allowing that Mr. Herbert had put no pressure on Mandy at all, he could hardly have chosen two places more psychologically advantageous for obtaining what he wanted.*

Then Mr. Burge took up the question of Mandy and the television set and the fact that because of it Mr. Herbert and Sergeant Burrows had gone out to London Airport to prevent her leaving the country. The answers were again somewhat equivocal.

"It is very exceptional for a uniformed Inspector to deal with a hire-purchase agreement or a question of larceny?"

"Yes, but I thought it was the duty of all policemen to investigate matters of crime."

"Are you saying you went to London Airport to detain Miss Rice-Davies because you considered there was a case against her in relation to the television set?"

"The allegations had been brought to my notice."

*For Mandy's version of her dealings with the police, see pages 245-247.

"Do you agree it was a subterfuge to prevent her leaving the country?"

"I felt she was leaving the country because of the larceny of the television set."

"Are you saying that a Chief Inspector went down to London Airport because you felt that a woman was leaving the country because she had stolen a television set?"

"Yes."

Mr. Herbert seemed quite unaware of the absurd position his answers had landed him in.

"Is that your answer?"

"Yes."

"And is it true?"

"Yes."

"What was the value of the television set?"

"£82."

"You took her into custody and as a condition of her liberty she was asked to enter into a recognisance of £1,000?"

"Yes. She had to appear at the police station at 9 a.m. on June 28th."

"It is quite clear that the reason that the 28th was selected was nothing to do with the television set, but was to make sure she should give the evidence you required from her in this case?"

"No."

But when Mr. Griffith-Jones was re-examining Herbert on this subject the next morning, a rather different picture emerged. The judge, aware no doubt that Herbert's—and indeed the Government's—insistence that Mandy was arrested because of a television set was increasingly making them a laughing stock, broached the matter himself.

"Let us be quite frank about this," he said to Mr. Herbert, "you found Miss Davies at London Airport about to go abroad. Was it then, knowing of the other charge that had given you powers, you decided to exercise those powers?"

But Mr. Herbert decided to appear to be frank without actually being so.

"The fact was that I had brought this matter to Miss Davies's notice just prior to her going to the airport," he said. "It seemed beyond coincidence after she had been acquainted with the facts of the matter that she had decided to leave the country."

"If you," said the judge helpfully, "by legal rights had certain powers that you could exercise, would you hesitate to exercise them in order to keep a witness in this country?"

Mr Herbert saw the proffered oar and grasped it.

"No," he said.

"Isn't it really the truth," continued the judge, easing Mr. Herbert towards dry land, "that it is a mixture of two things here?"

Mr. Herbert seized on this face-saving formula gratefully. "Probably that is so. Yes, sir," he said, thus admitting to the judge what a little while earlier he had strenuously denied to Mr. Burge.

It was left to Mr. Griffith-Jones to haul Mr. Herbert ashore. "Would you," he asked him, "have been doing your duty if you had failed to prevent her going abroad in certain circumstances?"

His wind and confidence restored, Mr. Herbert gave the answer expected of him. "I think, sir," he said, "I would have been failing in my duty."

In the embarrassing silence that followed this remark, an American journalist behind me whispered softly "Amen!"

But that was tomorrow, and tonight, as the court clock showed, there was still a few minutes left before we adjourned for the day. Mr. Burge asked some questions about Miss Ricardo to try and confirm Miss Ricardo's own evidence that police pressure had been put on her. Mr. Herbert denied that pressure had been put on her, as he already had done to Mr. Griffith-Jones. Mr. Burge was about to propose the adjournment when the judge said to him : "Mr. Burge, have you finished your questions in connection with Miss Ricardo?" Mr. Burge said he had. I wondered what was coming. The judge looked round the court and then said : "I think in justice to these two police officers certain questions should be put to them and I propose to do it now." Then he turned towards Mr. Herbert in the witness-box.

"It has been said here that in three statements you took from

Miss Ricardo that you, in fact, made up those statements and they were not the statements truly given by her. What do you say about that?"

Once again in his answer Mr. Herbert managed to avoid mentioning himself. "The statements taken from her," he said, "were taken at her dictation and read over to her. She was invited to make any alterations and she signed them."

"It is said" (the judge continued) "you wrote the statements down and you must have written the implication behind them and included in the statements matters which she had never spoken about. Is there any truth in that?"

"No truth at all," said Mr. Herbert. "Each statement was read to her, and she was invited to make any alteration she wished and she was asked to sign each statement."

And so Mr. Herbert was restored, if not to his former glory, at least to a position of comparative strength, and the doubts which the jury may have been having about him were dispelled like morning mist. Mr. Griffith-Jones had already put virtually the same questions and received the same answers. What need was there for the judge to put them again? What purpose did the asking and answering of them achieve other than to tell the jury obliquely that in the judge's view Herbert and Burrows were men whose word was to be trusted. But can a judge air his views publicly in this way and still claim to be impartial? Is it not rather his duty to regard all witnesses as equal, to weigh their words, prostitutes and policemen together, one against the other, to assess their worth privately, and to postpone judgement and comment on them, however marginal and oblique, until the end? A judge, to alter a celebrated phrase, must not only be impartial but must be manifestly seen to be impartial.

This was the third occasion when in the closing minutes of a session the judge had taken the wind from Mr. Burge's sails, had said or done something the effect of which was likely to damage the case for the defence and strengthen the case for the prosecution. Once again I was left wondering whether the judge had any idea of the probable effect on the jury of his questions, and whether he would have uttered them if he had.

PART IV

UNDAUNTED MR. BURGE returned to the attack in the morning.

"The statement that Miss Ricardo made on April 5th was a statement of four and a half pages—a short statement?"

Mr. Herbert hesitated. "A *reasonably* short statement."

"How long did it take?"

"The actual taking of the statement was between one and a half and two hours."

"Would it be right to say that the statement was not signed by her until 2 a.m.?"

"About 2 a.m., yes sir."

"And the taking of the statement started at 10 p.m.?"

"The interview started at 10 p.m.?"

"Just look at the statement. The final paragraph reads: 'Statement taken at Harrow Road Police station 5th/6th April 1963 between 10 p.m. and 2 a.m.', and signed by you."

"Yes, sir."

"Then is it true it was taken between 10 p.m. and 2 a.m.?"

"I was with Ricardo between 10 p.m. and 2 a.m., but I was not taking the statement the whole time."

Something that Ronna Ricardo had said in her evidence came back to me. *"I think at the police station I was kept so long I was ready to sign anything."* Suddenly this remark came to life. Why had the police chosen the dead hours of night, a time when the rest of the world was asleep, to interview and take a statement from her? It was an extraordinary thing to do. It was not as though there was any hurry: at the beginning of April they had only just started their investigations. But then, as we were finding out, the police had a habit of interviewing potential witnesses at times and places when they were most vulnerable.

Furthermore, although the police did not spare themselves when it came to getting statements from possible prosecution witnesses, interviewing between 125 and 140 people, sitting up till all hours, it was quite a different matter when it came to the defendant. Although Mr. Herbert agreed that he and Sergeant Burrows had questioned Ward for an hour and a half at Marylebone Lane Police station, he said that it "did not strike" him to ask Ward to make a written statement.

"During an interrogation of a man in custody for one and a half hours you never thought of a written statement?"

"No."

"Are you aware of Rule 9 of the Judges' Rules which says that whenever possible a statement should be taken down in writing?"

"Yes, sir."

"And there were clearly facilities and opportunity for taking down a statement, weren't there?"

"Yes, sir."

Then Mr. Burge put the question that many of us were thinking.

"Is it that if he had been asked to give a written statement and reduce it to writing, he would have appreciated that this might be something that might be given in evidence?"

"No, I don't think so," said Mr. Herbert, "it was merely I had not thought of taking a written statement." It was about the fourth time he had said this, and I found it no easier to believe. He added that after all the cautions Ward had been given, he should have realised that what he said *might* be used in evidence. True enough, yet one doubts if he did; a man at the time of his arrest cannot see as far ahead as his trial.

Mr. Burge was less successful in his efforts to show that Ward had not said some of the things that Mr. Herbert alleged he had. For instance he suggested to Mr. Herbert that when Ward was arrested, he had not said "Oh, my God, how dreadful! No one will come forward to say it is true", but "You have made a dreadful mistake". Presumably Ward had told Mr. Burge that he had said this. But it sounded more as though it was what *he would have liked to say*. "Oh, my God, how dreadful!" is what one would expect someone in Ward's position to say after the shock of arrest. "You have made a dreadful mistake" was too rational, too cool for the circumstances. Mr. Burge also took up a statement of Mr. Herbert's that during the interview Ward had said: "The more we discuss this the happier I feel. This has been worrying me for the past nine weeks." He suggested that what Ward had really said was: "The more you tell me about this the happier I feel. It all seems so trivial." Again Mr. Herbert's version seemed on balance the more likely. Expressions of relief and a strong desire for the sympathy of the interrogator are symptoms common to the majority of prisoners in their first interview after arrest. Presumably Mr. Burge was putting these questions on Ward's instructions. Yet I was sorry to see him do it; for while neither version of either incident made any difference to Ward's guilt or innocence, one had doubts for the first time of his reliability as a witness.

There was only one part of Mr. Burge's cross-examination which proved at all damaging to Ward. This concerned what Ward had said to Mr. Herbert about Mandy.

"Did you put a rather loaded question as to whether she had a number of boy friends?"

"I certainly did ask where she got the money from. He told me she seemed to have plenty of boy friends."

"I suggest you asked Ward if she had plenty of boy friends and he said 'Yes, sir'."

"No, sir."

"He absolutely denied anything was said about your statement as to sexual intercourse with different men at the flat?"

"No, I made that part particularly clear to him."

And yet was it so damaging after all? For in her evidence Mandy had said that she had slept with only three people during her stay at Wimpole Mews: Lord Astor, her boy friend and the Indian doctor; and that the Indian doctor was the only one who had paid.

In his re-examination Mr. Griffith-Jones laid a splendid red herring. He pointed out that the statement which had formed the basis of Mandy's evidence had been taken by Mr. Herbert on April 24th, and that as the matter of the television set had not then arisen, no pressure could have been put on her because of it. But Mr. Burge had not suggested this. What he had suggested was that the statement of April 24th was taken at a time when Mandy was extremely vulnerable because of the motoring offences; and he had also suggested that the alleged stealing of the television set was used simply as a pretext to take Mandy into custody and ensure, by the demand of extortionate bail, that she would turn up at the magistrate's court as desired. Which was rather a different matter.

The next witness was Mr. Herbert's henchman, Detective-Sergeant John Burrows, a spruce but melancholy bloodhound. He had a long, firm, sad face and his hair was thinning on top. He wore a natty blue pin-stripe suit with blue shirt, red tie and tie-link, and I suppose he was about thirty-five years old. I had seen him once or twice outside, puffing at an enormous pipe, a minuscule, embryonic Sherlock Holmes. Mr. Griffith-Jones did not keep him long, for his first question was whether his notes were the same as Mr. Herbert's. He said, a little cautiously, that they had made the notes together, whereupon the judge, who was now indulging in quite a few quips as and when the mood took him, said: "I shall be surprised if they are *not* the same," and we all had a good giggle.

Mr. Burge asked whether Sergeant Burrows had interviewed Ward on certain dates, and we expected a short affirmative answer. But Sergeant Burrows was not a man to be rushed, to say mad, wild things without first checking them. He pulled a notebook from one of his pockets, but it was the wrong one. He pulled another notebook from another pocket and it was still the wrong one. He tried a third pocket and drew out a third notebook with the same result. Soon the edge of the witness-box was supporting a small monument of notebooks. It was like watching a conjuring trick that has failed to come off. Sergeant Burrows smiled a little in embarrassment and a ripple of sympathy ran round the court. Then, from his vest, I think, he extracted another notebook. He studied it closely. "Yes, sir," he said.

Nothing much new arose from the rest of the cross-examination, apart from an interesting side comment on Mandy. Referring to an interview that Sergeant Burrows had had with Ward on March 22nd at his surgery in Devonshire Street, Mr. Burge asked: "Was there an allegation by Ward that Miss Rice-Davies had stolen an electric fire and a table?" and Sergeant Burrows answered that there was. A little later he agreed with Mr. Burge that Ward had told him that anything that Mandy said should be treated with caution. Neither of these incidents were referred to again, but it did strike one that here was some grounds for thinking Mandy had malice.

Mr. Burge also questioned Sergeant Burrows about the Gordon case.

"You were the officer in charge of the prosecution against Gordon?"

"I was."

"Is it right that at that trial the accused Gordon made application to call three witnesses—John Marshall, Pete Comacchio and Truello Fenton?"

"Yes, sir."

"Were you asked by the court to obtain these witnesses and you told the court you could not?"

"Subsequently, yes, sir."

"That was quite untrue, was it not?"

"Certainly not, sir."

"Comacchio was on bail at that time?"

"He was on remand on bail."

"Do you say that he, being on remand on bail, it was not within the powers of the Metropolitan Police to find him?"

"I do."

"He surrendered to his bail, didn't he?"

"Yes, sir."

"Did you say to Miss Keeler: 'It will be all right, I won't find them'?"

"Certainly not, sir."

This was as far as Mr. Burge could properly go. But as the facts about the Gordon trial were not then known, and as Mr. Burge had no supporting evidence for his claims (though he had not conjured them out of nothing), it did not prove anything one way or the other: that being so, the jury may well have resented aspersions on the integrity of the police.

Lastly Mr. Burge asked him about the one and a half hour interview with Ward. He said he had not written down anything during the interview, *because Ward spoke so quickly*. Yet surely he could have got *something* down? And the more he did get down, the greater would have been the chances of accuracy. It was impossible not to believe that the decision to wait till after-wards had been deliberate, because they thought that Ward would have been inhibited by seeing Burrows writing. If that was so, why not be frank and admit it? It was this seeming equivocation by the police that inevitably made one doubt them.

Two more police officers followed Sergeant Burrows into the witness-box. Their names were Eustace and Glasse, which seemed unlikely. They were the officers who had been detailed to keep an eye on Ward when he had been put in a room by himself after his arrival at Marylebone Lane Police station. They had come to confirm what Herbert and Burrows had said about Ward sending a message that he wanted to see Herbert, rather than Ward's version of Herbert sending for him. I was sorry to see Ward dispute this, as not only did it make no differ-ence to his case, but Herbert and Burrows' version was more believable. To put a man alone in a room immediately after his arrest is common police practice. The object of it is to quicken his desire to talk to someone as an alleviation from his loneliness and fear, and so get at the truth. Ward was gregarious by nature, and loquacious too; and I did not doubt that he wanted to speak to Mr. Herbert very badly. In a way it seemed that both versions of the story could be true, i.e. that after some time Ward had sent word to Mr. Herbert that he wanted to see him, and that after some more time Mr. Herbert sent for him.

But Ward had disputed the matter, and as he had disputed it, here were Eustace and Glasse (they sounded like a firm of estate agents) to back up Herbert and Burrows. They took their time over this, so that I was able to take stock of what was going on around me.

The central figure in the court was still Ward: yet in a curious way he seemed remote from it all, as though he, like us, was listening to the story of another person: somehow there seemed as little connection between him and the man we were hearing about as there is between the photographs of one's youth and the person one is today. He sat in the front of the dock on a hard, wooden chair, with one policeman behind and the other beside him. His eyes were focused downwards most of the time, but this was not due to shame or embarrassment, but because, to give himself something to do, he was drawing pictures of Mr. Griffith-Jones and Mr. Burge. Even in comparative repose he looked a very lively person.

Opposite him the judge scratched away with his pen in what looked like a vast ledger. It was odd, I thought, that modern recording techniques had not yet found a way of supplying judge and counsel with transcripts of each day's hearing. But lawyers are conservative people and innovations of this sort are anathema to them : was it not Mr. Griffith-Jones earlier who had contemptuously referred to the microphone in the witness-box as "that machine"? As it was, the scribbling often could not keep pace with the speaking, and counsel were obliged to interrupt with weird admonishments like : "Not so fast, Miss Barrett, please, my Lord is taking a note", which sounded like a negro spiritual. Yet old-fashioned though the note-taking may have been, it was highly effective. Hardly ever was the judge at a loss for a name, a number, a date, the smallest detail of what some witness had said perhaps two days before. With his pen and ledger and spectacles he was mole-sharp, accountant-quick. And every other day or so he would take off his spectacles for two or three minutes; and then he looked like an *old* mole, a mole gone to grass, heavy and tired and wise, full of understanding and compassion.

Immediately below the judge sat the Clerk of the Court at a little desk of his own. He also wore a wig but a yellow wig, I noticed, in contrast to the grey wigs of most other barristers, and I wondered if this denoted some peculiar hierarchical significance. There was a telephone on his desk and every now and again he used it. But where to and what for? It was remarkable how discreetly he used it. I sometimes saw his lips moving but, even when the court was at its most silent, I never heard him utter a word. In the chair on the judge's right sat a long, gangling man, who, I was told, was the judge's clerk. He pottered in and out, never staying for long, and using the opposite door to that used by the sheriff and aldermen. The sheriff himself came in occasionally and sat in the centre chair. The bench behind Mr. Burge and Mr. Griffith-Jones was packed with barristers, sardine-tight, some pink, some brown, all grey, the best advertisement for integration I ever saw. There was one woman among them, pink and pretty. Her hair was done in a beehive so that her wig lay vertically instead of horizontally. It made a bizarre sight.

And now, Messrs. Eustace and Glasse having gone out of our lives almost as quickly as they had entered it, the usher announced the return appearance, positively for this performance only, of the one and only Christine Keeler. Mr. Burge had set us all wondering the day before when it was announced that he wanted her recalled. "Why?" the judge had said, adding: "I have granted Mr. Burge many indulgences and I want to give him the biggest latitude possible." I could not recollect any indulgences that the judge had given Mr. Burge, if anything the opposite, but the unexpected generosity was none the less welcome.

She was dressed in a kind of all-yellow linen outfit, a spring wasp this time but still fly-blown; and when she reached the witness-box she was reminded that she was still under oath.

"Do you remember," said Mr. Burge (and for one mad moment I thought he was going to say "an inn, Miranda"?), "do you remember when you gave evidence you said quite clearly that the accused had not taken you to New Scotland Yard for an interview with an officer called Partridge?"

If Christine remembered it, most of us on the Press benches had forgotten it, if indeed we ever knew it.

Christine said: "No, well actually he asked me and I misunderstood it, to start with they came while I thought about it . . ." While we were trying to unravel all this Mr. Burge said: "Is it quite true that he took you to Scotland Yard to be interviewed by a sergeant, other officers and Partridge?"

"No, not for an interview," said Christine.

Mr. Burge held up a paper in his hand. "What I am asking you," he said, "and I am holding a copy of the statement of the police officer in my hand, is: Is it right that the accused Ward brought you to New Scotland Yard and you were interviewed by Detective Inspector Partridge and the Sergeant?"

"That is quite right," said Christine.

At this point Mr. Burge had proved Christine to be as barefaced, if not as frequent a liar as Vickie Barrett. It was a pity he could not have stopped there, for he had made the only point that mattered. But further questioning revealed that the officer

Partridge was to do with the Narcotics Squad, and this reminded us that earlier Miss Keeler had told Mr. Griffith-Jones that it was Ward who had introduced her to smoking marijuana cigarettes. This did not quite tie in with what she told Mr. Burge now.

"Is it right that the accused asked the police to advise you not to return to clubs that you had been going to where there were coloured men, and not to use Indian hemp?"

"As I said before, yes, he did say that, but Stephen was always saying something like that. It was something I couldn't understand because he as well as myself went to these clubs."

"The fact is that a man accused of living upon your immoral earnings took you round to the police and asked them to advise you not to frequent these clubs?"

"This was Stephen's way," she said, admitting, though not liking to, the truth of Mr. Burge's suggestion. And in answer to further questions by Mr. Griffith-Jones the wasp showed a vicious sting in her tail. Angered at being recalled to the witness-box to be shown up as a liar, she repeated with relish her earlier statement that Ward had first introduced her to smoking reefers, and with relish too she reaffirmed that he smoked them also. Although none of this was proof of his living on her immoral earnings, it was, *if true*, some evidence towards showing the control he had over her. Later Ward denied emphatically that he smoked marijuana himself or encouraged others to. Yet on balance and in retrospect, I think it would have been wiser not to have recalled her. That Mr. Burge had proved her to have lied on oath was in danger of being forgotten. Less easily forgotten were the reefers, and the clubs where one bought the reefers, and the *clientèle* who frequented the clubs. To most people in court, and this included the jury, lies were commonplace: they had told them and been told them themselves. But the taking of drugs by a teenage girl who counted black men among her lovers was then a thing that lingered in the mind: to many people, at that time, it would seem about as far in depravity as one could go. And whether Ward had any part in it or not, the association could do him no good.

When Christine had gone, Mr. Griffith-Jones said to the judge: "There is a matter on which I desire your Lordship's

ruling. Might I do so in the absence of the jury?" I wondered
what this was about. The judge said "Certainly" and the jury,
like prisoners in a chain-gang, shuffled out. When they had
gone Mr. Griffith-Jones said he wanted to talk about pornographic books, and although we were at the end of a very long
morning, there was a quickening of interest everywhere. It
seemed, according to Mr. Griffith-Jones, that some seventeen
pornographic books or pamphlets had been found. It was not at
all clear where they had been found, or when, or even who had
found them. I thought I heard Mr. Griffith-Jones say that at one
time they had been in Ward's flat, but that later he had got rid
of them. Whatever the background picture Mr. Griffith-Jones
wanted the books to be admitted as evidence and Mr. Burge
didn't: they were, he said, quite irrelevant to any of the charges
and would undoubtedly prejudice the jury.

After listening to both sides the judge said: "I suppose I'd
better have a look at them." The thought that the books were
close at hand and could actually be *seen* had not, I think,
occurred to many of us. The atmosphere in court suddenly
heightened. *The judge was going to look at some dirty pictures.*
What would his reaction to them be?

A very grubby brown paper parcel was produced from what
looked like the lower portion of the Clerk of the Court's desk. It
was handed over to Mr. Griffith-Jones who opened it and with
suitable gravity picked out a book or two at random. There was
not a sound in court. Mr. Griffith-Jones chose three books altogether and handed them up to the judge. A hundred pairs of
eyes watched the judge receive them. A hundred pairs of eyes
watched him put two of the books aside and open the pages of
the third. And a hundred pairs of eyes strained every optical
nerve they possessed to see if they could catch a glimpse of the
exhibits within. Needless to say none could. The judge's behaviour was a model of impeccability. He flipped through the
pages of each book at a pace which was fast enough to avoid
any accusations of indulgence and yet slow enough to obtain
a general idea of the sort of stuff they contained. His face remained inscrutable. Then he made up his mind. "I think," he
said, turning to counsel, "that strictly speaking these books are
admissible as evidence. On the other hand their effect on the jury

is in my view likely to be so prejudicial that I intend to exercise my discretion and not allow them—that is, unless a particular witness is concerned with them."

This ruling—the inadmissibility of evidence which is more prejudicial than probative—has been built into English law as a safeguard for the accused—in much the same way as Crown counsel's licence in his opening speech of making allegations against the accused which are not subsequently substantiated seems to be a sort of insurance for the prosecution. It was, in this instance, a sensible enough ruling. Although few dirty-book collectors in the land are likely also to be living on immoral earnings, Mr. Burge might have had a hard job convincing the jury of it. Their experience of *erotica* (apart from the woman, who would probably have been shocked) was likely to have been restricted to the bedside tables of tarts; and I could hear Mr. Griffith-Jones's voice awakening youthful memories for them. "For what purpose, members of the jury, was the defendant keeping these filthy books? Was it for satisfying his own depraved desires, or was it, do you think, for something far more sinister? Are not these just the sort of books that ponces supply to prostitutes as part of the goods and services of their trade, and was that not exactly what the defendant was doing?"

Later, after the trial was over, I was told that the books did not originally belong to Ward, but had been left with him by a friend who had gone abroad. But if the books had been allowed as evidence, would Mr. Burge have been able to convince the jury of that? It seemed unlikely. On such hairs does justice sometimes turn.

And with that ended not only the morning's session but the case for the prosecution. It was by any standards, a feeble case. It consisted mainly of uncorroborated statements by proven liars: it was a hotch-potch of innuendoes and smears covered by a thin pastry of substance. It was a tale of immoralities, rather than crimes. It had not seemed like that in the beginning, but that was because the gap between what Mr. Griffith-Jones had said he would substantiate in his opening speech and what in fact he had substantiated, had grown progressively larger. Later I made a list of the things which Mr. Griffith-Jones had said

Ward had done, yet which subsequent evidence failed to prove he had done.

1. *"Whatever the extent of his earnings for this period may have been, from the evidence you will hear, and indeed from what he has told the police, they were quite obviously not sufficient for what he was spending."*

No evidence had been brought to show that his earnings were not sufficient for what he was spending. Indeed the police admitted that they had been unable to ascertain what his earnings were.

2. *"He introduced Christine Keeler to one Peter Rachman, of whom you have read in the newspapers."* (This was said twice.)

He had not introduced Christine Keeler to Rachman. They had met Rachman together, and by chance, when they were looking for a flat.

3. At Comeragh Road Christine and Mandy "were frequently visited by the defendant, *he bringing on a number of occasions his men friends to see them."*

According to the evidence the only person named as having been once taken to Comeragh Road by Ward was Lord Astor —and on that occasion according to Mandy the girls were out. There was no other evidence that Ward had specifically brought his men friends on a number of occasions to see the girls.

4. Christine *"was being used by him ... to make a little money from intercourse she was having from time to time with men who visited the flat ..."*

No evidence was offered that Christine was being used by him in this way. There had been evidence that two men and two men only had given Christine money for intercourse at Wimpole Mews. One was Mr. Eylan, who said that it had happened three times, and the other was Mr. Profumo whom Christine said had once given her a present for her mother.

5. *"She has said that over a period, roughly speaking, she*

must have paid to the defendant about half of what her earn-
ings were from that particular exercise." (i.e. copulation.)

Christine's evidence was that she usually owed him more
than she ever made, and that she only gave him half *of that.*

6. *"Sometimes Ward would be hard up, short of cash, and
he would tell the girl to telephone one of the gentlemen who
was seeing her fairly regularly and who was paying her £20
a time. He would ask her to ring one of them up and go round
to see him, earn her money and then bring it back."*

Apart from the man Charles, whom Mr. Griffith-Jones
mentioned separately, no evidence was offered in support of
this claim at all.

7. *"Sometimes the man would go to the flat and Ward
would be there throughout . . ."*

Christine had offered no evidence in support of this claim.

8. The Indian doctor was paying Mandy between £15 and
£25 each time, *"out of which she said she paid Ward some
£2 or £3 a time."*

We had heard no evidence of this.

9. *"It was proposed to have it* (the two-way mirror) *put in
order again."*

There had been no evidence of it.

Many of the assertions in Mr. Griffith-Jones's opening speech
failed for one of two reasons; either they went very much further
than the subsequent evidence that emerged, or, contrarily they
were completely let down by it. The source of these assertions
was the depositions, that is the statements taken from
witnesses by police officers and put into court as evidence. The
fact that there were so many occasions when the spoken word
failed to match the written word meant that inevitably one began
to have doubts about the veracity of the statements. Time and
time again Mr. Griffith-Jones made assertions which no amount
of questioning could confirm, time and time again his witnesses
gave quite different, sometimes opposite answers to what he
expected. What was the reason for this? Was it simply that the
witnesses became nervous under examination and did not know

what Mr. Griffith-Jones was driving at? Or was there another simpler explanation? Long ago and far away had they told falsehoods to their interrogators and had they now forgotten what those falsehoods were? To many of us it seemed not only possible but likely. But what about the jury? Had they even noticed the discrepancies? I doubted it.

In the pub, whipping was the number one topic of conversation. *Q.* What happens when you dial the TIMe on the telephone? *A.* The voice says: "At the third stroke, it will be £3 precisely."

Mr. Burge began his opening speech by reminding the jury of the handicap they were under; that in a normal criminal trial they would not know beforehand either the charge against the accused or the nature of the evidence to support it. Here they had brought with them a background of knowledge. It would not be easy to dismiss it from their minds but they must try. Then he turned to what really mattered.

"My learned friend, when he opened the case, referred to introductions—introductions which were intended to bear sinister significance—the introduction of a man to a woman. He said the accused introduced Miss Keeler to Rachman and then he said 'Forget it'.

"You may have made a mental note that if it had nothing to do with the case, why was it mentioned at all, and why immediately after you were asked to forget it."

Some of us had indeed been wondering that very thing.

"If you read the Press you would have seen such headlines as 'Ward Introduces Rachman to Keeler'. That is the danger in this case. *There was no question* of an introduction of Miss Keeler to Rachman for the purposes alleged by the prosecution, and in fact it was a chance meeting.

"I won't go through every instance, but I only mentioned that in order to show the enormous danger of substituting fiction for fact in this case, rumour for evidence and prejudice for real substance, *because this case absolutely reeks of it.*"

This was good stuff. I looked at the jury. Their faces were masks. You couldn't tell what they were thinking.

"You and only you," said Mr. Burge, looking from one to the other of them, "preserve the balance between a man who is charged with a series of revolting offences and a prosecution which is based more largely, you might think, *upon prejudice than actual evidence*."

Then Mr. Burge referred to his own part in the proceedings. "You may have noticed," he said, "that I raised various objections during the course of the case and you may have thought 'Well, really, this is the sort of thing that doesn't appeal to us, a lawyer getting up and talking lawyer's points and interrupting the prosecution and so on'. I couldn't agree with you more. That is not the sort of thing that any sensible and experienced advocate would wish to do."

I was sorry to hear Mr. Burge say this. I know that none of us on the Press benches, and I would not have thought the jury either, had resented Mr. Burge's interruptions or felt that they needed an apology. Lawyers forget that laymen are ignorant of legal procedure: for all they know it is common practice for lawyers to interrupt each other incessantly. Personally I should have liked to see Mr. Burge challenge Mr. Griffith-Jones more often.

He went on to something else that was in many of our minds.

"For months on end following the declaration in the House of Commons on March 22nd, the police have combed the country in a frenzy in order to find evidence implicating the accused.

"You have heard of the number of witnesses that have been interviewed, and you have seen some of them, and you have heard the circumstances and places in which they were interviewed.

"If you analyse the situation, you will see that the evidence has cut this case down to its true proportions."

It had indeed. Mr. Burge went on to give an illustration of the sort of thing the prosecution had stooped to in its efforts to improve its case. It was an incident I had not noticed myself, and it had occurred in Mr. Griffith-Jones's gruelling cross-examination of Miss Ricardo.

"She was treated as a hostile witness and the statement made in April was put to her in detail. For over an hour she was cross-examined by the prosecution.

"One of the questions that was put to her, and of course it is not evidence and you will be warned it is not evidence—there must have been some motive for putting that statement sentence by sentence—was 'Did you not say in that statement that Ward had told you that he was introducing girls to influential men?'

"If one had not had a copy of the statement," he went on, "that would have gone by and could not have failed to make an impact on you. But it turned out that not only does she *deny* making that statement, but that the statement she *had* made was not that *this man (pointing to Ward)* had said it, but that someone called John had said it."

It was a good point, and I wished that while he was at it Mr. Burge had called the jury's attention to all the other prejudicial assertions, such as Lord Astor and the £100 cheque, Ward's expenses exceeding his earnings, etc. But perhaps at this stage he was right to keep his remarks brief. We had all just had lunch.

Next he spoke of the background to the case and the difficulties of proving Ward innocent. "After the publicity, before he ever had a trial, before any evidence was offered, quite obviously it was thought that he *was* a procurer and a man who lived upon the earnings of prostitution." When he came to give evidence, the jury would hear of his two lives, the first that of a skilled osteopath, the second that of a Bohemian artist "who will not flinch from telling you that he is very highly sexed and indeed has had affairs with a great many women". This led Mr. Burge on to the thing he had to say, perhaps above all others : "You are not concerned, I hope—because if you are, we might just as well plead guilty—you are not concerned with the standards of moral conduct of this man. That is far short, and the accused will be forced to admit it, of anything you will approve of."

But here Mr. Burge was wrong. The jury *were* concerned with the moral conduct of the man. Juries are : they cannot help it. Individually jurymen are as worldly wise as the rest of us : indeed when they are not being jurymen they *are* the rest of us. But once they have entered their little box and the lawyers start talking to them, they begin to lose their identity. Individually they are men who have masturbated and fornicated and committed adultery, shown each other dirty books and told each other dirty stories; and what they have not done they have dreamt of doing. But the lawyers impose on them a sort of collective morality, appealing not to the standards of them as they are but to the standards of the sort of people they think they ought to be (yet would hate to be if they ever paused to consider it). It is on this artificial ethos that judge and counsel batten, flattering it as Mr. Griffith-Jones had done and was increasingly to do, paying lip-service to it as Mr. Burge had just done (and had to do in view of the lead that Mr. Griffith-Jones had given him). This is one of the least attractive though perhaps inevitable aspects of any country's law, and of British law more than most.*

Mr. Burge ended his brief opening speech by echoing what many people were thinking. "Although public opinion has obviously been horrified by the scandal that was raised through no fault of this man, and therefore demands expiation, some speedy sacrifice, so the matter can be established and disposed of and forgotten, that is not a consideration that will affect you in deciding the issue here.

"Looking at it at its closest, accepting the fact that this man is an artist who lives with a number of women, sleeps with them, behaving perhaps outrageously, can you say he was a man really living on immoral earnings in the first place or that it has been established that he is a procurer?

"We may have one or two surprises for you in the form of evidence we shall call, and in particular you may have some evidence that will assist you over the remarkable testimony of Miss Vickie Barrett, of whom we first became aware as recently as July 10th.

"It is not possible to foreshadow the exact nature of that evidence. We are calling the witnesses. I shall now call the accused himself."

He was ushered out of the huge dock, along the well of the court and into the witness-box. He walked there with grace and a certain sort of dignity which, even in his most extreme moments, he was never to lose. He took the oath firmly, resonantly; and he faced us.

Anyone who visits the criminal courts regularly knows that the man in the dock is usually the least interesting, most inarticulate of those present. Here the opposite was true. This was not simply

*While I think this was true in 1963 I do not think it is so today.

because of the facts of the case, that such a person should be involved in such charges, but rather because of something in the man himself. One had heard of his charm and personality, and now one was experiencing them. It was difficult to pinpoint where they lay, for his features were not attractive. Mostly I think it was in the voice, a voice of quite extraordinary richness and resonance. When he was silent one hardly noticed him; when he was speaking, his voice transformed him, gave him life and magnetism. It was a voice which had been used to win friends and influence people—friends like Lord Astor and people like Christine Keeler. It was a voice which one could hear exhorting, persuading, demanding, and in the end having its way. It was undoubtedly his most precious asset. Now it was to be used—and no one was more aware of this than he—in defence of his life and career.

He started off quietly enough, answering in monosyllables Mr. Burge's inquiries as to his credentials as osteopath and artist. Some people can say more in monosyllables than others in whole sentences. Stephen Ward was one of them. All the time one had the impression of dammed waters, banked fires. As his tenure of the witness-box went on, one realised that behind this bland exterior, was a man of daemonic energy: indeed to have lived a life as full, if not as rich, as he did, to have run a successful practice, been a successful artist, and at the age of fifty to have put such frequent and unusual sexual strains on himself, called for more than ordinary stamina.

Sometimes the temptation to unbank the fires, open the floodgates, became irresistible. One felt that he had been warned beforehand that loquaciousness was his besetting sin, that if he said more in reply than the questions demanded, the jury would hold it against him. Yet clearly his whole being was crying out to speak, to explain, to justify, to see the old magic working on all of us. It was this struggle within himself to hold himself in check, to put a rein on his emotions, that made his giving evidence so fascinating to watch. When he did go overboard it was for one of two reasons; either he had become over-confident and felt he could afford a little levity, or else something was said which went to the very roots of his being. The first was as harmful to his case as the second was favourable. For instance he described with obvious enjoyment how Mandy had fallen down in a faint when he told her of Rachman's death : "when she had recovered, she opened her eyes and said 'Did he leave a will' ?" He told the story well, but the stony faces of the jury indicated that he was not the man, and this was not the time or place, to tell it. Similarly, when asked if he had said to the police "Mandy is not a prostitute, she is a nice girl", he was unwise to answer with a smile: "I hate to think I used those words, but I may have done." There are occasions in the witness-box when it does not pay a man to be himself, and this was one of them. Yet once when he felt goaded beyond endurance, he banged the side of the witness-box and shouted out : "Any little tart from the streets can come forward in this court and say I am lying. Apart from this case I am considered to be a truthful person." It was an impressive, because spontaneous, rejoinder.

On the whole he was a good witness, a little too plausible sometimes but clear and precise in most of his replies. Precision, even about the smallest detail, seemed important to him : perhaps he felt that while he clung to the truth he could not go far wrong. Asked if Mr. Eylan went out with Christine after meeting himself and Profumo, he said, as though it mattered: "Let us be quite clear. I thought he went, and that Miss Keeler went out with Mr. Profumo, but it could have been the other way round." Again, describing the incident at the Brush and Palette Restaurant when Christine was alleged to have made a pass at Sally Norie's friend, Mr. Longman, he said "I thought that Longman was after Keeler and not the other way round". His manners were impeccable. He addressed counsel as "sir" and the judge as "your lordship". His hands were seldom idle. Often while thinking out an answer he would turn his palms upwards and look down at them, as though inspiration lay there. Sometimes while counsel was addressing him, he would brush the fingers of his left hand across the top of the witness-box, gathering invisible dust. And when he wanted to emphasise a point in his reply, he would tap the wooden surface in front of him lightly with his fingernails. But then hands had always played an important part in his life. With them he had healed the sick, sketched the famous, excited women.

Mr. Burge took Ward through the Comeragh Road period

and got him to tell his own version of Lord Astor and the cheque for £100. This added little to our knowledge of the affair, except that Ward had known Astor closely for many years and was in the habit of borrowing money from him which he subsequently repaid. The £100 for the rent of Comeragh Road was one such loan. "I had seen the two girls were broke," Ward explained. "They were contemplating doing a moonlight flit and were anxious about it. I happened to mention it to Lord Astor in conversation one day—we talked about lots of things—and I said I had paid the rent for them. He said 'I will give you a cheque and you can pay me back later'. And he did. It was a personal loan to me and, in fact, I gave it direct to the landlord. It did not seem to have any sinister implication."

It may not have had; but the whole thing was just as far from being satisfactorily resolved as ever.

Mr. Burge then turned to Wimpole Mews and established the financial relationship between Ward and Christine.

"During that time, she was living rent-free?"

"Yes, she was."

Ward said that Christine did not seem to have much money. "She had a small amount when she came. She was given money by me and her friend Marilyn. She did not really *need* much money. She had clothes, and everything else was provided for her."

"You say you gave her money?"

"Yes, during the time she was at the Mews I gave her about £70 or £80." He added: "She gave part of that back."

"There was more outstanding from you than from her?"

"Yes, that is what she said."

Mr. Burge went on to the various men with whom Christine was said to have intercourse while at Wimpole Mews and here Ward was much less satisfactory. At first he said he had "no direct knowledge" of her having had intercourse at the flat, which could only mean that Christine had never told him she had, and this was almost impossible to believe. Later he admitted he had "a pretty shrewd idea". Asked if he knew that she was having intercourse for money he said that he had "not the remotest idea", and in answer to a further question as to whether he would have allowed her to continue living there if he had known, he replied "Certainly not". When Mr. Burge asked him if he knew that Profumo had given her money, he replied: "I did not hear about it until recently, and I was horrified." He also said "I disapproved, very strongly, of a person taking money for sex". These expressions of moral indignation did not tie up with what one knew of the man. He was, by his own admission, extremely immoral, and there were few sexual byways he had not explored: he consorted with prostitutes like Ronna Ricardo and if the evidence of Brenda O'Neil was true, he had paid her and Vickie Barrett £2 each for intercourse. His "horror" and "disapproval" then were largely contrived; and they were so, surely, because *not* to have expressed them would have been tantamount to admitting knowledge, and therefore condonation, of what Christine had done; and in law living *with* a prostitute and living *on* a prostitute are separated only by a hairsbreadth. This is not to say that I think that Christine Keeler told Ward of every occasion when men gave her money for intercourse, nor that he necessarily asked her; for many men slept with her who did not give her money. From a conventional viewpoint Christine was right when she said that she did not consider herself a prostitute, and Ward was right when he told her that she ought not to do so; for by her own admission she slept with more men for enjoyment than money, while those who did give her money had some relationship with her over and above the sexual act.

Mr. Burge ended this part of his examination by asking: "During that time when it is said you were living on her earnings, you have already pointed out you informed one branch of the executive, New Scotland Yard. (This was Inspector Partridge.) Did you in fact inform another branch of the executive?"

"Yes, I informed the Secret Service."

"Who did you inform?"

"Mr. Woods of Room 393 at the War Office."

"When did you give that information?"

"It would have been some time in early August 1961."

"Did you anticipate some observation being made as a result of the information to the Secret Service?"

"Yes, I did."

"Would you in those circumstances, having informed two

branches of the executive, have lived upon the earnings of prostitution at this address at that time?"

"There was no question of my having done that."

It was a good point though it only really showed that, even if Ward *was* living on the earnings of prostitution, *he did not think he was*. But some of the shine was taken off it by Ward's admissions of going to the authorities at all. For a man whose own life was such a moral swamp, these sneaking, tell-tale visits did not make him any more endearing.*

Before leaving Christine Mr. Burge asked one question about the mysterious Charles.

"The other man she referred to was Charles. Do you know of the man she was referring to?"

"No," said Ward, "I have been racking my brains and I cannot think of anybody."

More and more it seemed that Charles was a figment of Christine's imagination. I remembered what Ward had said earlier about Christine's claim to have slept with the Russian Ivanov: "I only have Miss Keeler's word for it. She said she would like to have had intercourse with him. I have always believed myself she never did. I think like a lot of people she tells a story often enough and comes to believe it and does tell lies." This was something that rang true.†

Mr. Burge now passed on to Mandy's six-week occupation of Wimpole Mews. He did not elicit much information from Ward about the vital matter of the Indian doctor, for Ward disclaimed all knowledge of the Indian doctor going there. But he did extract some interesting facts about Mandy's tenancy from a financial point of view. Ward agreed that Mandy had been living with Rachman for two years before she came to him.

"And obviously she was well endowed with the good things of the world?"

"Yes."

"What rent did Miss Davies pay you for the room at Wimpole Mews?"

"£6 a week."

"Was it worth £6 a week?"

"Well, obviously considerably more."

"What was she like on the telephone?"

*It has now been revealed, what the court did not know at the time, that Ward had been asked by M.I.5 to try and trap the Soviet assistant naval attaché,

"Very extravagant. I think the bill came to £54."

"Did you speak to her about the cost and about lights, fires and telephones?"

"Frequently."

"Did she pay you four weeks in advance?"

"Yes."

"Apart from that first monthly rent, did she make other payments to you?"

"Small contributions to the telephone bill, that is all."

"Did she make further payments for the rent?"

"No."

Mr. Burge referred to the time when Mandy's parents had come to stay with her at the flat after her attempted suicide. He asked Ward what Mandy's total contributions had been for herself and her father and mother.

"The total contribution," said Ward, "for the period of two months would have been £24, plus about £5 or £6 for the telephone."

This evidence was not subsequently challenged by the prosecution, and I thought when I heard it, how *could* they go on asserting that Ward was *living* on Mandy Rice-Davies's *earnings*? It seemed so utterly absurd.

Ward gave his own version of the Ropner story. ("Ropner is one of my oldest friends and if I had wanted money from him I would have asked him myself"); of Miss R ("I have never brought pressure upon anyone in their life to have sexual intercourse") and of Miss X ("I did not find her attractive. Her story puzzles me more than any of the witnesses because I cannot see any obvious purpose"). And then Mr. Burge brought him to the time of Vickie Barrett and Bryanston Mews. It was early in January, it will be remembered, that Ward had moved into Bryanston Mews; and according to Brenda O'Neil it was soon after her release from Holloway on January 27th that Vickie Barrett had come to stay with her.

Mr. Burge asked Ward if he had been seen by Sergeant Burrows on a number of occasions in the early part of 1963.

"Yes, sometimes at my own request."

"During that time the Profumo scandal was warming up?"

"Yes."

Commander Ivanov, into defecting. It might have made a difference to Ward's case if this could have been disclosed at the trial.

†c.f. footnote to p.54

"Is it right you were suddenly visited by a large number of journalists?"

"Yes, an enormous number. I sometimes had to fight my way into the flat."

"Did you on occasions send for the police?"

"I had to send for the police on more than one occasion to keep the crowds out."

Mr. Burge asked Ward how he spent his evenings and Ward said that he spent some evenings playing bridge in the flat, starting at about eight o'clock and ending about midnight.

"Was anyone living in the flat?"

"There was. Sylvia Parker."

"Do you remember when she came to live there?"

"It would be about February 10th."

"How long did she remain there?"

"About two and a half months."

This meant that if Vickie Barrett's story was true, she was coming round to Ward's flat for whipping and copulating two or three times a week from the beginning of February to the middle of April, at which time journalists and police were in and out of the flat, people were spending the evening playing bridge there, and Sylvia Parker was staying there. It did not seem very likely. Mr. Burge put Vickie Barrett's evidence to him direct, and he said, shaking with anger: "Her whole evidence was a tissue of disgusting lies from beginning to end." It was said convincingly but would have been even more convincing if he had said "malicious" instead of "disgusting". These attempts of Ward to put himself in a kinder light, to show himself as a better man than he was, did him no good. Nor was he in the least convincing in his account of how he picked up Vickie Barrett in the first place.

"I had run out of cigarettes late at night and I went to a place in Tottenham Court Road where you can buy cigarettes, and on the way back I was hailed by her. She asked for a lift and when she got into the car she made herself known as a prostitute almost immediately. I took her back to the flat and I drew her, had intercourse with her, paid her £2 and took her to a club called the Nucleus Club."

Ward said he had had intercourse with her for the same

amount on a second occasion, and he also agreed that he had picked up Brenda O'Neil in the same way and had had inter-course with her for £2. There were things here one could not quite swallow. Vickie *hailing* him, for instance. Ordinary women are not in the habit of hailing passing cars in the West End of London late at night; and since the passing of the Street Offences Act prostitutes have taken care to keep in the shadows. Surely the truth was that he had not liked to admit picking her up. Again, how had Brenda O'Neil come into the picture? Was it by chance that he had found her in the streets at about the same time? Or did she and Vickie and Ward know one or two things which they were not going to let on to any of us? There were odd pieces of the jigsaw that would not quite fit.

Mr. Burge had a question or two to ask about Ronna Ricardo and the four-way party, which I was glad to see Ward admit (it was obviously, painfully, true) and also about Rachman. Ward said that he used to send messages to Rachman asking him not to come down to his cottage because, as he put it, "he made finan-cial offers to the guests"—a charming reason for asking someone to stay away from one's house.

Finally Mr. Burge turned to the interview that Ward had had with the Marylebone police after his arrest. Not surprisingly Ward disagreed with the police account of it, though in a not implausible way.

"How came it that you went up to the office and saw Chief Inspector Herbert and Sergeant Burrows?"

"I was taken from that room and put in a cell, and I asked repeatedly to see a solicitor. Nobody turned up. I was taken up-stairs and shown into an office where the two officers were. In those circumstances you just go where you are told."

"Was it a question of you asking to go up and be interviewed by Chief Inspector Herbert or was it that you were sent for?"

"I must be perfectly fair. I was sent for, but I was certainly anxious to go."

"Did you say that you wished to discuss the case fully with him and would answer any questions he liked to ask?"

"I would not quarrel with that."

"Did he tell you that you need not answer any questions?"

"Yes."

"Did you say you could trust him and Sergeant Burrows?"

"I did." There was a pause and he added wryly: "I thought I could at that time."

"Of the financial position, you said that you had not the faintest idea and they put the figures to you of your rent and so on?"

"Yes, they put the figures. The interview was conducted in a completely different way than is described in the statement."

"Does it change the effect?"

"Yes, it does indeed—misrepresentation of what *was* said, and a great number of things which were *never* said are in there."

Knowing what one does know of the way police interviews are carried on, it did not strike me that Ward was necessarily lying. Luckily it did not affect the main issue whether one believed Ward's version or that of the police. Except perhaps for the Indian doctor whose ghost-like figure was destined to haunt the defence. It was with him that Mr. Burge concluded his examination.

"Is it right you did not wish to discuss the Indian doctor with the police?"

"Yes, sir."

"Will you tell my Lord and the jury why that was?"

"A friend of mine had telephoned me and told me this Indian is a married man and did not want to be involved in the case and I had been asked already to keep his name out of it."

"Did the officers tell you that the doctor had made a statement?"

"Yes, sir."

"Did you know whether or not the doctor had been going to 63 Great Cumberland Place?"

"Miss Keeler told me that took place."

"In fact he never came to your place?"

"Not to my house."

Or did he? Perhaps Mr. Griffith-Jones would have some questions to ask about this.

Mr. Griffith-Jones had a lot of questions to ask, about this and other matters too. All next morning he pummelled away at Ward mercilessly, looking at what at worst was grey, in clear black and white. Grey is where the truth lies, but the truth is not something with which prosecuting counsel—or defence counsel either for that matter—are primarily concerned: that is for the jury. There were times when Mr. Griffith-Jones's sarcastic probing threw Ward right off balance: there were other times when he became, as it were, the commentator in some mad Victorian melodrama, tracing Good and Evil in letters high enough for any child to see. His opening questions regarding Christine Keeler set the tone of the whole cross-examination; a cross-examination less about crimes than morals.

"Was it right that after you met this girl in Murray's Club you started telephoning her?"

"Yes, sir."

"Why?" *Why?* Well, why not?

"I liked her."

"What for?"

What does anyone like anyone for? But it was a trap of course and Ward fell right into it.

"I would have said at that particular time I was attracted by her, and to be honest I would say I would have liked to have had some sort of relationship with her."

"You mean," said Mr. Griffith-Jones, watching his ball roll into the hole, "a sexual relationship?"

"Yes, sir."

"You pursued her and telephoned her and went to her mother's house, didn't you?"

"Yes, sir."

"A man of forty-eight chasing a girl of sixteen who had just come to London?"

"Yes."

"Just so you could go to bed with her?"

"No, sir."

"What other possible interpretation is there?"

"I saw in Miss Keeler something that I felt I would have liked to have known longer. It was not just purely the idea of going to bed with her."

"What other than sex?"

"I thought she was a very pretty girl, and I just wanted to know her for a long time and I did."

Mr. Griffith-Jones changed tack but not general direction.

"Not so long after that she introduced you to the girl Davies?"

"That would have been quite some time after."

"And that girl was sixteen?"

"Yes."

"And you by now were a year or so older?" (Here I longed for Ward to say no, as a matter of fact he was now a year or so *younger*.)

"Yes."

"Did you ask her down to the cottage?"

"Yes."

"Why?"

"I was attracted by her."

"You wanted to go to bed with her?"

"Yes, sir."

Mr. Griffith-Jones looked at Ward with his cold blue eyes. "So we start this story, do we," he said, "with a man of forty-eight or forty-nine chasing two girls of sixteen?"

"Quite so, sir." Was there a slight mocking tone in Ward's reply?

"With nothing else in common except sex?"

"I wouldn't have said that, sir."

"And then these two girls went to live at Comeragh Road and you arranged to pay the rent for them?"

"Yes, sir."

"What were you arranging these two girls' rent to be paid for?"

"Well looking back on it I suppose my motives were mixed. Basically I wanted to be kind to them, but at the same time I was attracted by them."

Suddenly Mr. Griffith-Jones's voice took on a sharper edge.

"What are you doing, arranging for these two girls to live in a flat and have the rent paid? Why were you doing it?"

Ward reacted like a barometric needle. "I've told you already I was attracted by Miss Rice-Davies." He recovered his balance. "I had known Miss Keeler for quite some time then, and I wanted to be kind to them. They were in fact broke at that time."

"There are plenty of people who are broke but do not have the good fortune to have their rent paid for them?"

"That is true."

"Was the truth that you wanted to provide your friends with pretty girls?"

Ward had seen this one coming a mile away and was ready for it. "*That*," he said with emphasis, "*is completely untrue.*"

But Mr. Griffith-Jones had more cartridges in his locker, even if many were blanks.

"Then why," he said, "did you not pay the rent yourself?"

"But I did pay the rent myself. I borrowed the money and I paid it back."

"You borrowed the money from Lord Astor?"

"Yes."

"According to your evidence you happened to mention the girls to him?"

"Yes."

"Why?" (These persistent "whys" of Mr. Griffith-Jones were like steel on a decaying tooth.)

"We often talked over a wide field of things."

"The girls you had taken from a night club with the hope of seducing?"

"I did *not*," said Ward, irritated again, "as a matter of fact *take* them from a night club."

"Did you introduce Fairbanks to them?"

"Yes. I thought they were very pretty and I thought of films, and I asked him if they could have a film test, and I think there was a film test."

"Here you are having, as it were, befriended these two girls, arranging for them to live in a flat and you introduce them to Lord Astor. How old is Lord Astor, fifty?"

"Yes."

"And Fairbanks?"

"I don't know."

"He's nearer sixty?"

"I don't really know."

"Why did you introduce him to these two girls?"

"I thought I could help them."

"Did you introduce them to other men?"

"I think I must have taken friends of mine round there." (It would have been a better answer without "I think I must".)

"Miss Keeler has told us how she had intercourse with two of the people you took round?"

Now Miss Keeler had not *definitely* said that she had had intercourse with two of the men that Ward had taken round. Her actual answer was, "Maybe a couple", to a question as to whether she had intercourse with people Ward had introduced her to *while living* at Comeragh Road; but she was extremely vague and uncertain about it.

"Yes," said Ward, "they are obviously promiscuous."

Now Mr. Griffith-Jones was ready to tie the ends together. "Let's just get the picture," he said, "here are two thoroughly promiscuous girls set up in a flat for which you are arranging to pay the rent and introducing them to men much older than themselves, with some of whom they appear to have gone to bed?"

"It is," said Ward, trying to control himself, "a *false* picture."

Mr. Griffith-Jones moved on to the period when Christine was at Wimpole Mews. The day before Ward had told Mr. Burge that he had "no direct knowledge" of Christine having intercourse with anyone while she was at the flat. Now, under Mr. Griffith-Jones's relentless questioning he had to modify that answer.

"Did you introduce her to the man Charles?"

"I don't know who the man Charles is."

"Whether you introduced her or not, you know while she was living at Wimpole Mews she was having intercourse with a number of men?"

"One or two to my knowledge."

"Let us add up to see on the evidence how many there were in fact. With Mr. Profumo, did you know that?"

"I did not know that."

"You knew he had visited her?"

"Yes."

"But what do you think Mr. Profumo was visiting this girl for?"

"I had a pretty shrewd idea what was taking place, but I didn't know because I wasn't there."

"Are you telling the jury you did not know perfectly well that Miss Keeler was having intercourse with Mr. Profumo?"

"I had no direct knowledge but I *thought* they were having sexual intercourse."

Mr. Griffith-Jones went down the list: "Ivanov?"—"I don't think that she ever had intercourse with Ivanov": "Eylan?"—"I heard about this later": "A Mr. Charles?"—"I don't think she said at my flat": "Lambton?"—"I have met him subsequently but not at my flat": "Rachman?"—"Yes, but that was not at my flat": "A Persian boy?"—"Yes": "Another boy friend who stayed at the flat all night?"—"Yes."

"You knew she was having intercourse with him?"

"Yes."

The judge: "Was this young man a friend of yours?"

Ward, oddly: "He *is* a young man."

The judge, testily: "Will you answer the question? Was he a *friend* of yours?"

"Yes."

"Was he a person you had introduced Keeler to?"

"Yes."

"And a person you allowed to remain the night in the flat?"

"I don't think they stayed the night. He took her out."

Mr. Griffith-Jones asked: "Did your friends tell you when they had intercourse with a girl to whom you had introduced them?"

"Not always."

"How did this one come to tell you he had had intercourse with this girl whom you had introduced him to?"

"They both told me."

"Edgecombe, the West Indian negro?"

"It was not at my flat at that period": "Lucky Gordon, another West Indian?"—"Not while she was at my flat."

Mr. Griffith-Jones had catalogued Christine's lovers in this way to show not only the extent of her promiscuity but that Ward must have been aware of it. In this he succeeded admirably. Yet in another way he had defeated his own purpose; for the evidence showed that only about half of the ten people he had named had given her presents or money, and that only *two* of these, Profumo and Eylan, had slept with her in Ward's flat. And he denied he knew this.

"Miss Keeler has told us that on one occasion she did go round to see the man to whom she has referred as Charles?"

"No, sir," said Ward emphatically, "I would never suggest such a thing. That was quite wrong. *She is lying.*"

"Complete fabrication by that girl?"

"Complete fabrication."

"Did you tell her in effect it was all right to go with men for money?"

Ward almost shouted his answer: "NO SIR, I DID NOT." He added: "*I did not know* of the relationship with Eylan or the fact that he was giving her money."

Mr. Griffith-Jones said: "Don't you think control of a man aged fifty over a girl of eighteen in an atmosphere of immorality such as must have been the atmosphere in Wimpole Mews...?"

Ward interrupted him passionately, saying, "That was *not* the atmosphere in Wimpole Mews. You have described a sensational relationship which went on over a long time. Most of the time in Wimpole Mews I was playing bridge or drawing. You have concentrated all these incidents into a short time which gives a false picture, and I am not that sort of person at all."

Then Mr. Griffith-Jones went on to Mandy's tenancy of the room and made a similar catalogue of her lovers as he had done with Christine's.

"There were Astor, Fairbanks, the Indian doctor, Rachman, her Persian boy friend and Shepbridge. That is six."

"The only one I had any knowledge of," said Ward, "was Rachman. The Persian boy friend was before she came to my flat. I had no knowledge of the others. In fact I deny that she had a relationship with Lord Astor, and not only have I said that but Lord Astor has said it as well." In answer to another question Ward said: "During the whole of that three and a half year period, *she was in my flat for six weeks only* and you are now making me responsible for all the relationships during that period."

"She told us that it was normal for you to be in the flat when she was having intercourse with men in the bedroom. Is that not so?"

"Only in the case of one person," said Ward. "It was someone of approximately her own age after she left Rachman." Yet only a few moments earlier Ward had said that Rachman was the only one he had any knowledge of.

"That adds another name to the six I have mentioned," said Mr. Griffith-Jones, pointedly. "She is only eighteen now," he said, "and all this has happened since she met you. She was just over sixteen when she met you, and you were a man of forty-eight."

But this attempt of Mr. Griffith-Jones's to make Ward responsible for all of Mandy's life was more than even he could take calmly. "Sir, sir!" he pleaded, "I met her half a dozen times in Comeragh Road and for the next year barely at all."

But when Mr. Griffith-Jones had the wind in his sails, nothing could stop him.

"The whole story so far as Davies is concerned starts when you met her in Murray's Club and arranged for her rent in Comeragh Road? That is the start of this dreadful story?"

"No, sir, *no, sir*," Ward implored. Mr. Griffith-Jones's suggestion was so contrary to the evidence that Mr. Burge had to rise and point it out. Later Ward summed up his relationship with Mandy by answering a somewhat loaded question from the judge.

"What did you think the girls were having sexual intercourse with men *for*? They were not working and they were living at the flat. What did you really think they were *doing*?"

"In the case of Rice-Davies," said Ward, "she was in the flat for only a month before she attempted to commit suicide. She had come from a relationship which was an intended marriage with Rachman and she was not short of money and was well dressed. I provided food in the flat and she had few expenses. She was a pretty girl and she was taken out by people. There wasn't a question of living off her. *If anything she was living off me*."

Mr. Griffith-Jones said: "Even if you knew there was one man, what do you think she was doing it for? Pure love as you say?"

"No, not in this particular case," said Ward, "I think it was for enjoyment of the sexual act," which seemed fair enough.

"And living off your charity at the same time," said the judge, I thought unnecessarily sarcastically.

Mr. Griffith-Jones asked Ward how he had picked up Vickie Barrett, and he said: "I went out in the first place to get some cigarettes. She was there and I gave her a lift." I was wondering if Ward had forgotten what he had said about Vickie Barrett hailing him when Mr. Griffith-Jones suddenly said: "Are your sexual desires absolutely *insatiable*?" Ward said carefully: "I don't think I have any more sexual relationships than any other people of my age, but possibly the variety is much greater." The "possibly" was a nice touch. There was a little murmur in the court and several people smiled.

Yet it was in his evidence about Vickie Barrett that Ward was most convincing, not simply in his denials of what Vickie Barrett had said but in the wording of the denials and the tones in which they were spoken. When Mr. Griffith-Jones asked if Vickie Barrett was right when she said there was a man lying in bed in the flat, he said, in a loud and emphatic voice, stressing each syllable: "*She Is Lying, Sir.*" A little later he said: "If this girl is telling the truth, then I am guilty. My case must depend on saying that this girl is lying, and why she is lying, we must find out." And when Mr. Griffith-Jones asked him if it was not true about the cane and horse-whip he said: "May I appeal to your reason? Even with the somewhat disreputable pattern of my life, does it seem probable or possible?" This remark brought a caution from the judge that he would do his case no good by not straightforwardly answering the question, but in fact by answering as he did, he had done his case much good. For these answers were not *the sort of answers* a guilty man would give. They had, like one or two other answers in the case, the instinctive, spontaneous ring of truth.

Mr. Griffith-Jones questioned him about Sally Norie and Miss R and Miss X, and he said, as he had said to Mr. Burge, that his alleged proposal to Miss X about the two-way mirror was "disgusting"; and I thought, as before, that this was an unfortunate word for a man whose sex life included two tarts from Oxford Street and a four-in-hand. On the other hand Mr. Griffith-Jones did *his* case no good when he asked Ward if he realised "how startling" it was that the four-in-hand should be true. There was nothing startling about the truth of it at all.

Just before the court adjourned for lunch, Mr. Griffith-Jones asked Ward about Christine's assertions that he had introduced her to smoking marijuana. Ward again denied it, as fiercely as he had denied anything.

"She has written this in the *News of The World*," he said, "and is repeating it in order to give substance to it." Then in a rising voice, he said : "I have lectured about drug addiction and I have written to *The Times* about it, and it is completely and absolutely untrue that I have ever encouraged anyone at any time to take drugs. I would not and I could not do so."

"The suggestion was put to Miss Keeler," said Mr. Griffith-Jones, "that you had taken her to Scotland Yard because you were anxious to cure her of the habit?"

"No," said Ward, "it was not because I was anxious to cure her. *She didn't have the habit then.* She told me about the places she had gone to and what happened, and I asked her to take me there. I had a look, and when I saw what I saw, I took her to the Yard and asked them to give her a good talking to."

And that had a certain plausibility too.

The general feeling in the pub was that although there had been occasions when Mr. Griffith-Jones had rocked Ward visibly, he had done nothing to substantiate the charge of Ward's living on Christine's or Mandy's immoral earnings. Obviously the more that Ward admitted he knew of the girls' activities, the more chance the prosecution had of making the charges stick. That was why he had originally said he had "no direct knowledge" of Christine going to bed with men. Yet although it was obvious that Ward *did* know of their promiscuity, he was reasonably convincing that he did *not* know they were sometimes doing it for money (according to the evidence they weren't doing it for money often). And as for proof of him *living* on their immoral *earnings*, this seemed as far away as ever. Indeed it was with a slight sense of shock that one remembered that these were the charges against him.

Mr. Griffith-Jones, however, like all good advocates, was keeping his heaviest ammunition in reserve. After lunch he asked Ward questions about the police interview at Marylebone Lane, and Ward confirmed what he had said to Mr. Burge.

"The police went out and wrote down the form of words, and wrote them in the wrong order and the wrong tone. The questions were not in the form they were put to me. It was a quite distorted picture of what really happened."

Then Mr. Griffith-Jones came to what Ward had said to the police about the Indian doctor. Earlier in his cross-examination Ward had said that he had met the Indian doctor only once, at a coffee bar near Wimpole Mews. It was after Christine had left the flat, the room was vacant, and a friend of his called Mr. McKew had brought the Indian doctor along as a possible tenant. Mandy had arrived while they were having coffee, McKew introduced her to the Indian doctor, and soon after Ward left for his surgery, leaving the three of them in the coffee-bar. He had not seen the Indian doctor again : he had no idea that he had been round to the flat; and there was no question of him ever giving him money.

Now Mr. Griffith-Jones took up the Indian doctor again, and it will be seen from Ward's replies how unsatisfactory many of them were.

"Did the police mention Dr. Savundra?"

"Yes."

"Did you say, 'Do I know him?'?" (This is what Ward was alleged to have said about Eylan, and was possibly his way of borrowing time to think.)

"I said I had a recollection of a person of this name."

"You knew perfectly well who he was?"

"I had a pretty good idea."

"He was a man you had been in negotiation with about a room in your flat?"

"I can't be 100% certain about that . . . I now know this is the man in question."

"There are not all that number of people with that particular name, Savundra?"

"No."

"It was some time in December or January, was it not, that you were in negotiation with Dr. Savundra to let the room?"

"No, not at that time."

"At what time?"

"It was the summer about August or September."

"In May of this year you asked Keeler not to mention this man's name to the police, and you say that Mr. McKew had told you he didn't want his name brought into it?"

"Exactly, sir."

"But when the police asked you about Dr. Savundra, I suggest to you about three weeks after your conversation with Keeler, that you must have known to whom they were referring. Did you or didn't you?"

"Not instantly when that question was asked." He added: "I didn't tell Keeler not to mention *his name*. I said not to mention *him*."

"Isn't that the same thing?"

"No, not entirely, sir."

"You spoke to Keeler about it, asking her not to disclose his name?"

"Yes."

"Are you telling the jury that on June 8th, when the police asked you whether you could remember him, you *couldn't* remember him?"

"I was obviously anxious to keep, on reflection, this man out of it. I didn't discuss the matter any further."

It seemed that Ward was hiding something here; that he knew more about the Indian doctor than he was prepared to let on. But *what* he was hiding and *what* he wouldn't let on we never discovered.

Mr. Griffith-Jones was now ready to sum up Ward's evidence as he had assessed it under examination and cross-examination. His line of attack was in the classic prosecuting tradition, showing that if Ward was telling the truth, everybody else was lying. But he did not have it all his own way.

"Let us summarise the position. If you are telling the truth, Keeler is not speaking the truth?"

"Keeler is not speaking the truth, no."

"Although you had helped her from the beginning by getting her rent paid and had her to live with you?"

"Yes."

"Tried to stop her smoking marijuana, tried to get her out of the hands of this horrible Rachman, done everything you could for her, and now she comes to lie about you?"

But Ward had samples of *why* she had lied ready to hand. "Did you see the way she reacted to the police statement?" he said (referring to Mr. Burge's questions about them going to see Inspector Partridge). "This girl can be *extremely detrimental*," he went on. "It may be a variety of things which caused her to do this. She had committed certain stories in the papers . . ."

Mr. Griffith-Jones interrupted: "Davies is lying?"

"Davies is lying."

"Although you helped her with the rent in the early days?"

"Yes."

"And she attempted to commit suicide and you had her parents to stay? You have done all you could to help her?"

"We have," said Ward, "her own admission it was malice."

"Did you hear her say, 'I hope the defendant will be acquitted'?"

"I heard it," said Ward. "It was crystal clear. And I regard it as the kiss of death."

"Why should that girl lie?"

"Why? Because on her own admission she had shown malice and committed malice in the past, and she knows perfectly well that after she came back from Rachman I discovered that her character had changed quite rapidly. She had become changed in a way, and I told her parents, and she viciously turned against me."

"So viciously that she went to see your exhibition of drawings?"

"It was not out of love for me. She was getting her photograph in the papers."

Mr. Griffith-Jones decided that brevity might be more effective.

"If you are telling the truth, Miss X is lying about the two-way mirror."

"Yes." (Not lying but exaggerating, and it was a pity Ward didn't say so.)

"If you are telling the truth, Ricardo was lying when she gave her evidence to the magistrates?"

"Yes, sir."

"If you are telling the truth, Vickie Barrett is lying?"

"Yes," said Ward, banging the side of the witness-box again, "this is the bottom of the bucket. If they question 150 or 160 people it is easy to find at least half a dozen willing to come forward through some motive—malice, cupidity—who will make statements against a person who has some sort of irregularities in life such as I have and lays himself open to this type of representation."

Mr. Griffith-Jones allowed quite a pause after Ward had finished speaking, and then said in his familiar drawl: "Not only are you the victim of these perjured witnesses but also of a police conspiracy of four officers to lie against you?"

Mr. Griffith-Jones was a professor in the art of the loaded question. The word "conspiracy" was as damaging to Ward as it could be. Yet had not the judge himself said earlier that he would be surprised if the notebooks of Herbert and Burrows did not correspond? Policemen do "conspire" to give the same evidence about the same matter. They would not be of much use to the public if they didn't. The conspiracy in this instance amounted to their agreeing that Ward had asked to see Herbert rather than Herbert sending for him.

"Do you want me to make an accusation?" said Ward, angrily and a little unwisely.

The judge said: "Will you answer the questions and not ask them?"

"I'm sorry. I am saying that the statement I made is not as represented by Chief Inspector Herbert and Sergeant Burrows."

Nor by the old firm of Eustace and Glasse either. But did the jury know what statement Ward was referring to? Did they appreciate that it was about something trivial, that did not affect Ward's guilt one way or the other. Or were they thinking, as Mr. Griffith-Jones intended them to, that if Ward was telling the truth, then everybody else, *including four police officers*, were lying, and that this did not seem very probable.

Mr. Burge's re-examination was admirably brief and to the point.

"It is suggested you were chasing an innocent young country girl, Christine Keeler, who had just come to London. I think you purposely wanted this to be kept out, but there is no alternative but to raise it. Is it within your knowledge that there was a confinement at Windsor Hospital?"

"Yes."

"And before the period we are investigating?"

"Yes."

"In your view would it be right for the jury to have a picture of you aged forty-eight, corrupting an innocent girl of sixteen?"

"I did not corrupt her, and she was not innocent at all."

We had heard nothing about Ward's income during the case. The prosecution had not been able to assess it, and presumably Mr. Burge had not mentioned it before so that the prosecution should not cross-examine on it. Yet in the light of the two main charges, it was perhaps the most relevant single piece of evidence in the case.

"During the period in question, what income were you getting from your practice as an osteopath?"

"About £4,000."

"And from your drawings?"

"Another £1,500 or so."

"A total of between £5,000 and £6,000?"

"Yes."

How *could* the prosecution say that a man earning this sort of money was living on Mandy's or Christine's earnings? Mr. Burge put the point another way.

"If the prosecution's picture of a man procuring, and the picture of people in high places and very wealthy men was true, would you have needed to carry on your practice and work as an osteopath?"

"If that were true, evidently not."

"Would you have needed to do two drawings a day to earn money by this?"

"No."

Mr. Burge sat down and Ward was about to leave the witness-box when the judge turned to him.

"Dr. Ward," he said, "when do you say a woman is a prostitute?"

Ward hesitated, then said: "May I have a moment or two to think about it?" The judge nodded, and there was total silence while Ward, looking down at his feet, thought. A lot perhaps would depend on his answer. He thought for about half a minute and then he said : "It is a very difficult question to answer, but I would say when there is no element in the relationship between the man and the woman except a desire on the part of the woman to make money—when it is separated from any attachment and indeed is just a sale of her body."

"Do you really think," asked the judge, "that sexual intercourse that arises from pure sentiment and feeling could properly be paid for?"

"No sir," said Ward, "Indeed I have not said that." He might have added that in many relationships it is *because* there is sentiment and feeling that money and presents are given.

"If anyone does receive payment when the basis is sexual," the judge went on, "is she not in your view a prostitute?"

"If the relationship, my Lord," said Ward, "*were* purely sexual, she *would* be a prostitute. I did make it clear that where sentiment or other factors entered into that relationship, it became a more permanent relationship, like a kept woman. You cannot possibly refer to such a woman as a prostitute."

"That is your view?" said the judge.

"I cannot admit that a kept woman is a prostitute," said Ward, "because there is a permanence in the relationship which removes it from the status of prostitution."

What Ward was saying was an extension of what he had said earlier; that kept women are no more prostitutes than women who marry for money. This was his view. It was also my view, and as I knew, the view of many people. But was it the judge's view?

When Vickie Barrett had mentioned the name of Vasco Lazzolo, I wondered whether we would see him in the flesh. I thought probably not, unless he wanted to clear his name. So that when he took Ward's place in the witness-box, one had a fair idea what he was going to say. He was a square, burly man, wearing a double-breasted blue suit with blue tie and a blue handkerchief sticking out of his breast pocket like a tent. He had greyish hair and smallish eyes for so large a face, and he looked about fifty.

He said he was a painter and sculptor and lived at Edwardes

Square, Kensington. Vickie Barrett was brought into the court
and Mr. Burge asked Mr. Lazzolo if he knew her. Mr. Lazzolo
glanced at her as though she had just crept out from under a
stone, and then looked quickly away. "I believe," he said, "that
I met her once, three or four months ago." He said this in the
pained tones of one obliged to admit to having just trodden in
something nasty. "I was coming out of a bar in Soho," he went on,
"and there were two girls looking at my car. There were some
drawings on the back seat of the car and they were looking at
them. I had a conversation with one of them and she said she
wanted to do some modelling." He had given her his telephone
number and asked her to ring him. Later she did ring him and
came along to his studio. He had intended to do some drawings
of her, but he did not do so, and that was the end of the story.
It was an improbable story, and it was not improved by the
telling of it.

"Did you ever have intercourse with her?"

"Definitely not."

Mr. Burge then asked him about lying naked in bed in Ward's
flat, and not surprisingly he said this was quite untrue. "I have
only been in Ward's flat on one occasion, at about 9.30 in the
morning, and that was for less than five minutes. He was treat-
ing me as a patient. I had a twisted hip, and I came round to
his flat in my car to pick him up and take him to his surgery."
(Earlier Ward had said that Lazzolo was an old friend.)

Mr. Griffith-Jones asked the only relevant question which
in the circumstances he could ask.

"Is there anything you have done to this girl which causes
her to be spiteful towards you?"

"No, I am sure there isn't."

"Your telephone number is in her diary next to Stephen
Ward and in front of others who I gather were clients?"

"I gave her my number and she obviously put it in her book."
What did he mean *obviously*? Did he not see her write it down?
And if he didn't, was he expecting us to believe that she carried
the number in her head?

"You cannot help us as to why this girl should make these
gross allegations against you?"

"I have no idea why she should make these gross allegations."

Just before he left the witness-box Mr. Lazzolo said, without being asked : "May I say I would hardly have been mad enough to go round to Ward's flat at this time and behave in this manner, knowing there was a case pending against him."

He said this with emphasis and conviction. It was the most convincing thing he said.

The defence were taking Vickie Barrett's charges seriously, as indeed they had to. For the rest of the afternoon a succession of witnesses took the stand to refute her evidence, to testify that she couldn't have been in Ward's flat at the times she said she was, because they were there themselves.

The first was an elderly author called Mr. Edward Warwick, who had a green suit, a sad tortured face and a bald head. He was a loquacious man but stubborn, and not to be deflected by anyone from what he wanted to say. He and his wife had been to Wimpole Mews frequently, mainly in the evenings, and they had met other men and women there : they would not have continued going if they thought there was anything improper. He himself had often been to see Ward at Bryanston Mews. From January until the end of March he visited the flat four or five nights a week some weeks, and once or twice a week other weeks. There were often Pressmen there, and he had also seen a girl called Sylvia Parker. Vickie Barrett was led into court for him to examine like a prize ewe. He said he had never seen her.

"Is it right to say," said Mr. Burge, "there would not be people there after 12.30 in the morning?"

"Not really, because one went to the flat intending to stay half an hour, and one went on talking, talking, talking (*I could just hear him and Ward at it like a pair of old crows*). I went there intending to stay half an hour one night and stayed all night waiting to see the papers come out. Whenever one saw a light in the place one went in. There was no lock on the door."

I think Mr. Warwick would have gone on talking all afternoon, but his place was taken by Mr. Barry O'Brien, a journalist from the *Daily Telegraph*, a youngish, clean-shaven man in a charcoal suit and blue tie. He gave a variation on the same theme. From March 22nd (the day after Mr. Profumo had told his lies to the House) he was round at Bryanston Mews constantly. He too met Sylvia Parker there and his impression was that she was staying there. On the evening that Miss Keeler had come back from abroad (March 28th) he was at the flat from 8.30 p.m. until after 1 a.m., and the following night (March 29th) he was again interviewing Ward, arriving at the flat at 10 p.m. and not leaving until after 5 a.m. He confirmed that there was no lock or handle on Ward's front door and that anybody could walk in.

Then came Vickie Barrett to be confronted with Mr. Burge's accusations of her lies about Douglas Burns, and after her the long awaited Sylvia Parker. She was a tall willowy girl with a mass of red hair parted in the middle and wearing a smart biscuit coloured outfit. She leaned on one of the pillars of the witness-box in a languid sort of way and thought herself very *blasé* and sophisticated. Despite a tendency to give much of her evidence down her nose, she was easily the most audible of all the female witnesses. She chattered away about boy friends and girl friends and Mayfair, and Stephen being very well known "around town". Her own life had been plagued with disasters: her father had been sick, her boy friend had been shot, she herself had had problems and bad publicity. She struck so many attitudes that at one moment the judge told her not to pose. In loud forthright tones she told us that she had never wanted to be brought into the case, and the only reason she had consented to appear was because "things have been written down which are completely and utterly untrue". She had stayed at Bryanston Mews for five or six weeks "at about March" as a guest: she had slept on the living-room sofa and gone to bed each night at about eleven—"a perfectly respectable time"; and she had not had any "illicit association" with Ward. She seemed particularly anxious to defend any imputations on her virtue. She said that if Vickie Barrett's story of being brought in for sexual intercourse after 12.30 a.m. were true, she would have known of it; and she described her evidence as "a complete load of rubbish". All this was very convincing, but it would have been even more convincing if, as Mr. Griffith-Jones was quick to point out, Mr. Warwick had not just said that he was in the living room four or five nights a week into the small hours of the morning. I wondered whether Sylvia Parker had not perhaps slept chastely in Ward's room, yet for fear of misinterpretation had not liked to admit it.

It was now after four o'clock, and soon the court would rise for the day, not to meet again until Monday. The name "Frances Brown" was called. It was an ordinary enough name and it did not make any impact. A small bird-like woman with a pale face and a fringe teetered down the court and into the witness-box. She was wearing a dark blue dress with a white bow, and I had a feeling, which turned out to be correct, that we were back in Vickie Barrett land. Yet that was all one could have foreseen.

She gave her address as Great Western Road, Paddington, and said that she had come to court because she had read the evidence of Vickie Barrett in the newspapers.

"Did you," said Mr. Burge, "know her?"

"Yes."

"For how long?"

"Since January this year."

"Where were you living at that time?"

"St. Stephen's Avenue."

She was not all that easy to hear but quite definite in her answers, quite sure.

"Would you recognise Vickie Barrett if you saw her?"

"Yes."

The prosecution's prize exhibit was led into court for the third time that day.

"Is that the girl you are talking about?"

"Yes."

Vickie Barrett was led out.

"Did you ever see her at an address in Leighton Road, Kentish Town?"

"Yes, a few times."

Was Frances Brown a member of Mr. D's little establishment too? It was a small world.

"Did she ever come to St. Stephen's Avenue?"

"I got her a place above me in St. Stephen's Avenue."

As on one or two other occasions during the trial, there was now almost complete silence in court. Everyone felt that we were on the brink of further startling revelations; and we were.

"What were you both doing during that time?"

"Soliciting."

"Were you aware of her activities, whether they were small or great, and what she was earning?"

"She was earning about £9 to £15 a night."

That worked out at fifty to eighty pounds a week: yet according to her own evidence she had been content to go round to Ward's flat three nights a week for two and a half months for nothing.

Mr. Griffith-Jones got up and said: "In the course of soliciting with Vickie Barrett, did you ever meet a Mr. Vasco Lazzolo?"

Presumably this question was a shot in the dark, as Mr. Griffith-Jones had no knowledge of Frances Brown appearing. If so, it found its mark.

"Yes."

"Where did you meet him?"

"In Shaftesbury Avenue."

"Yes, go on."

"Well he asked us if we'd like to go back to his flat with him, and we said we would."

"And did you go back to his flat?"

"Yes."

"And what happened there?"

Now there was dead silence everywhere.

"Well he gave us a few drinks, and then Vickie Barrett did business with him."

A long pause.

"Were you present in the room together?"

"Yes."

Another pause.

"You saw it?"

"Yes."

"What, if anything, did you do?"

A small pause this time, but it seemed like eternity.

"I helped."

God, what a multitude of things those two words covered! *I helped.* It should be engraved on her tombstone. "She also served who only stood and helped."

Yet even that was not all.

"Were you soliciting with Vickie Barrett regularly before the incident you have just described?"

"Yes."

"Did you ever see her picked up in Oxford Street by Dr. Ward?"

"Yes, I was with her."

With her? There seemed no end to the coincidences.

"How many times did you see her picked up?"

"Twice."

"Not more?"

"No."

Well, that tied in with what Ward had said.

"Were you ever with her when she telephoned Dr. Ward?"

"Yes."

I felt my heart racing again. She had already confirmed what Vickie Barrett had said about Mr. Lazzolo. Was she now going to confirm what she had said about Ward?

"How often did she telephone Dr. Ward?"

"Twice."

"Where from?"

"Once from Mr. Lazzolo's place, and the other time from a phone box at Marble Arch."

"And did she speak to him?"

"No. She wasn't able to get through."

"Neither time?"

"No."

"What time did she telephone him?"

"Between half past twelve and half past two at night."

Why hadn't she been able to get through? Perhaps Mr. O'Brien and other journalists had been using the telephone.

"Did you yourself ever visit Dr. Ward's flat?"

I felt it was a question asked more as a gesture than anything else.

"Yes. With Vickie Barrett."

The suspense was almost too much to bear. What new revelations were we going to hear now?

"How many times did you both go there?"

"Twice."

"When was that?"

"Between the middle of March and the week the Pope died."

It was as good a way of pinpointing it as any.

"And what happened when you were there?"

"Well the first time Vickie did business with Dr. Ward."

"And what did you do?"

Oh, God, I thought, not helped again. But she said: "I looked on".

"And the second time?"

"We just had coffee."

Soon after this Frances Brown stood down, and the relief was tremendous. There had been moments during her evidence when it had seemed as though she was about to unlock the door to the whole case. In the end she had proved little, yet added further complications to an already complex situation. If she was telling the truth when she said that Vickie Barrett had intercourse with Mr. Lazzolo, then Vickie Barrett was *half* telling the truth and Mr. Lazzolo was lying. If she was telling the truth when she said that Vickie Barrett had had intercourse with Stephen Ward, then Stephen Ward was telling the truth, Brenda O'Neil was telling the truth, and Vickie Barrett was lying. But Ward was only *half* telling the truth when he said he had intercourse with Vickie Barrett, for he had made no mention of Frances Brown. And again he was only *half* telling the truth when he said he had had Vickie Barrett twice when according to Frances Brown he had had her once and had coffee with her once. Unless, of course, unknown to Frances Brown and Brenda O'Neil, he had had her a third time. Yet in all the muddle and confusion one thing seemed clear. There was no corroboration at all of Mr. Lazzolo having waited for Vickie Barrett naked in Ward's bed, or of Vickie Barrett having attended to him, or any other men, there.

PART V

OVER THE WEEKEND a man walked into the Bloomsbury
art gallery where they were selling Ward's pictures and bought
up all his drawings of the Royal Family for over £5,000:
these included Prince Philip, Princess Margaret, the Duchess of
Gloucester, and the Duke of Kent. The man would not give his
name. He paid the money in fivers which he was carrying in a
briefcase and he took the pictures away with him. Ward himself
went off for a day in the country with his latest girl friend Julie
Gulliver, who had been hanging round the Old Bailey all week.
They were photographed in rustic style leaning on a gate. The
News of the World carried a feature article on Christine Keeler's
life in the flat of her friend Paula Hamilton-Marshall, and the
Mirror showed pictures of her being tested for a film which I
doubted would ever get made. The *Observer* published a picture
of Wayland Young and myself coming down the Old Bailey
steps, which apparently is forbidden and nearly resulted in the
regular cameramen having their facilities withdrawn and the
Observer cameraman being lynched. And then almost before we
knew it, it was Monday morning.

The next, and as it turned out, last witness for the defence
was a young man called Noel Howard Jones at whose flat in
Chelsea Ward was staying. He described himself as an advertis-
ing executive and looked not unlike a successful pop singer. He
gave his evidence modestly and quietly (so quietly that Mr.
Burge constantly had to ask him to repeat his answers) and for
most of his time in the witness-box he impressed the court by
his sincerity. He said he had visited Ward at Wimpole Mews
and Bryanston Mews frequently. He confirmed Ward's dislike
of Rachman, that Sylvia Parker was staying at Bryanston Mews,
and that there were many people coming and going there. He
told Mr. Burge that he had no idea Christine Keeler was taking

men back to Wimpole Mews for intercourse, and he would not have brought his wife round there if he had known.

"Do I understand," said the judge, "that during the frequent visits to Wimpole Mews and Bryanston Mews that you never had the slightest suspicion that anything of an immoral nature was being carried on?"

"I knew perfectly well," said Mr. Jones, "that Ward had a number of girl friends and I knew perfectly well that he was not a moral man. I found him extremely kind and entertaining. I never had the slightest suspicion that he was doing anything of the sort with which he is charged."

All this was good stuff and valuable to the defence. But Mr. Griffith-Jones must have known a thing or two which we didn't. With a few deft jabs he set the whole edifice rocking.

"Did you have intercourse with Miss Keeler?"

The question was tossed lightly, like a shuttlecock. But it shook us all, not least Mr. Jones.

"Yes, sir."

"On how many occasions?"

"Two or three occasions, I believe, sir."

"At the flat?"

This was the same flat, of course (though Mr. Griffith-Jones did not say it) to which Mr. Jones would not have taken his wife if he had thought anything of an immoral nature was going on.

"Yes."

"Was Miss Keeler introduced to you by the defendant?"

"No."

"How did you meet her?"

"I met her accidentally in a coffee-bar."

A pick-up?

"How old are you?"

"Twenty-four."

"You, a man of twenty-four, attended Wimpole Mews for the purpose of having intercourse with Miss Keeler, who was living there?"

"I did not attend the flat for that purpose, but that is how it transpired." Mr. Griffith-Jones looked at his papers and said nothing, and oppressed by the silence Mr. Jones said: "I went to visit Miss Keeler and this happened". Mr. Griffith-Jones let the silence hang heavy, let it dot the i's and cross the t's of what Mr. Jones had been saying. Mr. Jones spoke again. "May I say that this was before my marriage, when I met Miss Keeler?"

But as far as Ward was concerned it did not matter greatly now *how* Mr. Jones had met Miss Keeler. For Mr. Griffith-Jones had partly discredited him as a witness, just as Mr. Burge had discredited Vickie Barrett. Yet when all was said and done, what did Mr. Jones's admissions amount to? That Christine Keeler was a promiscuous girl which the defence had been maintaining all along. The prosecution could not claim Mr. Jones for their own, for they had not asked him whether he had paid Christine for her services: and it was on that sort of evidence that Ward's guilt or innocence largely depended. Why had they not asked him? Presumably because they knew the answer was in the negative.

Mr. Burge said that that concluded the case for the defence, and one realised with a little chill that the trial was almost at its end, and Ward within measuring distance of knowing his fate. For weeks now, it seemed, we had been coming here daily to watch the witnesses parade before us, and there seemed no reason why we should not go on doing it for ever. But now the last witness had come and gone, and only counsels' closing speeches and the judge's summing up separated us from the verdict.

All the defence witnesses had been concerned with challenging the evidence of Vickie Barrett, and in view of the gravity of the count, I supposed this was inevitable. All the same I wondered if the defence had been wise to produce no witnesses at all for Counts 1 and 2. Admittedly most of the evidence on these counts amounted to choosing between Ward's word on the one hand and Christine's and Mandy's on the other. But there were two witnesses whom one would have liked very much to see called, who could perhaps have lightened our darkness. One was Lord Astor, the other the Indian doctor. The first could have laid to rest our doubts about the cheque for £100 for Comeragh Road, the second could have categorically denied that he had paid Mandy for intercourse at Wimpole Mews. I had heard it said that Ward wanted to spare his rich friends the embarrassment of appearing in court, and that they had expressed a similar wish. I had also heard that the Indian doctor had issued a statement denying what Mandy had alleged. But all this was rather unconvincing. Here was a man virtually on trial for his life. The law in justice to him had given him the power of subpoena. He had not chosen to use it. One could only regretfully assume that his advisers considered that when it came to the push Lord Astor and the Indian doctor might prove more of a liability to them than an asset.

The judge turned towards Mr. Burge and Mr. Griffith-Jones, and said that he would tell the jury that corroboration would be required on all five counts, and so he hoped that they would deal with corroboration in their speeches.

Mr. Burge said he thought the prosecution might indicate what names were relevant to what charges, and I thought it a peculiar thing that they had not been obliged to do this long ago. Mr. Burge said he presumed that Count 1 was concerned with Keeler, Count 2 with Rice-Davies, Count 3 with Barrett and possibly Ricardo, Count 4 with Miss R, and Count 5 with Miss X. Mr. Griffith-Jones indicated that he would not quarrel with that and that possibly Brenda O'Neil might be added to Count 3. *Brenda O'Neil?* I could hardly believe my ears. Why didn't he throw Frances Brown in for good measure too?

At eleven o'clock Mr. Burge rose to make his closing speech. "If this trial," he said, "was concerned with establishing that Ward led a thoroughly immoral life, a demoralised and undisciplined life, your task would be a simple one. No one has thought to disguise that fact from you. If you were to make sure the public conscience was shamed by a major scandal and should be appeased, and the penalty should be paid, you would hardly find a more suitable subject for expiation than Ward, who has admitted he is a loose liver and his conduct is such as to deprive him of any sympathy from any quarter."

He turned again, as he had done in his opening speech, to the way the prosecution had presented its case. "You will have noticed the method of approach by the prosecution in the cross-examination of the accused. The events of three years have been so contracted and so selected by the prosecution as to give you an impression that there was nothing going on over that period except repeated acts of sexual intercourse with different women. They have selected only the parts of those years that suit their case and have left out all those matters which do not suit their case."

I glanced at Mr. Griffith-Jones. He was busy writing. Not once during the whole of Mr. Burge's closing speech did I see him look his way or give any indication that he knew he was there. (Ward on the other hand was looking at his counsel constantly : he was in the act of sketching him.)

The prosecution, went on Mr. Burge, had tried to make out that Ward was living on Christine Keeler's earnings. If that were true, one would have expected her to be loaded with money and not having to borrow off him. Certainly Christine had had a large numbers of affairs but they had covered a period of three and a half years, from Comeragh Road in 1959 down to the present day. The prosecution had also tried to make out that Ward was intimately associated with Rachman and had introduced Keeler to him. In fact the opposite was the case. They had met Rachman by accident and Ward strongly disapproved of him.

"Be on guard against an attempt to select and to contract isolated incidents in this case. Also be on your guard against the suggestion that these two young girls were completely innocent persons who were caught, as it were, by the accused for the purpose of his trade or business of procuring.

"Because they were seventeen or eighteen and the accused was fifty, it does not mean that everything he did was from a corrupt and repulsive motive, and everything they did was out of complete innocence. You can have a girl of eighteen or even younger who is highly sophisticated and experienced. You can have a man of fifty who never seems to grow old and certainly whatever one says about the accused, he certainly has the secret of eternal youth in one respect."

He warned the jury against the unreliability of many of the prosecution witnesses. "Witnesses of that type when they go into the witness-box may have all sorts of reasons for the things they say. A woman who is living with a man may have some spite against the man, or some sort of financial or mercenary motive for telling a story, and it might be of financial advantage to her to say such a thing."

He turned to the evidence of and about Vickie Barrett, and dealt with it at length—to my mind almost too great a length, for it had been demolished already. Yet it was the most potentially dangerous of all the charges, and for this reason presumably he could take no chances. Not only did he remind the jury of all the contradictions and inconsistencies within her evidence, but he showed how suspect was the background picture.

"She turned up, did she not, members of the jury, at a very opportune moment for the prosecution. She comes out of the blue, just when she is wanted, on the very day of the accused's committal. She tells the story of an absolutely conventional ponce, which is entirely different to anything else in the history of this case. And then she happens to have a diary somewhere, which is found by a police officer.

"A key witness emerges for the prosecution because there were great difficulties about the case of Miss Keeler and Miss Rice-Davies. What a turn up for the book! Members of the jury, I suggest to you it is too good to be true."

He drew the jury's attention to the contract that Vickie Barrett and her mother had made with Mr. Burns. "That fits into the picture of a woman hearing of the vast sums paid by the Press to other witnesses in this case, and jumping in on the bandwagon. She and her mother are out to make money, members of the jury, like so many people in this case. Whether that would be wrong would not be for me to say, but what is wrong is to lie about it. She was hiding the fact that she was lying about the financial advantages."

With the police coming to Bryanston Mews in the daytime and Sylvia Parker and other people being there at night, it was, said Mr. Burge, "an extraordinary time and place to start living upon immoral earnings". Vickie Barrett's evidence was quite unreliable and he asked the jury to reject it.

Mr. Burge then turned to Counts 1 and 2, and he had this important thing to say about prostitution generally. "The fact that a prostitute has money in her handbag which she has earned by prostitution and that money finds its way into the pocket of another person does not necessarily mean that the other person is living on her earnings. She has to live, she has to buy food and clothes and pay for her lawyers, and possibly doctors, and they are paid inevitably out of her immoral earnings." Turning to the £6 a week which Mandy paid Ward for the bedroom at Wimpole Mews, he said: "It is a reasonable rent for a West End furnished flat, to have also the use of the telephone, hot water, heating and lights", and he went on: "As a lawyer or a green-grocer who receives a reasonable remuneration for services they are giving to a prostitute—not *as* a prostitute but as an ordinary person—is not guilty of living on her immoral earnings, so in my submission, whatever the view one takes in this case, this man was *not* living on her immoral earnings, *if* she was a prostitute". This of course was the heart and core of the matter, on which, depending how they looked at it, the jury would convict or acquit.

Mr. Burge dealt with all the various men, real and imagined, in Christine's life, and reminded the jury that they would require corroboration of both her and Mandy's evidence. There were many reasons why Christine should not tell the truth, and they should hesitate a long time before accepting what she said. He reminded them of when he had confronted her with her lies about Inspector Partridge. "Immediately she was on the defensive and denied the whole thing and spat out manifestly what was untrue. *There is nothing to support it in the whole of this man's history or in the character given him by Chief Inspector Herbert that in fact he was a drug-taker and had introduced that to her.*" There were other reasons, he said, for disbelieving her evidence. One was to justify what had already been written for her in the Press. Indeed after all the interviews she had had with the police and the Press she might, quite genuinely by now, be unable to distinguish between truth and fiction. A third reason for doubt was the fact that she believed she had committed an offence (in helping to procure Miss R) and, though Mr. Burge did not specifically say this, could thus have been susceptible to police pressure. Finally there was the Lucky Gordon appeal, now pending, and the allegation of her giving perjured evidence at the trial. "If that conviction against Lucky

Gordon had been quashed, and if the allegation was correct that she had given perjured evidence, think of the assistance it would have been to the defence." It would have been of even more assistance to the defence if the court had known not only that Lucky Gordon's conviction was about to be quashed but that three months later Christine would stand in the dock and hear herself sentenced to nine months' imprisonment for perjury.

The stories in the pub had changed slightly in character. They were what you might call 'slogan' stories. *Q.* "What is Christine's slogan?" *A.* "Life is better under the Conservatives." *Q.* "What is Vickie's signature tune?" *A.* "Just a thong at twilight."

After lunch Mr. Burge dealt with Mandy's evidence and the suspicious circumstances in which it had been obtained. "You have to decide, members of the jury, whether when Miss Rice-Davies gave evidence, she was in that state a witness should be in; and that is, *whether she was free to decide whether or not she could give evidence and what that evidence was, completely without any pressure from anybody.*

"She was stopped at London Airport and questioned about a suggestion of her stealing a television set, and she was taken to Marylebone Lane Police Station. She was kept there until midnight and only released after she had entered into a recognisance of £1,000. The day selected for her to answer her recognisance was June 28th, the day she happened to give evidence in this case.

"Now both she and the officers in charge of the case, members of the jury, knew that her evidence would implicate Ward concerning the Indian doctor. Indeed you may think that there was *little to implicate the accused without that.* Accordingly *something was wanted from Miss Rice-Davies,* just as something was wanted from Miss Keeler.

"She went into the witness-box with that hanging over her head and she gave evidence implicating Ward. After finishing her evidence, the possible charge of stealing the television set *was removed at the psychological moment when she had completed her evidence.*"

Mr. Burge also reminded the jury that Mandy had made a statement to the same police officers in Holloway Prison on April 25th, and that their inquiries concerned a forged driving licence and a car registration book. "She was in fear, under pressure of consequences that might happen to her, and self preservation is one of the first rules of conduct in many walks of life."

Mr. Burge had put this part of his client's case brilliantly and with immense conviction. Now he summed up the position regarding Mandy and Christine.

"The prosecution will say that all they have to prove is that he was living with a prostitute, and then the defendant has to prove that he was not living on her earnings.

"In the context of this case, we have undertaken that burden, and it is perfectly clear that in neither case was he living on the earnings of prostitution. There can be no question of his own earnings being substantial. He was earning an income which would amply provide for the circumstances of his living."

When I heard Mr. Burge say this, I could not see how any jury could bring in a verdict of guilty. Guilty of associating with prostitutes, certainly, but of living on their earnings, no. But I had not reckoned with what was to come.

Mr. Burge dealt with the remaining three counts. In asking the jury to disregard completely the charge concerning Miss X, he brought up a telling fact which I had not heard before. This was that Ward was only a weekly tenant of Bryanston Mews and on such a temporary basis would be extremely unlikely to instal a two-way mirror there, as Mr. Griffith-Jones had suggested. Then he came to Sally Norie, and for the first time in the trial he allowed some of the fire within him to break through the surface of his otherwise bland exterior. "That the Central Criminal Court," he said, "and Court Number One, and all the temporal majesty of a High Court Judge and Senior Treasury Counsel should direct your attention to the incident such as took place in the Brush and Palette Restaurant *beats one's comprehension. . . . It is horrifying.*" He almost spat the words out, he was so angry. It was admirable to see; and I only regretted that we could not have had more of this anger and more of this contempt before. Summing up the three procuring charges he said that there was "a complete lack of evidence of any wholesale introduction or procuration by Ward, which would have been inevitable if one tenth of the allegations by the prosecution and one tenth of the investigations over several months had any basis at all". He ended angrily: "There is not a vestige of truth in the fact that he introduced any of these women to other people at all."

Lastly Mr. Burge tackled, with absolute candour and great courage, the evidence and indeed the conduct of the police.

"An important element in this case is that at the time the investigations started, public indignation had mounted, following certain scandals. It was quite clear that something had to be done. Obviously the highest authorities were concerned with this investigation.

"It was," he went on, "a situation in which officers *can either make their names or sink into oblivion*. It is obviously a matter which they could go into with the knowledge of what was behind it and the knowledge that they have to do their very best to provide a case."

I looked at where Sergeant Burrows was sitting at a table in the well of the court. He had his hand under his chin and was looking at Mr. Burge intently. "A man would be clearly not human," Mr. Burge went on, "if he were not influenced in the enthusiasm of his inquiry by these considerations. *They have allowed their enthusiasm, and possibly the fear of the possibilities of failure, to spur on their investigation of the various witnesses* and to colour their evidence in the interpretation of facts that are alleged to have been said on June 8th."* (This was the date of their interview with Ward after his arrest.)

Referring to the police and Ricardo he said: "She is a prostitute. In the relations of such a person with the police they are vulnerable, and they are liable, in fear of consequences to themselves, to succumb to the temptation to think they are assisting the police and that therefore their position may be improved." He went on: "Whatever she is, or whatever she says, there is one thing that cannot be denied, and that is that she is a woman of the most enormous courage because she came here and went back on certain evidence that she had given at

---

* In plain language, though obviously Mr. Burge could not say so, the police has been pressurising witnesses.

the Magistrate's Court. One can only assume that she, at least, is not prepared to go as far as to tell lies against this man at the Central Criminal Court, realising what it may mean."

Regarding the police account of their interview with Ward, he reminded the jury that in spite of the Judge's Rules, it had never occurred to Mr. Herbert to make a written statement of what Ward had said, and that his own version of what had been said had been written an hour and a half afterwards. "They had been working on the investigation for a long time. Their minds were running along a particular line which they were wishing to establish—*desperate to establish, you may think*—so where you get a slant on the record of the answers it is not always reliable to accept it as being fully accurate."

Now Mr. Burge was at the end. "Was this life of Ward's," he said, "led for fun or profit? That is the key to this case. Was he conducting a business, living as a parasite on the earnings of prostitution? It is a very, very wide gap and a big step between a man with an artistic temperament and obviously with high sexual proclivities leading a dissolute life, and saying he has committed the offence here of living on the earnings of prostitution.

"On a fair and impartial view, I will ask you to say these charges have not been made out and find him not guilty."

It was half past three in the afternoon when Mr. Burge sat down, his task now ended. He had done everything for his client he could have done and said everything, or almost everything, he could have said. And he had done it well. Perhaps his closing speech might have been improved by more pace and variety, perhaps his words would have carried greater weight if delivered with greater passion; but he had made all the points that mattered. When he sat down I felt like giving him a small cheer; and I am certain as I can be of anything that if at that moment the jury had been asked for a verdict, they would have found Ward not guilty on all counts. But another two days were to go by before the jury were asked to retire, two days in which the defence could only look and listen; and by the end of those two days Mr. Burge's words, vivid though they had been at the time, seemed as remote and intangible as yesterday's dream.

Mr. Griffith-Jones's opening speech was like a mild sermon compared to his closing speech.

"A reference has been made," he said, referring to some remarks of Mr. Burge, "to what has been called my mission, my divine calling to see that this defendant is convicted. I do hope that you will not put that against any responsible member of the Bar who happens to be instructed on behalf of the state to place before a jury the evidence of a man's alleged offences."

Having thus insured himself for what was to follow Mr. Griffith-Jones plunged straight in.

"Mr. Burge has warned you properly that because Ward may be said to be a filthy fellow, it does not necessarily mean he is guilty of the offence with which he is charged.

"I hope that nothing I have said or shall say will suggest that is the way in which I put this case before you." This was an odd thing for Mr. Griffith-Jones to say. His whole case had been based, as far as I could see, on the premise that the more dissolute Ward's behaviour, the greater the likelihood of his guilt. Then he qualified this: "I do not say for one moment that the fact that he is a filthy fellow, to use his counsel's expression, is wholly irrelevant. You may think it is highly relevant in this case." Mr. Griffith-Jones appeared to be saying one thing in one sentence and the very opposite in the next.

But this was merely the overture and soon we were into the opening aria. "This filthy fellow," he said (he seemed obsessed by the phrase), "this thoroughly immoral man took a flat which had an aperture equipped for a two-way mirror ... and I believe that some suggestions were made about restoring it to its former use." This is what he had suggested in his opening speech, but it had already been disproved and it brought Mr. Burge to his feet. No such thing, he pointed out, had been said: Ronna Ricardo in her evidence had suggested that she had a piece of *ordinary* mirror in her flat which could be put over the hole. Mr. Burge sat down, whereupon Mr. Griffith-Jones, not to be defeated, said to the jury: "You may think it odd that he did not have the hole filled up." But as Ward was only a weekly tenant, why should he have it filled up?

"How do we start? We start with two girls of sixteen, just over, recently in London from their homes in the country (*homes*

*in the country was a nice emotional touch, suggesting log fires
and soda bread—a far cry from Christine's prefab at Staines),*
two girls who, if not then, and it may well be then, were already
promiscuous, certainly were afterwards, two girls at that age
promiscuous and without any means of their own at all.

"Coupled with those two girls we have this man over thirty
years their senior, then forty-eight, a thoroughly immoral man,
and a man who was himself on the evidence, you may think,
always hard up, whatever the money was that he in fact was
earning. . . .

"You find these two girls leaving that night-club and being
set up in a flat and the rent was paid for. The rent was paid for
by Lord Astor at the instigation of this defendant. Ward said:
'I happened to mention the girls to Lord Astor one day'."

Now Mr. Griffith-Jones's diapasons went to full stretch.

"It is no good approaching a case like this with one's eyes
shut to reality. What is this doctor, so called, of forty-eight
doing when he happens to mention these girls to Lord Astor
one day? I do not know. Two penniless promiscuous girls who
are performing in a night-club, and this man happens to mention the matter to Lord Astor one day who immediately coughs
up £100 to pay the rent. Why? I do not know. What is the
inference?"

Now the sarcasm came creeping into his voice, but his face was
still expressionless, like a mask.

"Is this mere friendliness? Is this really brotherly concern
about those two girls who are broke? Or do you think, with any
knowledge of human life, and the ways of a thoroughly immoral
man, the inference is that there was something far more sinister
than that.

"And that is the picture upon which all else builds in this
case. And having got the flat and their rent paid for them, Ward
pays them frequent visits, as he has admitted, and he introduces
a number of his friends, Astor and Fairbanks and certainly two
others—according to Miss Keeler she had intercourse with two
others (*her actual words were, 'Maybe a couple'*).

"Where are we getting to, members of the jury? Do you think
if this is just brotherly interest and kindliness he is going to take
his friends round to those two girls in the flat?

"Being a thoroughly immoral man he may be paying them visits himself in the hope of getting something in exchange for the rent he has arranged, but is he going to bring his friend Douglas Fairbanks, junior, aged between fifty and sixty, to the flat too?" He looked round the court. "Those two penniless, promiscuous little girls, setting up as they were, and then this West End osteopath, Dr. Stephen Ward, trotting round there with his middle-aged men friends." It sounded dirtier by far than it could ever possibly have been.

He reminded the jury of what Mandy had said about giving sex in exchange for what she was to get financially, and then he said : "If you accept Miss Davies's evidence about that, fitting as it does with the background, then, members of the jury, it carries you the whole way. Almost by itself it carries you home on the question of whether this man was subsequently living on her immoral earnings"—an assumption which was perhaps rather stretching it. I wondered again, as I had done during Mr. Griffith-Jones's opening speech, why, if he was so certain about what had gone on at Comeragh Road, a charge relating to it had not been included in the indictment.

Then he turned to Keeler and somewhat exaggerated the truth by saying of her lovers that "a good many of them" had had intercourse with her at Ward's flat and "a good many of them" had done it for money. The facts were that out of the thirteen men said to have had intercourse with her *during a three year period*, five or six were said to have done it at the flat (Ivanov?, Profumo, the Persian boy friend, another boy friend, Jones and Eylan) and four or five were said to have given her money (Charles?, Profumo, Eylan, Lambton, Rachman); but the only two who had both had intercourse with her at the flat *and* given her money were Eylan (three times) and Profumo (once): furthermore with *all* the lovers who paid her, she seemed to have some sort of relationship over and above the sexual act. I was also surprised to hear Mr. Griffith-Jones say that "the defendant agreed that his relationship to Keeler was that of a brother". Certainly Christine had said that, but I seemed to recollect that Ward had denied it. Had he not said : "I was not posing as her guardian at all"?

As Mr. Griffith-Jones droned on, and the afternoon drowsed to its close, I could not but admire the skill with which he managed to convey two distinct but opposed ideas; that Christine was a brazen hussy who slept with all and sundry for money, and that she was a poor little waif in need of care and attention. It was the latter theme that Mr. Griffith-Jones trumpeted during the closing minutes of the session. "This little girl," he said of Christine Keeler, "and I repeat the use of the word little, because she was still only seventeen and he was old enough to be her father—was living in this flat with his permission (*she was hardly likely to have been there* without *his permission*), carrying on with one man after another, and apparently never a word being said by him or to her parents whom he had visited.

"The evil of this, members of the jury, and it is evil, you may think, goes very deep. You remember after his first meeting in the club, when he is trying to get his hands on her, this respectable Dr. Ward not only rings the girl up, but goes and sees her little people down at Staines." He made them sound like two distressed dwarfs. I looked at Ward, half expecting to see a pair of horns on him. His eyes were fixed on his tormentor, fascinated, incredulous, as hypnotised by the performance as the rest of us. "What for?" said Mr. Griffith-Jones, "unless to deceive?"

For the last few minutes of the day Mr. Griffith-Jones concentrated on Ward's character, and let the jury go away with this image of him.

"What do we find Ward saying to the police. 'Christine had a lot of boy friends. I was not always there when they called. Sometimes I would go round to the surgery. I know they used to go into the bedroom and sometimes they would be in there when I returned.' " Was he really expecting us to believe that Ward had said these words, in that order, voluntarily to the police? I believe he was; and the jury, who by now must have been very confused as to who said what when, may well have thought they were hearing the literal truth. Then without warning Mr. Griffith-Jones shot back to Comeragh Road. "How was she living?" he asked. "She had no income and she was dressing herself. A penniless creature who could not even afford, with another girl, her rent. What was the answer to this by a thoroughly immoral man? What must have struck him? What was happening between the girl who had no cash, and these men who were continuously going in and going to bed with her? This was the girl to whom he himself had introduced some of his middle-aged rich friends."

It was a vivid picture that Mr. Griffith-Jones was painting, but not one that was even remotely recognisable from the evidence we had heard. I wondered if the jury would be proof against it.

Now that the chorus had passed from the stage and the principal actor had played his main scene, there was a sharp drop in attendance. Next morning, for the first time during the trial, the crowd had thinned and there were only a handful of cameramen. It was the same inside the Court. The Press benches were three-quarters empty, and you could count the Ascot hats on the fingers of one hand. In the dock Ward appeared as self-possessed and detached as usual. It was the last day any of us would ever see him.

Mr. Griffith-Jones lost no time in picking up the threads of the day before, and was soon warming to his task. There were echoes of his famous question to the *Lady Chatterley* jury in his emphasising the difference not only in the ages of Christine and Ward but in their *education*: he seemed to think that society should be divided into the privately educated and the publicly educated, and never the twain should meet. He garnished his speech with more choice expressions: "Two-way mirrors and practically the whole gamut": "a couple of West Indians thrown in": "promiscuity plus Indian hemp": "funny business if I may use that expression"; but far and away the most unattractive thing he said was that during Ward's tenancy of Wimpole Mews he had lived with a different woman and "changed mounts" half-way through. There had been no evidence at all that Ward had slept with either Christine or Mandy during his tenancy of Wimpole Mews.

It was this sort of thing that characterised much of Mr. Griffith-Jones's closing speech. Mr. Burge was only one of many people in court who seemed unable to take his eyes off him:

it was like watching a very skilful conjuror. Sometimes Mr. Burge rose to protest, at other times he sat bewildered in his seat, vigorously shaking his head. Like some thick-skinned politician Mr. Griffith-Jones forged steadily ahead, oblivious to everything but the sound of his own words.

"This case," he said, referring to Mandy's occupation of Wimpole Mews, "must be an eye-opener to some of you as to how some people live. Again there is the picture of a man years older than this girl who was having her there living in this flat cheek by jowl, *and it was quite normal for him to be there while she retired with the man she had with her to the bedroom leading off that sitting room next door to his own bedroom.*"

This was a typical example of how Mr. Griffith-Jones exaggerated the facts. What he had said gave the impression that there were strings of men in and out of Mandy's bedroom, and that Ward was in the flat for most of the time this was going on. In fact she had only given evidence of having had intercourse with three people during the two months she was there: the Indian doctor, Lord Astor (both of whom denied it) and a boy friend: she had said that Ward was in the flat *once* when she was having intercourse with Lord Astor, and Ward had admitted to being in the flat *once* when she was having intercourse with the boy friend, while she herself had said that she had had intercourse with the Indian doctor in the daytime while Ward was at his surgery.

A little later, when talking about the procuration charges, Mr. Griffith-Jones ran together several quite separate pieces of evidence in order, presumably, to make a greater impact.

"May I remind you," he said, "of the words Keeler used in her evidence: 'It became like an understanding between us that I used to go out and find girls for Dr. Ward. *This is because* I was highly influenced by Dr. Ward and I would do anything he asked me to do.'" (She had certainly said that Ward had asked her to find girls—which he denied—and she had also said that she was influenced by him, but, according to my notes, she had *never* said that one was because of the other; and *if* she had never said it, then surely the prosecution had no business to say she had. For undoubtedly the jury would think the words were true.)

Again, a little later, Mr. Griffith-Jones said: "Are you to disbelieve Keeler when she says that the real purpose of her going modelling was to get girls back to introduce to him?" According to my notes Christine had not said this. Mr. Griffith-Jones had asked her: "Did you in fact meet girls modelling and bring them back?" and she had answered: "On a few occasions, yes"; which was rather a different thing.

Yet almost his most startling suggestion was that there was some connection between the lunatic Miss X episode and the coming of Vickie Barrett.

"It is a curious thing, you know, this suggestion that he put to her about that matter. He is just going into Bryanston Mews. But she happily turned the suggestion down. What do we find almost as soon as he is in Bryanston Mews, within a day or a week or so?

"We have on her evidence, Barrett being taken back there night after night to serve men, friends of the defendant. (Apart from Lazzolo, Vickie Barrett had offered no evidence that the men were friends of Ward.) Is that pure chance that this girl should tell you that just as he was going into the flat, this proposition is put to her and we find within a week or so another girl being taken back to that flat for just the same purpose?"

This brought him on to Frances Brown, a witness who, as he inevitably pointed out, had been called by the defence and not the prosecution.

"And she gave the lie, didn't she, to Mr. Lazzolo?

"Can you believe Mr. Lazzolo now when he tells you it is untrue that he went to the defendant's flat and had intercourse there? Can you honestly look at that evidence in the face of his lying evidence to you about what happened with Miss Barrett at his own studio?"

The jury may well of course have been wondering why, if Mr. Lazzolo could entertain Vickie Barrett in the comfort of his own studio, he should want to cross London in the early morning to have her in Ward's flat. But Mr. Griffith-Jones was on to a new thought.

"So it came about, perhaps unexpectedly, that Miss Frances Brown let the side down. The real purpose of her evidence was to refute Miss Barrett's, not confirm it—refute it by saying:

'She and I were soliciting together every night and I know in effect Miss Barrett did not go back night after night to Bryanston Mews.'

"What is the truth of that? Again it has become quite apparent. *Miss Frances Brown is talking of a different period of time to that which Miss Barrett was talking about.*"

It had never occurred to me that Mr. Griffith-Jones might try to explain away Frances Brown's evidence in this sort of way, and it said much for his bottomless ingenuity. He went into the question of the dates in detail and gave a plausible but quite unconvincing explanation of them.

"Does that make sense, do you think?" he asked. To Ward it made no sense at all and from the dock he shouted out "No". Mr. Wheatley rose from his seat and had a word with him, but a few moments later, while Mr. Griffith-Jones was still discussing Vickie Barrett and Frances Brown, Ward again shouted out, this time the words "Except she was *not* soliciting!" The judge said: "This is the third time you have interrupted and I will take action if you do it again." Ward, trying to control himself, said: "I'm sorry, my lord. It's a great strain." This was the cue for Mr. Griffith-Jones to take the knife which he had already firmly lodged in Ward's body, and give it a few twists. "Of *course* it's a great strain," he drawled, "for a *guilty* man to *hear* the *truth at last.*" He spoke the words very slowly and deliberately, and I felt quite sick that any man should be able publicly to humiliate another man so. No doubt Mr. Griffith-Jones would say that he was only doing his duty.

It must have been about half-way through the morning when the woman sitting next to me, an American magazine writer, handed me a note which read: "Lucky Gordon has just been freed." This news came as a surprise to most of us, as we did not know his case was being heard. The question immediately was, had the Court of Criminal Appeal said *why* he had been freed? Would *this* court, and above all *this* jury, be told that Christine Keeler had given perjured evidence?

The answer to that came towards the close of Mr. Griffith-Jones's speech at the very time when he was discussing the truthfulness or otherwise of Christine's evidence.

"Gordon was tried here for assaulting Miss Keeler and

appealed against his conviction at the Court of Criminal Appeal, Miss Keeler having given certain evidence against him. As I understand it, the basis or the grounds of that appeal were that her evidence was not true and that there were two witnesses Gordon desired to call but were not at the trial and were not available. . . .

"That appeal has already been heard and Gordon's appeal has been allowed.

"*That does not of course mean to say that the Court of Criminal Appeal have found that Miss Keeler is lying. As I understand from the note I have, the Lord Chief Justice said that it might be that Miss Keeler's evidence was completely truthful,* but in view of the fact that there were witnesses now available who were not available at the trial, it was felt that the court could not necessarily say that the jury in that case would have returned the same verdict as they did if those two witnesses had been called.

"That," he concluded, "is all it amounts to. The Court of Criminal Appeal have *not* found whether Miss Keeler was telling the truth: they have allowed the appeal simply and solely because these two witnesses were not there."

At the time we were all a bit gulled by these words. There had been so many lies and half-truths already that no one was prepared to declare anyone else a liar without firm evidence. Later on we found out that the evidence was there but that the public were denied hearing it. Yet if it *had* been heard publicly by the Court of Criminal Appeal (and many lawyers think it monstrous that it was not heard), if the Ward jury *had* known that Christine had lied on oath in the witness-box, not only at Gordon's trial but at this trial too, where she had repeated the lies, it is inconceivable that they would have brought in the verdict they did.

Mr. Griffith-Jones now brought his two and a half hour peroration to an end. "Members of the jury," he said, "you will no doubt be glad that this case is drawing to a close, and it will no doubt be a relief to get back to the clear air of one's home and away from the atmosphere of those flats.

"Certainly we have come from what you may think were the very depths of lechery and depravity in this case—prostitution,

promiscuity, perversion, and getting girls to go out and borrow
money by giving their bodies for it. . . .

"You won't convict the defendant just because he was at the
centre of all this, and just because his homes at Wimpole Mews
or Bryanston Mews were the pivot upon which all this turned.

"But, members of the jury, while you do not convict for that
reason alone, you may think that the fact that he was the centre
of it in itself lends the strongest influence that these charges
which are now laid against him are true bills—that in fact he
was taking money from these various women, money earned by
prostitution.

"You may think that the defendant is a thoroughly immoral
man for no other reason than he was getting girls for himself
and his friends.

"If you think that that is proved, members of the jury, you
may think it is in the highest public interest to do your duty
and return a verdict of guilty on this indictment."

It was just after noon that Mr. Griffith-Jones sat down and
as he did so, I could not help reflecting how grossly unfair it
was that the prosecution should have the advantage of both the
first and the last word; of, so to speak, establishing the accused's
guilt before they had led evidence to prove it, and then, right at
the end, of reaffirming it. Perhaps the jury would not be prepared to accept all of Mr. Griffith-Jones's theories—though
they would undoubtedly swallow more of them than the Press
benches—but he had made some good points too. What would
count with the jury was not an assessment of each individual
incident but, as Mr. Blom-Cooper said, "general impressions".
And, there was no burking it, the general impression of Ward
as portrayed by Mr. Griffith-Jones was that he was a sexual
monster whose activities were no longer to be tolerated. Now it
was up to the judge and his summing up.

But first, one's own summing up.
There were, I think, no doubts at all about Counts 4 and 5
which were an insult to the intelligence and too absurd to consider: indeed they should never have been brought. Nor was
there much doubt now about Count 3 in view of all Vickie
Barrett's lies and the implausibility of her story in relation to the

general pattern of Ward's life and the other evidence concerning him. If he had been a professional ponce, as Vickie Barrett was suggesting, then the 130 or so interviews conducted by Herbert and Burrows would almost certainly have revealed more of his activities than the single, isolated story she had alleged. And the evidence of Frances Brown and Brenda O'Neil especially went a long way towards corroborating the defence's assertion that Vickie Barrett had not done what she had said.

There remained Counts 1 and 2, living on the immoral earnings of Christine and Mandy. Now for these two charges to stick, it was obvious—indeed Mr. Griffith-Jones had said it— that three things had to be proved. Firstly that Christine and Mandy were prostitutes, secondly that Ward was living with them knowing them to be prostitutes, and lastly that he was actually living, wholly or in part, on their earnings as prostitutes. The prosecution had to prove the first two things : and then it was up to Ward to refute the third.

It might be thought in the light of Mr. Eylan's evidence, and that of Mandy about the Indian doctor (if one believed it), that there could be little doubt that these two women were prostitutes. But were they? The definition of a prostitute is a woman "who sells her body indiscriminately for sexual intercourse". Now there are several things to note here. The first is the inclusion of the word "indiscriminately", which is of great significance. For where a prostitute fundamentally differs from other women is that she exercises little or no selection in the choice of her sleeping partners. But could this be said of Christine or Mandy? Certainly Christine had had a liberal assortment of lovers, *but she had slept with most of them for pleasure not money*; and even those who had paid her, like Eylan and Profumo, had a social relationship with her as well. Profumo had taken her for drives in his car, and to his own home, while Eylan used to take her out to restaurants and to theatres over a period of several months. In other words, while there was plenty of evidence that she had behaved promiscuously, there was no evidence that she had slept with people *indiscriminately for money*. It was the same with Mandy. She also had shown selection in whom she took to bed. Had she not said of Mr. Ropner : "I liked him but I didn't fancy him", meaning she liked him as a person but did not fancy going to bed with him?

But the most important ingredient in any definition of a prostitute is one that at present the law takes no cognisance of, and that is the strictly temporary nature of the sale of her body, combined with the fact that *the terms of sale are agreed by both parties beforehand*. It may be £5 for straight intercourse, or £1 a stroke for whipping, or whatever it is. But there is *a contract of sale*, and there seems no reason why this should not be written into the definition of the word for legal purposes, i.e. that a prostitute is a woman "who contracts to sell her body indiscriminately for sexual intercourse". Indeed this *ought* to be written into the law if it is to be just, for it is with the common prostitute as such that the ponce associates, and it is with the ponce's relationship with the common prostitute that society, and the law, are concerned. Indeed without the conditions contained in the definition, the ponce would not exist; for he is usually, and paradoxically, the one stable element in the shifting sands of the prostitute's life. Now such conditions simply did not apply to Christine and Mandy. There was no evidence at all that they had *contracted* to sell their bodies to strangers. Mr. Eylan had given Christine money on each occasion he had had intercourse, but one cannot say for certain that he would have been denied the intercourse if he had not given the money. When Mr. Griffith-Jones asked the jury whether they thought Profumo would have given Christine money if he had not been getting sex, he was bargaining they would answer no. But it was common ground that Profumo had had intercourse with Christine several times *without* giving her money; so that one cannot assume that if he had not given her money once, that she would therefore have withheld her favours.

To sum up, I would say that Christine and Mandy were not prostitutes within the *intention* of the Act. But they may have been within the *meaning* of the Act as then defined, and therefore one must assume that the prosecution had so proved. But had the prosecution also proved that he knew they were prostitutes, and had the defence proved that he was not living on their earnings?

Here it seemed to me the prosecution was on much shakier

ground. Ward himself had emphatically denied that he knew
that either of the girls was getting money from anyone in return
for sex, and he had said that he would have turned them out of
the house if he had known. While I think that this posturing was
exaggerated, I could recall no evidence to suggest that
Ward *knew* of the occasions when money passed. Indeed it
would have been surprising if he had, for the bulk of Christine's
lovers *were not giving her money*. I see no reason at all why one
should assume that Christine told him of every occasion when
she was given money or presents, or of the more frequent
occasions when she wasn't. It cannot have been all that
interesting.

But even although we allow that the prosecution had proved
that Ward was knowingly associating with prostitutes, it was
surely a very different matter when it came to the question of
living on their immoral earnings. Christine had said, and
Ward had said, that *she owed him more than she ever
gave him*. Now this, by itself, I should have thought, was all the
proof one needed that Ward was *not* living, even in part, on her
earnings. And it is *living* on the prostitute's *earnings*, not con-
sorting or associating with her, with which the law is concerned.
It is a law which has been framed, as all good laws should be, to
meet society's demands in a certain respect; and those demands
are that pimps that exist in every big city should not batten on to
prostitutes, sending them out into the streets or cafés night after
night, themselves living in idleness on the proceeds. Ward did
not come remotely within this category. He was earning as an
osteopath and artist *between £5,000 and £6,000 a year*, and he
had no wife or family. He hardly even came within the category
of "necessary traders", hairdressers, doctors, etc., with whom
prostitutes must deal and who inevitably live partly on their
earnings, because Christine was not even paying him rent.
Although Christine's residence at Wimpole Mews lasted over a
year, the prosecution had only produced evidence of four occasions (three with Eylan, one with Profumo) when she had
received money after intercourse. The total for this was not more
than £65. Ward himself had said that he had given Christine
£70 to £80, and she agreed that she had not paid more than
half of it back. If, on this information, it could be said that Ward

was living on Christine Keeler's earnings, then with equal
justification it could be said that the moon is green.

So one was left with Mandy and the Indian doctor. And if
what she had said about the Indian doctor was true, was Ward
guilty of partly living on *her* immoral earnings? What she had
said was that the Indian doctor had given Ward £25 to use her
room for sexual purposes in the daytime (this in addition to the
£6 a week rent she was paying) and indeed had actually shown
her the notes the doctor had given him. She had also admitted
she had had intercourse with the doctor four or five times at the
flat and been paid a minimum of £15 and a maximum of £25
a time. She had given Ward small amounts of money from time
to time, amounting in all to some £25, and she had also paid
for the food. Against this she agreed that Ward himself had
given her money, had paid the other household expenses, and
had had her parents to stay free of charge. There could not have
been more than a few pounds in it.

But allowing that there *was* a few pounds in it, then tech-
nically speaking it might be said that Ward was guilty of partly
living on her immoral earnings—provided the story was true. But
was the story true? This was the crucial question, and the more
one looked at it, the more reasons there seemed for doubting it.

The first and perhaps the best reason for doubting it was
quite simply that it was uncorroborated (unless one were to
attach weight to Christine's flimsy evidence on the subject); and
the judge had said that each count had to have corroborative
evidence. Also the Indian doctor had himself denied it. We had
had evidence of Mandy's malice already, both as regards Douglas Fairbanks and Ward himself, and there were therefore *prima
facie* grounds for thinking that she had cause to do him hurt.
Nor, for a female witness in a sex case, would this have been
anything unusual. Towards the end of a long life at the Bar the
great judge, Sir Travers Humphreys, said that miscarriages of
justice were almost always caused by either unforeseeable circumstances *or perjury by women*. He added that he himself had
encountered so many instances of perjury by women that he had
come to regard them as commonplace. "I have never known,"
he said, "and found it very difficult to imagine, the case of a man
who from envy, hatred, or malice, deliberately charged another

knowing him to be innocent, and supported the charges with his own false evidence; on the other hand perjury of that nature by women has been proved in several cases, it can occur almost any day in any society and unfortunately it is quite likely to be successful." We had had proof already that Christine had perjured herself, in relation to the visit to Scotland Yard, and there were suspicions (at that time unconfirmed) that she had perjured herself in the Gordon case. This did not incline one to attach much weight to her corroborative evidence about the Indian doctor.

But Mandy as well as Christine had been proved a liar. "Did the learned magistrate," Mr. Burge had asked her in relation to the motoring offences, "say to you that if you wanted to get something and get it by a lie, you would lie?"—and Mandy had answered "Yes". Had Mandy lied about the Indian doctor? And if so what had she wanted to get? Money from the newspapers, as Mr. Burge had suggested? Or, as he had also suggested, favours from the police?

It was the conduct of the police in the case that really gave one most cause for alarm. Mandy herself had admitted to Mr. Burge that pressure had been put on her so that things would be difficult if she did not give evidence against Ward. In view of this admission, one would have thought that her evidence should be discounted altogether. Certainly the circumstances in which she had been interviewed seemed to bear out what she had said : first in Holloway Prison, again in the courtroom before the hearing of the case, arrested at London Airport at night on a doubtful charge of stealing a television set, freed on £1,000 bail conditional on appearing at the Magistrate's Court at the time of the hearing against Ward, and taken to a room at the Magistrate's Court while still under oath and interviewed by a representative of the television company in the presence of the police. Nor was she the only one. Christine Keeler had been interviewed by the police *twenty-four times*. Why? She had been told that she had committed an offence in helping to procure Miss R, so she was extremely vulnerable to police pressure. Vickie Barrett did not speak of the police pressure put on her until after the trial but when she made her first statement at Marylebone she was in a vulnerable position because of the soliciting charge against her. John Hamilton Marshall had said at the Magistrate's Court that he had signed a false statement against Ward, and had given as explanation of it that he was kept at the police station six hours. Ronna Ricardo had first been interviewed in the middle of the night, and made no bones about the pressure the police had put on her: they had put words into her mouth, she said, both then and on a later occasion, and she had let them do so because they had threatened to send her sister to a remand home and take away her baby as being in need of care and protection. She had inferred that even then she would not have signed the statements if the police had not given her a promise, which they subsequently broke, that she would not have to appear in court.

Naturally the police denied all this. But their denials were not all that convincing. Mr. Herbert's replies about his mentioning to Christine the possibility of proceedings being taken against her had been equivocal; and he had waited until the judge practically dragged the story out of him before admitting his real reasons for taking Mandy into custody at London Airport.

To sum up then, two of the prosecution's four main witnesses, Mandy and Ronna Ricardo, admitted that the police had put pressure on them to say what they wanted, while the other two, Christine and Vickie Barrett, had been placed in positions where they were very susceptible to pressure (and one of these admitted pressure later). Ronna Ricardo agreed she had lied at the Magistrate's Court, Mandy Rice-Davies was proved to have lied, Vickie Barrett's evidence was a series of lies and Christine Keeler had lied about going to Scotland Yard to see Inspector Partridge. The evidence of one of the police officers involved had been very much less than frank. Indeed, the more one looked at the prosecution's case, the more dubious a thing it appeared. I hoped the judge would open wide the windows and throw the whole mess out.

But the judge had other ideas. Until now he had been, as it were, the stage director, flitting busily about the wings, occasionally seen, sometimes heard, always felt; restraining some players, giving others their head, guiding, encouraging, admonishing, warning, impressing with his own stamp everything that was said or done. But now the principals and chorus had departed, leaving the epilogue to him alone. It was a moment, one felt, for which he had been waiting; an occasion, a personal challenge perhaps, a footnote or even a paragraph in history. He was nervous as he came out from the wings, washing his hands with invisible soap, an hygienic Heeplike mole. He knew, as we all did, that the spotlight of the world was on him. He addressed the rude mechanicals casually, conversationally; but his opening words were for other breeds than them. "There have been, as we all know," he said, "repercussions arising out of what we have to investigate which have widely spread their tentacles across the public life of this country and have aroused great interest in foreign countries. One would have thought from what we have all been faced with in the national newspapers that this country has become a sort of sink of iniquity. But you and I know that the even tenor of family life over the overwhelming majority of our population goes quietly and decently on." As he said the words one could see in his mind's eye a million telegraph wires zinging them across the world to far-away places like Cork and Alice and Dusseldorf; and, in one's own mind's eye, their arrival there with all the impact of stale and soggy bread.

His was an elfin, workaday mind: even his clichés lacked the distinction and originality of those of Mr. Griffith-Jones. "The heart of this great metropolis": "One crowded hour of glorious life": "a great power sometimes known as the fourth estate": "justice is not a cloistered virtue". And yet one could not but marvel, as in our courts I have always marvelled, at the spontaneous combustion of English prose, the creation of sentences and paragraphs, the placing of colons and commas, the effortless jam session of an English judge in the groove. He looked at the jury and his notes, rarely elsewhere; and the jury, on the look out for portents to let them do the right thing (whatever that might be), looked at him. He had few mannerisms. Sometimes at the beginning, when he was still nervous, he gave his left hand, almost lost in the huge sleeve of his robe, a little shake, as a woman does to free a bracelet. His diction was orthodox: only a soft "a" in "example" and a long "e" in "period" hinted at the incubator in which he had first been hatched.

"One of the great tasks of a tribunal," he said, "is to seek to

keep the atmosphere down as we consider the facts dispassion-
ately", and for an hour or so it really seemed as though this were
happening. The bitter taste in the mouth left by Mr. Griffith-
Jones's words was slowly dispelled. The judge praised those
attributes ("artistic talents of no mean quality"—"job is to heal
and make whole") he believed the defendant had; he praised too
Mr. Burge and Mr. Griffith-Jones for their professional skills;
he praised the jury for their patience. Suddenly all was summer
and singing, as though we loved one another, so that it seemed
almost a shame that we could not now call it a day and go home,
hand in hand, to Pimm's and Shepherd's Pie. But already the
judge had turned to those things to which every judge turns—
the jury were the sole arbiters of the facts, they must disregard
his views if they conflicted with theirs, reasonable doubts were
not fanciful doubts, etc. This routine was familiar to most of us,
and to the judge more than any of us; yet he made the words
sound fresh and alive, as though he was saying them for the first
time.

It is difficult in retrospect to say at what moment one became
aware that the sun had dipped behind the hill, that the air had
an evening chill to it. There is no clear dividing line in the text.
Indeed the more one reads the Press accounts of the judge's summing up, the more fair and reasonable it seems. But this was yet
another example of the difference between how things sounded
at the time and how they read afterwards. Mr. Burge read far
more effectively than he sounded: Mr. Griffith-Jones sounded
much more hostile than he read. And now here was the judge
who at the time sounded totally unsympathetic to the accused,
yet who read so sweetly afterwards. When I first saw the summing up I could hardly believe I had an accurate report of it, so
great was the gulf between the words and my memory of them.
Yet I was certain my memory was not playing me false. I
puzzled over the discrepancy for a long time, and it was not until
after the trial, when I came across an account of it in—of all
places—*France-Soir*, that I found the explanation. This extract
is from the issue of August 2nd, 1963.

If Ward had not attempted suicide, we would have known
Judge Marshall's sentence yesterday evening, the sentence of a

judge who—it must be said—however impartial he tried to be, was betrayed by his voice over and over again.

Mr. Marshall is a puritan, and Ward, the debauched, cynical libertine, gave him the horrors. Admittedly, the final summing-up expressed perfect impartiality—on paper: the arguments for the defence come out a good deal better than those for the prosecution.

But each time Mr. Justice Marshall raised questions which the jury would have to resolve, his voice revealed the fact: Mr. Marshall did not like Ward, for Ward had brought scandal to Britain.

When I read this and applied it to my memories of the summing up it fitted into place. It was not that the judge had omitted what was favourable to Ward—the record belied that. It was, simply, a question of emphasis. When the judge was pointing out to the jury those things in Ward's favour, he often did so in a flat matter-of-fact voice. He appeared so uninterested in what he was saying that one could not be interested oneself : the mind automatically shut off from him. Yet when he came to matters which told against Ward, his tone changed : his voice and bearing became brighter, livelier; he held the attention where elsewhere he had lost it. It was this that made the summing up sound so one-sided. Now I do not for a moment think that the judge was conscious of what he was doing. But with his particular background, it would perhaps have been surprising if something of his own attitudes had not trickled through. Impartiality and objectivity are at best relative terms; we are all prisoners of our pasts more than we like to think.

As for the content of the first day's summing up, it is difficult to comment on it without the official transcript, which the Lord Chief Justice of the time denied me. I cannot categorically say that such a thing was omitted, when in the truncated press reports it may well have been omitted. All I can say is that I had the impression that many things that could have been said in Ward's favour were not said. For instance, I have a note that the judge read out Christine's evidence in relation to Mr. Eylan, but I have no note that he read out Ward's evidence.

I have a note that the judge spent some time in discussing Christine being introduced to Rachman and subsequently becoming his mistress, but no note that she and Ward had both first met Rachman accidentally, when looking for a new flat. I have no note of the judge stressing that Christine had had a child before she met Ward (and was therefore not the young innocent Mr. Griffith-Jones tried to make out), or of her saying that she owed him more money than she ever gave him. I have no note either of the judge saying that she was a liar and that Mandy was a liar and that the evidence of both of them should be highly suspect. Nor have I a note of him referring to the many and various pressures alleged to have been put on witnesses by the police. It is possible that all these things were said; but, as I say, I have not got a note of them.

As for what *was* said, there is little to complain about. Dealing with the two procuration charges the judge said that the jury must not convict unless they were satisfied of two things; that Ward was endeavouring to get Miss R and Miss X to sleep with people other than himself, and that there was corroborative evidence on both counts. I wished he had added that neither of these conditions had been met. I was also sorry that he did not say that such footling charges should never have been brought.

Regarding the first two counts, the judge said that the jury had to ask themselves three questions. Were Christine and Mandy prostitutes within the definition? Did Ward know they were? Did he knowingly receive from them or others money for "the introduction and facilities for sexual intercourse which he provided?" If, he went on, the jury were satisfied that the girls *were* prostitutes and that Ward *knew* they were, how was one to define the so-called "facilities"? How to distinguish between the milkman and doctor who lived on the prostitute's earnings, and the ponce? The test which the House of Lords had laid down, said the judge, was one of *assistance*. For a man to be proved guilty of living on a prostitute's earnings it had to be shown that he was *assisting* her in her trade. Three other things also had to be proved. That such assistance, whether in goods or services, was supplied by him to them for the purpose of prostitution; that they would not have been supplied but for the fact that they

were prostitutes; and that he received payment for such assistance out of their earnings. "If you are satisfied," said the judge,
"that the evidence has proved him to have acted in a way that
satisfies those four ingredients, then the charge of knowingly
living on the earnings of prostitution has been made out and
your verdict will be one of guilty." I could not see how anyone,
even with the worst will in the world, could say that the evidence
had proved that: to suggest that Ward was supplying Christine
and Mandy with goods and services for carrying out prostitution
was tantamount to saying he was running a brothel, which was
plainly absurd. The judge must have seen this himself, for he
now apparently added these significant words—I say apparently because at the time I did not hear them, or even hear
them remarked on: *"It may well have struck you that these are
matters which are very difficult to prove."* Did the jury, like
myself and others, miss these words too? Were they uttered so
casually or quietly that they were lost on the wind? And were
the judge's warnings to the jury that they must find corroboration *on every count* lost on the wind too? In the light of their
subsequent conduct, even in the light of Ward's subsequent conduct, it would seem that something of this kind must have happened. For all the people I talked to who were in court that day
were agreed that we had heard a "hanging" summing up. Ward
himself seemed certain of it.

To Ward, the most wounding thing the judge said about him
that day was that he had been abandoned by his friends. He
referred to the matter twice. "There may be many reasons," he
said, "why Ward has been abandoned in his extremity. You
must not guess at them, but this is clear: if Stephen Ward was
telling the truth in the witness-box, there are in this city many
witnesses of high estate and low who could have come and testified support of his evidence." And then a little later he said:
"Many witnesses who could have been called have not been
called in connection with the defence. They could have enormously strengthened the case concerning the earnings of prostitution." Some lawyers have told me that they were surprised the
judge should have said this, but as a layman I would only partly
agree with them. The nearer the law is to what ordinary people
are thinking then, in my view, the better law it is. The judge

was only echoing what was in all our minds. Where was Lord Astor? Where was the Indian doctor? They had issued statements and denials, but that was not enough. There could be little doubt that if they had taken the stand to support Ward's evidence, they would have enormously strengthened the case for the defence. Equally there could be little doubt that the reason they had not been called was that the defence considered them too great a risk; that after they had sung their songs of praise for Dr. Ward, Mr. Griffith-Jones might have cut them into little pieces.

If the judge had stuck to Lord Astor and the Indian doctor, then I would have had no quarrel with him. But he went further than that. He referred to "many witnesses of high estate and low". Apart from Lord Astor and the Indian doctor, who were they? Just *how* many of them were there? And—most important of all—what evidence could they have produced to show that they knew for a fact that neither Christine nor Mandy had given Ward money? It was this assertion of the judge's, this inference that Ward was lying because certain people had not supported him—yet not naming the people or the sort of people he had in mind, that seemed to me so unfair. And I had no doubts at all of the effect of such a remark on the jury.

To Ward though, it was more than unfair. It was the final twist of the knife. It was a reminder to him of what was the most painful aspect of the whole affair—the fact that his rich friends had left him to face the music alone. Lord Astor was not the only one: there were others whose names had not appeared in the case. And the reason they had left him was not simply one of self preservation, but that they did not think of him in the way he hoped and perhaps believed they did. For years, poor innocent, he had deluded himself into thinking that Lord Astor and others were his friends; and now had come the shattering awakening. He was not their friend at all: he was the court jester, the grand eunuch, the private medicine-man whose usefulness was now over.

There were two other things the judge said that day which, while not directly relevant to the issues before us, were immensely revealing of the judge himself. Referring to Mr. Eylan as a witness who had had the courage to come forward and publicly admit to having paid Christine for her favours, the judge said: "and in doing so, you may think, he regained his self respect". It was an illuminating remark and pinpointed not only the huge gulf separating Ward's world from that of the judge, but the judge's world from that of many of the rest of us. The other remark occurred at the end of a long day, when no doubt the judge was tired and his powers of concentration waning. Instead of "Marilyn Rice-Davies" he said "Marilyn Monroe". The slip was interesting; for one would normally expect the mention of such a sex-symbol in court to arouse the judicial comment, "And who, pray, is Marilyn Monroe?" Yet this latter-day Harlow, this Anglo-Saxon Bardot was so far to the front of the judge's unconscious mind that she actually spilled over into speech. He corrected himself with a little moley smile. "I am going back," he said, "to my youth." And that was interesting too. For the judge was sixty-four. Marilyn Monroe did not become a household word in England until about 1949, at which time the judge was fifty, the same age as Ward now. Was this what he considered his youth? (One would have liked to hear Mr. Griffith-Jones on the subject. "Members of the jury, you have heard evidence that the accused, Sir Archie Marshall, considered himself still in his youth when he was fifty. And you have also heard evidence, members of the jury, that when he was fifty, he was having thoughts about a beautiful young film actress called Miss Marilyn Monroe. He a man of fifty, members of the jury, and she a young girl, lately arrived in Hollywood from the country, and only just out of her teens. Members of the jury, what was this man of fifty *doing* thinking about this young girl in Hollywood? I suggest that the evil of this—and it is evil, you may think—goes very deep. . . .")

The court rose as usual at half past four. As usual Ward was smiling, hiding from the world whatever he was feeling inside. I never saw a man put such a brave face on things. He chatted briefly to Mr. Burge and Mr. Wheatley, and when his bail had been renewed for the last time, he left as usual by taxi. By then his mind must have been already half made-up. The rest of us drifted out into the street, uneasy, depressed. Some of us were going home to work, some to dinner or the theatre, others to books and an early bed. But Ward, already half-way to Chelsea

in his taxi, had had his fill of all these things. Ward was going
home to die.

When I went through the swing doors of No. 1 Court the
next morning, the policeman on duty said to me: "And what
flowers will you be sending along?" I have always believed in
life that when someone says something incomprehensible, it
usually saves time and energy to pretend one understands. "Oh,
roses, I expect," I said and went towards my seat. It was not
until I had been there five or ten minutes that I heard the news:
during the night Ward had taken an overdose of sleeping tablets
and been rushed to the aptly named St. Stephen's Hospital,
where his condition was said to be serious but not critical. Mr.
Burge entered and left. The time for the sitting of the court
came and went. It was rumoured that Mr. Griffith-Jones was
in the library, busily looking up precedents. The journalists
huddled together, exchanging gossip like flies. Would the trial go
on? What would happen if Ward died? Why had he been given
bail last night when it was always possible that something like
this would happen? Was it true that he wouldn't have been
given bail if the Clerk of the Court had not gone on holiday?
Did anyone know what sort of pills he had taken? Just before
eleven Mr. Griffith-Jones came back into court, and the two
duty policemen took their places in the dock. The rude mechanicals filed in and sat down, and soon after them the judge,
looking pale and nervous.

Mr. Griffith-Jones outlined what had happened and said (and
God knows one believed him) that there were few precedents to
go by. He said that latest reports indicated that with the Bank
Holiday ahead, Tuesday of the following week (it was now
Wednesday) would be the earliest date on which Ward might be
expected to be fit enough to appear. The judge asked Mr. Burge
for his views, and Mr. Burge said that without Ward in court,
it would be impossible for him to take instructions. The judge,
looking very unhappy, said that the time for taking instructions
was now past, and he therefore proposed to continue the trial
until the point where the jury reached a verdict but not beyond.
The fact that the case was a misdemeanour and not a felony
entitled him to do this, and that, when you came to think of it,

was a nice little paradox in itself. The judge added: "I give instructions that the defendant shall immediately be put under surveillance. I shall give instructions for bail to be withdrawn from now on and normal steps to be taken for greater security." No expression of sympathy for the plight of an, as yet, innocent man, no regret: simply a bolting of the stable door after the horse had gone.

The decision to continue the trial was one which some lawyers have since contested. It seemed to them yet another example of the haste which had characterised the proceedings ever since they had started, the reflection of an official wish to get the thing over as soon as possible, to bring on a verdict which promised catharsis all round. Certainly the atmosphere in court had changed dramatically. There was a sense of anti-climax, the knowledge that Ward now had no interest in the result of the contest, not even an interest in life itself. There was talk then of his recovery, but the general consensus was that by contracting out as he had done, Ward had immeasurably lessened his chances with the jury. For over a week we had watched with admiration the way he bore his huge burden, the strength and vigour with which he met his enemies. His dynamic and lively presence in the dock was a constant reminder to the jury that it was to *this* man, to *this* fellow human before them, that they were there to do justice. But now only his ghost was there, and perhaps the jury could relax a little, as people do when the man one is talking about goes out of the room, feeling the responsibility lift from them a little, knowing that when the time came for him to hear their verdict, they would not have to endure his searching eyes. They could even ease their consciences a little—and who knows, perhaps they did?—by telling themselves that the attempt at self-destruction was in itself evidence of a guilty mind. Even if his absence was Ward's own fault, it must have put him at a disadvantage. It would have been fairer, I think, to have postponed the trial until such time as he could return.

But the decision had already been taken, the judge was already gathering up yesterday evening's threads. "In this case," he said, "we have heard nothing from the Indian doctor, and that is a matter which you yourselves should keep in mind and consider." He reminded the jury of what Ward was alleged to have told the police about the Indian doctor, and he read out bits of their evidence. If what Mandy had said about the Indian doctor was true, and if the jury were going to follow the letter rather than the spirit of the law, it was difficult to see how they could avoid finding Ward guilty on Count 2. *But was what Mandy said true?* We had heard evidence of police pressure on her, of the statement in Holloway Prison, of the arrest at London Airport, of the charge of stealing the television set being brought and mysteriously withdrawn, of her own admission that the police had told her that things would be difficult for her unless she gave evidence against Stephen Ward. We had some reason to suppose that she had malice towards Ward, and we had heard that the West London magistrate had said of her that if she wanted to get something by a lie, she would lie. There were doubts then about the story of the Indian doctor, and what I wanted to hear was an expression of these doubts by the judge. But I did not hear them. I do not think the jury heard them. For if they had heard them I think that they would have been bound to give the defendant the benefit of their reasonable doubts.

Elsewhere the judge was full of implication. He referred to Ward's income of £5,500 or so a year, and after reading out some of his outgoings, suggested that the net figure must have been fairly substantially less. If the object of saying this was not to suggest that the net figure was so much less than the gross that Ward had need to supplement his income by living on immoral earnings, then I do not know what the object was. And if that *was* the object, then why not say so? He told the jury that they must disregard Ronna Ricardo's evidence altogether, but he did ask them if "events such as happened in the foursome would have occurred if the relationship had not been a close one". Probably not; but the fact that the relationship was a close one did not mean that Ward was living on Ronna Ricardo's earnings. I do believe that the judge found it impossible to imagine any sort of social non-professional relationship existing between two people so superficially disparate as Stephen Ward and Ronna Ricardo. Then he came to Vickie Barrett and instead of saying to the jury that she had lied in her teeth over and over again, he asked them: "Am I misrepresenting Barrett when I

say she answered her questions quietly and straightforwardly?"
Of course not: it was this that had fooled us in the first place.
But not to add that she had told one whopping lie after another,
not to say that the crucial parts of her evidence were wholly un-
supported by other evidence, this surely was a deficiency in the
summing up.

We went to lunch just after one o'clock. There were no jokes
in the pub that day. After lunch the judge quickened his pace
a little, as though he were running behind time and had received
orders to have everyone out by nightfall. Unbelievably the two
policemen who had been guarding their non-existent prisoner
in the dock all morning were still stoically sitting there in the
afternoon. I suppose it had not occurred to anybody to remove
them.

The judge dealt with Counts 4 and 5 and told the jury that
they must only convict on Count 4 if they were thoroughly satisfied with the evidence. Miss X, he said, "never fell to the sexual
blandishments of Stephen Ward", which brought Mr. Burge to
his feet to say that she had never said that Ward had made any
blandishments. Well, said the judge, the jury would decide
whether there had been blandishments or not. At 2.34 his mara-
thon solo came to an end. His closing words were in character.
"The ball," he said to the jury, "is in your court."

The ball remained in their court all afternoon and early
evening. When they had gone, the Press benches emptied reluc-
tantly, as though hostile to this break in the customary routine.
I went downstairs to the canteen for a cup of coffee and sat at a
table next to Mr. Herbert and half a dozen other officers. Mr.
Herbert said to one of them: "You've got to take the dirty books
to Lord Denning." The afternoon passed slowly. In the hall outside No. 1 Court we formed into little groups like strands of sea-
weed in the tide, drifted apart, came together again. There were
about fifty of us: Sergeant Burrows puffing lugubriously at his
pipe, George Gale of the *Daily Express*, newly-arrived and
padding about like a hungry Boxer in search of something for
tomorrow's paper, Sybille Bedford, her night editor's green eye-
shade now discarded, Dominic Elwes, Michael Corkery, Rebecca
West. Christine Keeler's solicitor, a tall, bald man, was there
too, John Mathew, son of the Director of Public Prosecutions

and now keeping a watching brief for Lord Astor, Mr. Wheatley, the red-haired shorthand girl, the friendly talkative matron. The lawyers said they had never known such a hum of conversation while awaiting a verdict and that if Ward had been in court, it would have been much quieter. We talked, walked, sat down, got up, telephone, yawned, made notes. A man from one of the dailies organised a sweepstake on the time the jury would return. The tickets were a shilling each and I bought two, at 4.17 and 5.17.

But it was at five o'clock exactly that we heard they were on their way back. As we scampered for the doors I became aware that my heart was pounding: this was the moment for which we had been waiting for eight long days. I looked closely at the jury while they were taking their seats. Two of the younger members were talking together and smiling, and the woman was smiling too. Did this mean that they had cleared Ward on all counts? The judge came in, and was handed a note. Now there was a cold silence, not a sound anywhere. I found my hand shaking. The judge said: "I have received a note from the jury. I haven't read it. I will just read it and pass it to both of you." It was a very long note covering two pages, and it took the judge about three minutes to read. There was no sound, no movement, all the time he was reading. I looked at the jury to see what their faces were saying: they said nothing. At last the judge finished the note and handed it down to Mr. Griffith-Jones. He put it on the little table in front of him and he and Mr. Corkery read the note together, standing up. Then he passed it on to Mr. Burge and he read it too, and during all this time, which must have been about seven or eight minutes, the silence was unbroken.

Yet when it was broken, it was something of an anti-climax. For it turned out that the jury did not fully understand the position about establishing the fact of prostitution and the shifting of the burden of proof. With great care the judge explained it to them. Then he said that he understood that the jury wanted some refreshment. He would give orders for this, *but they would have to pay for it themselves to avoid any suspicion of favours*. When I heard this I was sorry Ward was not with us. He liked a good joke and this, I think, would have delighted him.

So we all went away for another two hours, and paced up and

down outside, and smoked and gossiped and generally tried to forget the deep depression that was stealing over many of us. And then, soon after seven o'clock, we heard that the jury were coming back for the second time. Inside the court I looked at their faces as they filed into their seats, and from the suitable solemnity on all of them—quite different to when they had reappeared for the first time—I knew that on at least one count they had found Ward guilty.

"Members of the jury, are you agreed upon your verdict?"

"We are." This was said by a little man with pink cheeks, rimless glasses and (so far as one could see) no eyes.

"And how say you on Count 1?"

"Guilty."

"Count 2?"

"Guilty."

"Count 3?"

"Not guilty."

"Count 4?"

"Not guilty."

"Count 5?"

"Not guilty."

The guilty verdicts came as a shock. In the light of the whole course and conduct of the trial, they were, I suppose, inevitable, but they were not the verdicts I or the people around me would have given, and the saying of them was quite numbing. The judge, business-like as ever, said he would wait until Ward was physically ready to appear in court, and he would then come back and deal with him. The two charges concerning abortion would stand over until the next session ("I feel we have all had enough"). He thanked the jury for their attendance and excused them further service for twenty years ("That may let some of you out altogether"). And then, almost before one was aware of it, he was on his feet and through the door and gone.

Slowly, wearily, the court emptied. Papers were stuffed into pockets, pipes and cigarette packets fondled, ties adjusted, glasses put on and taken off. We pushed open the swinging glass doors for the last time and spilled out into the hallway. High up on the wall I read: "Right lives by law, and law subsists by power." You could certainly say some of that again. We pushed on along the hallway like a sort of ragged army, separate but together, each alone with his thoughts yet driven, I think, by a common purpose, which was to get away from that place as quickly and decently as possible. We went down the great marble staircase and out into the evening street. As I remember it, nobody said anything. It wasn't surprising. There wasn't, then, anything more to say.

PART VI

IF WARD WAS as plainly not guilty in law on Counts 1 and 2 as I and many of those present believed, why did the jury find him guilty? There were several reasons. Firstly, the fact that the jury either did not know, or where they did know, could not accept, that the police had pressurised many of the witnesses into giving false evidence. Secondly, the prejudicial effect of the committal proceedings at the magistrates court which were heard and reported in full in those days (they are no longer) and which—including Ronna Ricardo's original false evidence—may well have influenced the jury. Thirdly, the partisanship of Mr. Griffith-Jones's conduct throughout the trial, deplorable in Crown counsel, and in particular the many allegations which in his opening speech he said he would prove against Ward and then failed to prove. "Whatever other impressions the jurymen may have when they first take their seats," Mr. Louis Blom-Cooper Q.C. has written, "the first words of the trial are likely to make the most lasting impression." And he quotes an advocate in Scotland, where they dispense with opening speeches in order to go straight to the first witness, saying: "The risk, as I see it, is that the jury at the end of the day will be unable to distinguish between what they have been told will be proved and what has in fact been proved." And finally there was the judge's less than impartial summing-up.

The trial ended on Wednesday July 31st, and for the next three days Ward lay in St. Stephen's Hospital, hovering between life and death, unaware of the verdict against him. He must have had a strong constitution, for he did not die until the Saturday afternoon. His death was not a great tragedy, for he had brought too much on himself; yet there were many people in Britain who, on hearing the news felt a little ashamed, a little diminished. For a man who loved life as much as he did, it was a miserable end; but an end to agony too, peace from a persecution which would have broken many people earlier. His had not been a morally good life, nor a fulfilled one, but I do not think even in the loosest sense of the word, that he was a criminal. He surrounded himself with girls for pleasure, not profit; some were already profligate, others not; but there is no evidence that he ever forced anybody to do anything against their will. If John Profumo had not lied to the House of Commons it is unlikely we would ever have heard of him.

Since the trial many people have asked who it was who was responsible for Ward's persecution. I think the answer lies not in the specific orders of any one person but in the spontaneous actions of many. When the establishment closes its ranks, when authority takes arms against what it mistakenly believes to be a sea of corruption, there is no need for the posting of battalion orders. Within the hierarchy each member knows what is required of him, what he must do; and during the long investigation and trial each man did it. The proceedings against Ward had a certain inevitability. Once put into motion, they gained a momentum of their own which it subsequently became impossible to stop.

His death had a curious effect on some people, generating in them an almost psychopathic desire to share his tawdry glory. Miss Julie Gulliver announced that she was carrying his baby. A Mr. Joe Wade, a professional gambler, in a state bordering on hysteria, revealed that he had evidence which would have cleared Ward if he had had the courage to come forward earlier. Mr. Wade may well have been right, for his evidence was corroborative proof of malice on behalf of one of the key witnesses. Lord Astor had maintained a silence during the trial which had at least been consistent: now he broke it by issuing from Ireland an epitaph on Ward of quite staggering unsuitability, the sort of thing one would expect from a Head of State on the death of a distinguished specialist (". . . possessed remarkable gifts of healing . . . those who were fortunate enough to have been treated by him will remember him with great gratitude . . . his readiness to help anyone in pain is the memory many will treasure . . ."). No one should be too hard on Lord Astor, for God knows he had problems of his own; but the offer of his London house or car to Ward for the duration of the trial might not only have impressed the court, it would have been an elegant gesture by a man who, on any account, knew Ward a great deal better than his shabby little requiem suggested.

Ward left a number of suicide notes. The recipients included the judge, Mr. Griffith-Jones, Mr. Burge, Mr. Wheatley, and Lord Denning, who had recently been appointed by the Prime Minister to inquire into the Profumo affair. The letter to Mr. Howard Jones ran as follows:

Dear Noel,

I'm sorry I had to do this here! It's really more than I can stand—the horror day after day at the court and in the streets. It's not only fear—it's a wish not to let them get me. I'd rather get myself.

I do hope I haven't let people down too much. I tried to do my stuff, but after Marshall's summing-up, I've given up all hope.

The car needs oil in the gear-box, by the way. Be happy in it.

Incidently (sic) it was surprisingly easy and required no guts. I'm sorry to disappoint the vultures. I only hope this has done the job. Delay resuscitation as long as possible.

He also left letters for Julie Gulliver, Ronna Ricardo, and Vickie Barrett. He thanked Ronna Ricardo for having told the truth at the Old Bailey, and he left instructions for her to receive £500 from his estate. He also asked for £100 to be left to Sylvia Parker.

The letter to Vickie Barrett was rather different.

I don't know what it was or who it was that made you do what you did. But if you have any decency left, you should tell the truth like Ronna Ricardo. You owe this not to me, but to everyone who may be treated like you or like me in future.

About half an hour after Ward had died, Mr. Barry O'Brien, the *Daily Telegraph* journalist who had appeared as a witness for the defence, called at the address at Clanricarde Gardens, Notting Hill, where Vickie Barrett lived, taking with him (with Mr. Wheatley's approval) a photostat copy of this letter. What happened when he arrived there is described in the statement he gave later that day to Chief Inspector Thomas O'Shea at Scotland Yard.

Having arrived at the address I telephoned the office and was told that Dr. Ward had died. I then returned to the adjoining house, No. 35, and saw Vickie Barrett in a room on the upper floor about 4.30 p.m. We were alone in the room. I told her that Dr. Ward had died and that on the night he had taken the overdose he had written her a letter. I told her that I had a photograph copy of the letter with me and gave it to her. She was greatly shocked at learning Dr. Ward was dead. She sat down and read the letter and remained for some moments silently crying. She looked at me and said: "It was not lies". After a few more moments of silence I told her that Dr. Ward had consistently maintained that she was lying in her evidence against him. She told me that her evidence was the truth.

After another silence I asked her how she came to be a witness in the case. She told me she had been interviewed by two police officers after she appeared at Marylebone Magistrate's Court on a soliciting charge on July 3rd. I would add that it was I who mentioned the date by asking her if it was the day when Dr. Ward was committed for trial. She said she had heard Dr. Ward was in another court on the same day. I asked her why they had interviewed her. She said she had been arrested for soliciting in Notting Hill late the previous night and police at Notting Hill had taken possession of her handbag and its contents including a diary. She said Dr. Ward's telephone number was in the diary. She said that the handbag and its contents had been returned to her after her appearance in the court. I asked her how the police officers had known about the diary. She said she assumed Notting Hill Police station had told them about it. I asked her if she still had the diary. She said that a week after her appearance at Marylebone the police officers had asked her if they could have her diary and she had handed it to them. She said that it had not yet been returned to her though she had seen it when she appeared at the Old Bailey.

At this point in our conversation her landlady came into

the room and gave us each a cup of tea. The landlady asked if we would like her to stay. I asked Vickie Barrett if she would like her to stay. She declined the offer and the landlady left. After another silence Vickie Barrett began sobbing violently. She suddenly looked up at me and said: "It was all lies. But I never thought he would die. I didn't want him to die." At this point her whole body was shaking and convulsed with sobbing. She then said: "It was not *all* lies. I did go to the flat but it was only to do business with Stephen Ward. It was not true I went with other men." I reminded her she had said that she had whipped men there and that Dr. Ward had been handing out contraceptives. She said that it was not true that he had done this. I asked her why she had given evidence that was untrue. She said she had told one of the police officers when he had asked her what she had known about Dr. Ward, that she was a friend of his and had visited the flat two or three times a week to do business with him. She said: "I told him that I had whipped Dr. Ward at the flat. He said: 'Wouldn't it be better if you said you whipped other men at the flat?' I said: Why should I say that? He told me that if I didn't say that, I will never be able to show my face in Notting Hill again. He said that girls could get very heavy sentences for soliciting." I asked her if the police officer had mentioned how long a sentence. Miss Barrett said "He said I could get nine months or more".

All this time she was crying and clutching the photograph copy of the letter in her hand with a cigarette burning between her fingers. As it was burning close to her fingers I took it away from her and stubbed it out. She began sobbing violently again and said "I didn't want him to die. I never thought he would die." As she seemed so upset I put my hand on her arm and told her to drink some tea. After another silence I asked her if she was telling me the truth. She said that she was. I repeated this question several times and each time she said she was telling the truth. I told her that if she was now telling me the truth it was a very wicked thing to have done. She said: "Yes, and I did it". I told her that what she had just told me was a very serious accusation against two police officers. She said she knew that but she had told the truth.

She said: "I will now get into trouble won't I?" I said: "Perhaps but you are only 20 and if what you say is true the fault was only partly yours". She said: "They will send me to prison". I said: "I don't think they will do that. Ronna Ricardo also said that she had lied in her evidence and she has not been sent to prison." I asked Miss Barrett if she knew Miss Ricardo. She said she had never seen her before they were both at the Old Bailey.

I then told Miss Barrett that I would take her to Dr. Ward's solicitor, Mr. Wheatley, and she agreed to come with me. I told her that if she had lied at the Old Bailey she must now tell the truth. She said she realised that. I told her that I did not think that any harm would come to her because she had told the truth. She said she would go to her room to powder her face, which she did. While she was away I telephoned Mr. Wheatley and told him I would be bringing her round if he was agreeable. He said that he was. While I was telling him on the telephone that Miss Barrett had lied at the Old Bailey the landlady came out of her room and went to the room next door where Miss Barrett was. A few moments later the landlady came out and said that Miss Barrett was not going anywhere with me and was very upset and was not seeing anybody. The landlady said: "I told her I had just heard you telling someone on the telephone that she had said she had told lies. She (Barrett) said he is telling lies" (meaning me, O'Brien).

I then telephoned Mr. Wheatley and he said he would come round. When he did so the landlady said Miss Barrett would not see him. The landlady said that Miss Barrett had telephoned one of the police officers and he was coming round. The landlady said: "I hope we are not going to have another suicide". I told her that she should stay with Miss Barrett and impressed on her the importance of doing so if she was worried about her. Mr. Wheatley and I then left and he told me that I ought to make a statement to Superintendent Axon at Scotland Yard. We called at my office on the way to Scotland Yard and the News Editor of the *Sunday Telegraph* asked a colleague of mine to accompany me. I did not make any record of my conversation with Vickie Barrett while it was in progress. I have given an account of her conversation to my office and she signed no (repeat no) statement. I did not tell Vickie Barrett I would be going to the police or tell her to do so.

Vickie Barrett, who, like all prostitutes, was scared stiff of the police and the possibility of a prison sentence, later retracted her admission and affirmed that what she had said at the Old Bailey was true. Another prostitute who was equally frightened of the police was Ronna Ricardo. I saw her briefly at the trial when she was clearly in a state of terror at what the police might do to her for having gone back on her original evidence. After the trial she seldom stayed at one address more than a few nights for fear the police were looking for her. I managed to get in touch with her through her solicitor, as I wanted to test her evidence for myself, and I took her to lunch at the Cumberland Hotel on the same day as she testified before Lord Denning. She was still very frightened. I assured her that now the case was closed and Ward convicted, the police had no further interest in her: they were on to other things. She would not be reassured, and thought that it would be only a matter of time before they took their revenge.

The following are notes I made of our conversation at the time.

"R says police originally heard of her connection with Ward through a friend called Barbara. Police raided Barbara's place and found a picture by Ward on the wall. Barbara mentioned that R also had a picture by Ward on her wall. This was her West Indian friend who took part in the foursome in Ward's flat. She says the picture was stuck to wall with cellotape.

"She says police interviewed her altogether nine times. She was living earlier in the year in a flat at St. Irvines Road, and she says that a police car was constantly outside her flat. She says the names of the two officers in the police car were Slade and Ellis. She thinks they were kept there to frighten her and she says they did frighten her.

"She says Ward liked her and she liked him, but sometimes he could be a dreadful bore, and she had to 'sling him out' because he would go on talking. Says Ward couldn't manage normal sex any more. He was keen on her West Indian friend, which confirms rumours that Ward was homo as well as hetero. I asked R what else Ward liked and she said 'Sometimes he used to have the vibro'.

"R says that police put tremendous pressure on her to say what they wanted, and threatened to take action against herself and her family if she refused. She had one sister, Gwen, living with her, about sixteen I gathered, and very intelligent. Another sister, Dorothy, aged thirteen, lived with her mother at Vauxhall. She says police got both sisters to make a statement, and threatened to send Gwen, who was on probation for C.N.D. activities, to a remand home. She also says the police told her that Dorothy had been seen with Ward and going into Ward's flat with men, which she says 'quite untrue'. She says Ward had once given Dorothy £1 for her birthday when she was visiting Ronna, and police 'tried to make something of it'.

"She finally agreed to say what police wanted because she was 'completely fed up' and one of the officers promised that she would not have to appear in court. She says he promised this several times, and it was repeated by two other officers who came to take final statements at her new flat in Queensway. She says she did not read statement through before signing it because she wanted to 'get it over with'. Police told her she *would* have to appear in court only twenty-four hours beforehand. She says that when she reminded the officer concerned of his promise, he said that if she didn't come to court, he'd take Dorothy along there instead. She says that what she said about Ward asking her if she knew of anyone who could help a girl with an abortion was quite true, but not the rest of it.

"She says that when she disappeared before the Old Bailey trial, having decided to admit she had been lying at the Magistrate's Court, that one of the police officers had turned up at her mother's house at Vauxhall. According to her mother he was 'foaming and frothing at the mouth' and threatening to take Dorothy away as being in need of care and protection unless her mother told him where R was."

Without checking everything that Ronna Ricardo told me, it is impossible to say what was true and what not. I formed the impression that she was trying to convey to me an accurate account of what had happened. Her answers were too spontaneous and unsophisticated for any attempt at prolonged and consistent lying. From the conversation as a whole, I found it difficult to accept the only alternative explanation, i.e. that she had told the truth at the Magistrate's Court and lied at the Old Bailey.

In September Lord Denning's Report was published as a White Paper, and turned out to be a racy, readable and in parts rather nasty document. It was nasty in a number of ways. There were several occasions when Lord Denning could not resist the temptation to regale his readers with gossipy titbits of the women's magazine variety which had no bearing on his brief at all. For instance, he informed us in detail of how and where Mr. Profumo had told his wife that he had been lying. It was in Venice. "...they had a quiet dinner first. After dinner Mr. Profumo told his wife the truth—for the first time—that he had had an illicit association with Christine Keeler. He told her all the details. They talked over it most of the night. Mrs. Profumo said 'Oh darling, we must go home now just as soon as we can and face up to it'." It is difficult to read these words without acute embarrassment; one would have thought that Lord Denning might have spared the Profumos the revelation of personal intimacies which were the concern of them and nobody else, and did not help the inquiry at all. It was also unnecessary, one would have thought, to publish the detailed account that Christine Keeler gave of the inside of Profumo's house. ("The stairs bend to the left and on the wall is a picture, of all the things that Valerie likes and dislikes including pigeons and jewellery"..."there were a lot of mirrors in the bathroom", etc.) Lord Denning's excuse for publishing this tittle-tattle and embarrassing the Profumos further is that "she described the house so exactly that one would think it was not likely to have been invented". But no responsible person publicly suggested that the incident was invented. It was not in public controversy, and even if it had been, it had nothing to do with the matters to which Lord Denning had been asked to apply himself. It was gossip and nothing more. A last example of the somewhat curious quality of Lord Denning's mind occurred in paragraph 58 of the Report where he referred to a photograph of Christine Keeler in the *News of the World* of February 3rd and said that most people seeing it "would really infer the avocation of Christine Keeler". The photograph showed Christine posing in a swimsuit, but it was presumably not that avocation that Lord Denning had in mind. What he had in mind, one imagines, was the avocation of being a whore. But there are many girls who earn a living by posing in swimsuits, and to assume that all of them, or even most of them, are also necessarily whores, seems to me to be assuming rather too much. This was another indication, if any were needed, of how remote from the rest of us are the worlds in which some judges live.

But the nastiest part of the Report concerned Lord Denning's assessment of the characters in the story. In a high-falutin' introduction he announced the high principles by which he would be guided. Where the facts were beyond controversy, he said, he would state them as objectively as he could, irrespective of the consequences to individuals; but when the facts were in issue, he would always remember the cardinal principle of justice—that no man was to be condemned on suspicion. "The interest of justice to the individual," he wrote, "overrides all other." As far as the living were concerned Lord Denning carried out this noble precept faithfully. He went to some pains to tell us that Profumo was loyal to his country, which few had ever seriously doubted. He told us that Lord Astor had done sterling work for hospitals, refugees and charities, which was no doubt true, but irrelevant to the matter in hand. Even Christine Keeler was not to be judged too harshly because of her youth: at that time she had not been sent to prison for perjury.

But with the dead it was a different matter. When it came to discussing Ward, Lord Denning's flowery phrases about justice to the individual and not condemning on suspicion flew smartly out of the window. Ward, he said, "procured girls of 16 or 17 to be mistresses for his influential friends". Did Lord Denning not know that despite interviewing nearly 140 witnesses, the police had only found enough evidence to bring two charges of procuring against Ward, and on both of these the jury had found him not guilty? "Ward," he went on, "also catered for those of his friends who had perverted tastes. There is evidence that he was ready to arrange for whipping and other sadistic performances." The only evidence that had been produced at his trial to support this allegation had been that of Vickie Barrett, and on that charge also the jury had found him not guilty. Lord Denning then said that within "a very few days" of meeting Christine Keeler at the Cabaret Club "Ward asked her to go and live with him. She went. She ran away from him many times but she always went back." This gave the impression that Ward plucked Christine, as it were, straight out of the Cabaret Club and set her up in his flat, where she lived semi-permanently ever afterwards. The facts of the matter as disclosed at Ward's trial were that Christine did not go to live with Ward in Wimpole Mews until almost two years after she had first met him. She stayed for weekends with him at Orme Court and at the cottage at Cliveden, and then she went to live at Comeragh Road with Mandy and at Bryanston Mews with Rachman. Lord Denning continued: "He introduced her also to the drug Indian hemp and she became addicted to it". On balance the evidence at the trial was that he had *not* introduced her to it, and indeed tried to discourage her from taking it. In any events the facts would seem to meet Lord Denning's own definition of being in issue and therefore best left alone. Later, turning to Mandy, Lord Denning said that Ward "found another girl to live with him in place of Christine Keeler. He *got* (my italics) Marilyn Rice-Davies to live with him in Wimpole Mews." This suggests that the only reason that Mandy came to stay at Wimpole Mews was for procuring purposes. In fact the evidence at the trial was that Mandy had had a quarrel with Rachman, and Ward had offered to put her up temporarily because she was upset and had nowhere else to go. Finally Lord Denning stated that Ward "was known to be involved in a call-girl racket"—known, that is, by the Security Service. They must have known something that other people did not know, for no evidence of a "call-girl racket" as such, was produced at Ward's trial.

When I read these allegations of Lord Denning's about

Ward, I was astonished. I assumed that the only possible explanation of them was that Lord Denning had heard fresh evidence for which there had been corroboration, and that if only this fresh evidence had been produced at the trial, Ward would have been found guilty of several more charges. So I telephoned one of the officials who had assisted Lord Denning in his inquiry. I am not able to give his name for he asked me not to. To my further astonishment he told me that in fact there had been no fresh evidence (in the sense of evidence from witnesses whom the police had not already seen) and that most of the allegations about Ward *had been supplied by Christine, Mandy and other prosecution witnesses*. I asked for the source of the allegation about Ward arranging whipping parties, and I could hardly believe my ears when he said "Vickie Barrett". I pointed out that these and other allegations had not been proved at Ward's trial, to which he said "Well, I daresay we were a bit unfair to Ward there. We were under a lot of pressure, as I expect you know, and we didn't really have time to read the report of the trial in detail." We have reached an odd state of affairs in England when a judge with the reputation of Lord Denning can state hearsay as fact, and in the same breath as it were, say that he would never do any such thing. The Denning Report was criticised for whitewashing the living: a less attractive feature of it is that it also defamed the dead.*

In January 1964 Mandy Rice-Davies's memoirs were published by Confidential Publications, Ltd. under the title of *The Mandy Report*; and her account of the events from the time of her first arrest do much, if true, to confirm the suspicions already expressed about the statements taken from her by the police and the unreliability of her subsequent evidence.

Rachman was dead but I had not heard the last of his name. Attempting to leave London Airport on April 23 I was arrested whilst passing through Passport Control and taken by police car back to town. Then I was charged with driving under a forged licence, whilst uninsured, and making false statements to obtain insurance. This was all to do with the Jaguar and the phoney licence that Peter had provided for my birthday.

That night I slept on a hard straw mattress in a prison cell at Holloway. The next morning I appeared in a magistrate's court where police opposed bail on the grounds that I might try to leave the country. It was a fantastic situation and quite impossible to understand. You would have thought I had stolen the Crown Jewels or something like—or stopped a mail train in Buckinghamshire. My solicitor objected to the police statement and finally bail was set at £2,000. But when friends came up with the money the real significance of the case came to light.

A detective told me: "You'd be well advised not to accept bail. As soon as you're released we're going to arrest you on another charge. In fact we've got two warrants for your arrest. One of them is a bench warrant for parking in a wrong street and not turning up at court. If we re-arrest you, it'll mean finding another £2,000 bail. Take my advice and stay inside for another week. It'll cause you less trouble in the long run".

On two previous occasions the police had been to see me about making a statement on my relations with Stephen Ward. Each time I had refused. Clearly these proceedings were related to my refusal to co-operate and this was why I had to be kept behind bars. Well, back to jail I went. Holloway Prison must be one of the last places that God ever made on this earth. The conditions I thought were absolutely vile. I was turned out of my bunk every morning at 6 a.m. and locked up for bed again at 9 p.m. Compared with what I had been accustomed to, the food was like pigswill and tasted every bit as vile as it looked . . .

After a day or two of this I was ready to do anything to get out. I am sure that this was the way the police had planned it. They came to see me and asked if I would like to reconsider my refusal to make a statement about Dr Ward. The prospect of perhaps having to spend a further spell in Holloway over the motoring offence was enough to convince me that I had better keep on the right side of the police. I felt like a cornered animal. I told them all they wanted to know . . . and slowly the noose began tightening round Stephen's neck.

When my case went into court I was let off with a £42 fine and a warning. I left at once for Majorca. . . .

After spending some time in Majorca Mandy flew home.

At the airport I was met by two detectives from the Yard. "Oh no", I said. "Not again". They wanted to grill me further about Stephen's life but I told them that everything I had to say had been said when I was in Holloway. Their faces looked a little strained at this news and I had the feeling that we would meet again . . .

A few days later I was again called in by the police and interviewed for four-and-a-half hours, going all over the same ground again. I was getting pretty sick of this and decided that Majorca was the place to be. Things were moving very quickly.

On June 4, Jack Profumo resigned as War Minister and as an M.P. Three days later, Stephen Ward was arrested and charged with living on immoral earnings. And on the 16th, again on my way to Majorca, I was stopped and arrested for the second time whilst passing through London Airport. Again the police were about to pull a fast one on me.

I was driven to Marylebone police station and charged with the larceny of a TV set. The police asked me to enter in recognisances of £1,000. The condition of this was that I was to appear at Marylebone Court. By "coincidence" it turned out that I was to appear on the same day as the start of the hearing against Ward!

(The television set I was supposed to have stolen was removed from Peter's flat at Bryanston Mews after his death. They claimed that I had taken it. This was completely and utterly untrue and, in fact, nothing ever came of this charge. But it had enabled the police to take away my passport until after the Ward hearing.)

The preliminary hearing of Stephen's case opened on June 28.

Frankly, I thought the whole business was a farce. No one would deny that Stephen was a depraved and immoral man. But to suggest that he made a living out of it is nonsense. Much was made of the fact that I was paying him a few pounds a week whilst I was living in Wimpole Mews. But I said before and say it again—Stephen never did anything for nothing and we agreed on the rent the day I arrived. *He most certainly never influenced me to sleep with anyone, nor ever asked me to do so.*

It is this last sentence which is almost the most significant and revealing of all. For if it is true, it is nothing more nor less than an admission that her evidence of Ward's proposals regarding Ropner and the Indian doctor—the evidence which resulted in his conviction on Count 2—was untrue. Certainly what she said in evidence and what she says here cannot *both* be true.

If we accept what is said here as true, then the main prop in the prosecution's case falls from under it. But Mandy has a further astonishing revelation which also runs counter to the evidence she gave in court. This is that while she was at Wimpole Mews, Rachman, although no longer living with her, "continued to pay me my £100 a week allowance". She did not say this in the witness-box, though she had an opportunity to say it when Mr. Griffith-Jones asked her what other income she had at Wimpole Mews and she replied "What Stephen gave me" (see page 72). Clearly neither prosecution nor the defence knew about the £100 a week. If they had known and it had been put into court as evidence, it would have been impossible for the jury to have convicted Ward of living on Mandy's immoral earnings: indeed, taken in conjunction with the other, the case against Ward on that count would have collapsed altogether.

THE FILE ON THE TSAR
Anthony Summers and Tom Mangold

The definitive investigation into the fate of the Romanovs, in particular the Grand Duchess Anastasia, by two of Britain's most respected investigative journalists.

"A superb, real-life unputdownable mystery" – Len Deighton

ISBN 0 575 04128 5

NICHOLAS AND ALEXANDRA
Robert K. Massie

The internationally bestselling biography of Russia's last Tsar and his family, whose violent deaths still provoke speculation and debate.

"An exquisite story of love and compassion" – *The Times*

ISBN 0 575 03589 7

BIRDMAN OF ALCATRAZ
Thomas E. Gaddis

The extraordinary true story of life imprisonment, on which the famous film was based. This edition contains new information on the prisoner, who, in solitary confinement, reared hundreds of canaries and became a world authority on bird diseases.

"The most remarkable record of a human life that anyone is likely to read for years" – *Observer*

ISBN 0 575 03710 5

YEARS OF WRATH
A Cartoon History 1932–1945
David Low
Introduction by The Rt Hon. Michael Foot, MP

A powerful visual history of events leading up to and during the Second World War by the most influential political cartoonist of the day.

"Absorbingly interesting" – *BBC*

ISBN 0 575 03822 5